What's all this about, then? *The l*

Maybe it's one of those libera ... e floating on clou ... e.

But it could be like the lie of ... 's saying the opposite: 'This is wha

Or maybe he's saying good riddance to the old 'fire and brimstone.' Which I think is a shame, because we certainly need a stronger way to teach morals today.

I wouldn't be surprised if he is trying to chart again the old territory of souls in the eternal fire. But basing a religion on fear is crude and counter productive.

He's an Anglican! They've never really done hell-fire. And he's a Canon. That's like having a merit badge for saying the right things and not upsetting anyone. An establishment type.

He's a Canon in Uganda. They're more conservative there.

He's still more likely to be saying 'Let's pretend we'll all be nice to each other in the end,' and 'No one's going to come to any harm with us.'

Why would he write a book to say that? It's not as though there are many people stuck in the old thinking about devils and pitchforks.

This vicar must think there's something new to say.

That's the oddest thing. How can there be something new to say about hell after all these years?

Other experts have said this book is 'fresh and provocative' or 'a fresh perspective.' There must be something here that other people haven't said before.

It looks worth a read...

'Bible-believing scholars are increasingly rejecting as unbiblical the old picture of hell as everlasting conscious torment. In its place most often they offer a biblical vision of evil made extinct, along with those people who prefer to perish with evil rather than to let it go.

Leading the way in this important work have been a cadre of British biblical scholars: F. F. Bruce, John W. Wenham, Richard Bauckham, John Stott, J. I. Marshall, Michael Green, and N. T. Wright—to name but a few.

With this book we welcome to the conversation the fresh perspective of Anglican rector Roger Harper. Utilizing what some have called 'red-letter hermeneutics', Harper begins with the teachings of Jesus himself, then he uses those teachings as a lens through which he reads biblical writers in general. The result, whether right or wrong, is a stimulating and nuanced form of conditional immortality likely to invigorate Bible students of all persuasions.'

Edward William Fudge, author of *The Fire That Consumes: A Biblical and Historical Study of the Doctrine of Final Punishment* (3rd edn, Cascade Books/Wipf and Stock, 2011).

A movie, *Hell and Mr. Fudge* (2012), has been made of Edward's life and work. See www.hellandmrfudge.com

The Lie of Hell

Roger Harper

Rob,
Cheers mate!
Roger

Roger is Vicar of Burton Joyce with Bulcote
and Stoke Bardolph near Nottingham,
Canon of West Ankole, Uganda,
and a recent regular contributor to *Christianity* magazine

Ladder Media Ltd.
a Christian Equitable Company
www.laddermedia.co.uk

First published in Great Britain in 2012

This paperback edition
1

Copyright © Ladder Media Ltd. 2012

ISBN: 978-0-9561848-1-8

Roger Harper asserts the moral right
to be identified as the author of this work.

All rights reserved. No part of this book may be reproduced or transmitted in any form or by any means, electronic or mechanical, or by any information storage or retrieval system, without permission in writing from the publisher.

Every effort has been made to seek permission to use copyright material reproduced in this book. If any required acknowledgements have been omitted , or any rights overlooked, this has been unintentional. Please notify the publisher of any omission and it will be rectified in future editions.

All Scripture quotations are from New Revised Standard Version Bible: Anglicized Edition, copyright © 1989, 1995 National Council of the Churches of Christ in the United States of America. Used by permission. All rights reserved.

A catalogue record for this book is available from the British Library.

Cover design by Russell Wallis, RJW CREATIVE DESIGN
© Ladder Media Ltd. 2012
Photograph of Anastasis fresco in the Chora, Istanbul
by Gunnar Bach Pedersen (Public Domain)

Printed and bound in the UK by MPG Books, Bodmin and Kings Lynn.

For my father and his family,
who came closer to hell on earth
than anyone should experience.

Their Jewish heritage has formed this book.

CONTENTS

INTRODUCTION

Enter through the narrow gate; for the gate is wide and the road is easy that leads to destruction, and there are many who take it. For the gate is narrow and the road is hard that leads to life, and there are few who find it.

Matthew 7:13,14 (NRSV)

'Or else!' is a common human motivator. We hope that we will always choose the good for the sake of the good, but we know that, without a credible warning or deadline, our determination may be too weak. Hell has served as the ultimate 'or else!' Hell has motivated people to live with care, care for their own souls and care for others. It has been a useful, some would say, necessary part of the Church's teaching. William Booth, founder of the Salvation Army wrote: 'Send me some bare thoughts, some clear startling outlines. Nothing moves the people like the terrific. They must have hell-fire flashed before their faces, or they will not *move.*'[1]

For people today, however, hell is an incredible and despised motivator. Very few people believe in hell, and certainly not as a realistic option for their own future, if they are not careful. Early in the 20th century George Bernard Shaw wrote: 'belief in . . . hell is fast vanishing. All the leaders of thought have lost it; and even for the rank and file it has fled to those parts of Ireland and Scotland which are still in the XVII century . . . Even there it is tacitly reserved for the other fellow.'[2] Belief in hell has only diminished over the following century.

Hell is no longer generally believable philosophically. Hell is often now seen as incompatible with the God of love, the Father of Jesus. Rob Bell writes 'Of all the billions of people who have ever lived, will only a select number "make it to a better place" and every single other person suffer in torment and punishment forever? Is this acceptable to God? Has God created millions of people over tens of thousands of years who are going to spend

[1] H. Begbie, *Life of Wiliam Booth* (Macmillan, 1920), vol. 1, p. 228.
[2] G.B. Shaw, *Androcles and the Lion*, Preface (1915).

eternity in anguish? Can God do this, or even allow this, and still claim to be a loving God?'[3]

Many would agree with John Stuart Mill: 'Any other of the outrages to the most ordinary justice and humanity involved in the common Christian conception of the moral character of God sinks into insignificance beside this dreadful idealisation of wickedness.'[4] The threat of hell is seen as empty, a desperate attempt to frighten people into religion. Any religion founded on such fear is unacceptable.

Hell is therefore no longer preached and taught by the Church. Hell is understood by many to be still 'part of the package', part of the fundamental world-view of Christianity, but this part is well hidden and never talked about. The Church now has a dual problem: people are put off Christian faith because of the hell that they 'know' is lurking in the background, and yet the Church is unable to issue any lasting moral warning. Many today would agree with Bertrand Russell that, 'for all that might be said positively about the teaching and character of Jesus Christ, it was overshadowed on the negative side by his belief in hell.'[5] Yet because the Church has, in the past, proclaimed hell as the true 'or else!' it has no other message of eternal warning to give.

Jesus, on the other hand, often gave warnings, warnings of a good, ultimate future which could be lost. Even the Parable of the Prodigal Son, with its wonderful picture of the accepting, patient, welcoming, non-judging love of the Father, ends with the exclusion of the older son, not by his father's choosing but by his own choice. The warning in this, as in other parables, is simple: 'You could be left out, shut out.' How has the Church put itself in such a position that it cannot preach and teach ultimate warning as Jesus did? This book addresses this question, and some others: What exact warning did Jesus give? What warning comes through the rest of the Bible? Do we need to reinvigorate the traditional concept of hell or proclaim something else which is truer to Jesus and Scripture?

[3] Rob Bell, *Love Wins* (Collins, 2011).

[4] J. S. Mill, *Three Essays* (1874), p. 74f.

[5] Russell, *Why I am not a Christian* (Simon and Schuster, 1957), p. 17, quoted by B. Milne, *The Message of Heaven and Hell* (IVP, 2002), p. 144.

Although hell is generally not seen as credible, it is still understood. Hell is a common metaphor for the worst place a human can find themselves, much used in films and songs and books. The accepted definition of hell is:

- A place of torment, were people burn in a fire that never goes out, where people are lacerated forever by devils with pitch-forks, shut out from the mercy of God. (Some people question whether these pictures are real or metaphorical, whether the torment is physical or mental/emotional. The particular type of torment is of secondary importance to the primary assertion that people will be tormented for ever.)
- A place which continues to exist for ever, as eternal as heaven.
- A place from which there is no escape. No one can leave hell. All who enter have to abandon all hope.
- A place presided over by the devil, Satan. Hell is the domain of the devil.
- A place to which people are assigned after death. Eternal destiny, in heaven or hell, is fixed the moment we die.
- A place, according to Christians, for unbelievers. As the majority of humankind have not been believers in Jesus, they are 'the lost'. Hell probably has more inhabitants than heaven.

All the above is what is commonly understood as hell. All the above is also the theological definition of hell. The UK Evangelical Alliance in 2000 published a report called *The Nature of Hell* which began with this definition: 'The "hell" which awaits such people ['impenitent' 'unrighteous' or 'wicked'] is the domain of the devil and his hordes – a sphere of damnation, punishment, anguish and destruction.'[6]

Yet within the wider Christian tradition there are pointers to a contrary picture of hell. The great Welsh hymn, *Guide me O Thou great redeemer*, speaks to the redeemer as 'death of death and hell's destruction'. Will hell really be destroyed by Jesus? Will it not be as eternal as heaven? The medieval Advent hymn, *O come o come Emmanuel*, contains the plea 'from depths of hell thy people save'. Can Jesus save people from hell? Is there a way out of hell? *Ye choirs of new Jerusalem* is from even earlier in the Middle Ages. Here we sing

[6] ACUTE, *The Nature of Hell* (Paternoster Press, 2000), p. 1.

For Judah's lion burst his chains,
  and crushed the serpent's head
and brought with him from death's domain,
  the long–imprisoned dead.
From hell's devouring jaws the prey
  alone our leader bore;
his ransomed hosts pursue their way
  where he hath gone before.

Are there hosts of people released from hell by Jesus?

The words of *Ye choirs of new Jerusalem* describe 'The Harrowing of Hell', the tradition strongly depicted in Western Passion Plays and Eastern icons that Jesus did and can rescue souls from hell. Here we have an understanding that is at odds with the commonly accepted definition of hell, although the eternal, no-way-out hell remains the dominant understanding. Because of this dominance, little attention is paid nowadays to the Harrowing of Hell. Sermons are preached on neither the traditional hell nor the harrowable hell.

The Church's inability nowadays to preach and teach either hell or another 'or else!' is only part of the 'problem of hell.' E. W. Fudge comments: 'this subject is important for it colors our view of God's character and human nature and it shapes our attitude towards others and the way we share the good news of life in Christ.'[7] What we believe has a strong effect on how we live our lives. It is not true that we can believe anything we like as long as we don't harm others, as modern Western culture encourages us to think.

If hell is part of the Christian world-view, then it is clear that the Christian God, through His eternal proxy the devil, is a torturer. If the Christian God is a torturer it is not surprising that some Christians, and others, find it hard to believe that God is truly and always loving. If the Christian God is a torturer it is not surprising also that some Christians have also found torture in this life an acceptable tool to be used in certain extreme circumstances.

[7] E. W. Fudge, *The Fire that Consumes* (Paternoster Press, 1994), p. xii.

If the Christian God imprisons people for ever in the 'care' of vicious demons, it is not surprising that some Christians consider it appropriate to imprison criminals in nasty punitive conditions in this life.

If the Christian God can turn His back on the majority of the people He has created, it is not surprising that some Christians show little concern for the majority of the world today, especially the hapless poor.

If the Christian God condemns all unbelieving sinners equally, with no regard for individual differences and circumstances, it is not surprising that some Christians preach to these sinners in a formulaic and threatening way.

It is of great importance that what we Christians believe is true, true to Jesus and His Holy Spirit, true to Scripture, and leads to the increase of true faith, hope and love in this world.

This book has been written to help people understand and live in the truth as it is in Jesus, pointed to by the Holy Spirit, particularly through Scripture. Other books have been written on this subject, especially in recent years, and a number of them are reviewed in Chapter 6. This book uniquely builds from scratch a Christian doctrine of what happens beyond this life to wicked people who do not repent of their wickedness – the impenitent wicked. Instead of starting with the various understandings and positions taken by other writers and teachers, it starts with the primary sources of Christian doctrine. First it explains the method of 'construction' that will be use and then it starts building from the words of Jesus, the foundation and cornerstone of all our thinking, believing, and living.

CHAPTER ONE

BUILDING CHRISTIAN DOCTRINE

Six days later, Jesus took with him Peter and James and John, and led them up a high mountain apart, by themselves. And he was transfigured before them, and his clothes became dazzling white, such as no one on earth could bleach them.
And there appeared to them Elijah with Moses, who were talking with Jesus.
Then Peter said to Jesus, 'Rabbi, it is good for us to be here; let us make three dwellings, one for you, one for Moses, and one for Elijah.' He did not know what to say, for they were terrified.
Then a cloud overshadowed them, and from the cloud there came a voice, 'This is my Son, the Beloved; listen to him!'

Mark 9:2-7 (NRSV)

Listen to Jesus

This amazing encounter on the mountain is recorded in Matthew and Luke as well as Mark. Each time the point, the punch-line, is the same, 'Listen to Him.' A voice from a cloud speaks: 'Listen to Him.' To Jewish people a cloud, especially a speaking cloud, was a reminder of the cloud of God's presence which went with the people of Israel through the wilderness. They would understand that the voice from the cloud was a voice from heaven, the voice of God himself. This is how Peter explains the voice in his second letter:

For we did not follow cleverly devised myths when we made known to you the power and coming of our Lord Jesus Christ, but we had been eyewitnesses of his majesty. For he received honour and glory from God the Father when that voice was conveyed to him by the Majestic Glory, saying, 'This is my Son, my Beloved, with whom I am well pleased.'

We ourselves heard this voice come from heaven, while we were with him on the holy mountain. So we have the prophetic message more fully confirmed. You will do well to be attentive to this as to a lamp shining in a dark place, until the day dawns and the morning star rises in your hearts.

2 Peter 1:16-19 (NRSV)

The voice from the cloud is the voice from heaven. Voices from heaven are unusual even in the Bible. This is an extraordinary communication. The point, though, is not to say 'Wow!' or to keep expecting more voices from heaven, from clouds. The point is to be attentive to Jesus. God Himself says, 'Listen to Him.' Listening to Jesus is like welcoming a light shining in a dark place. Where it is hard to see even close around, let alone some way in the distance, we need a light shining so that we can see better. 'Listen to Jesus and things will become clearer.' Peter takes this as the voice of God to himself, James and John, and then to all Christians. 'If you want to see, want to know, listen to Jesus.'

Christians need to listen to Jesus – full stop. The voice did not add anything else. We are to listen to Jesus at all times and in all places and in all circumstances and for all questions. We are to listen to Jesus when we think we know what the answer is, 'taking every thought captive to him.'[1] We are to listen to Jesus, Peter says especially, when we are in a 'dark place'.

Hell is indeed a 'dark place'. When we think of hell, we think of deep darkness (as well as, oddly, fire – more on this in the next chapter.) Hell is dark in being gloomy, depressing, dispiriting. Hell is dark in being unclear. Hell is a subject of intense debate. There seems to be no one clear understanding of hell. Into this dark place, we trust, the words of Jesus shine like a lamp.

The lamp that is lit when we listen to Jesus does not, however, according to Peter, give us the absolute final word. Listening to Jesus lights a lamp which is sufficient for us 'until the day dawns . . . ' Peter, like all the early Christians, lived with the expectation that there would be greater clarity beyond the life that we now live. The day dawning is this new life, the life of heaven, the life that would begin with Jesus coming again. Jesus will return to put everything right. Jesus will return as the light which outshines the

[1] 2 Cor. 10:5 (NRSV).

sun and even makes it redundant.[2] In the life that begins when Jesus returns, the life of heaven, there will be no more darkness and we will see and understand clearly. 'Then,' wrote Paul, 'we will see face to face. Now I know only in part; then I will know fully, even as I have been fully known.'[3] Compared to the full knowledge and understanding which we will have beyond this life, the best that we can know and understand now is only 'in part.' Listening to Jesus is like having a lamp lit. But the lamp does not show us everything. When the day comes, when the light of heaven dawns, then we will see and understand fully. Now our knowledge of everything is partial. How much more so our knowledge of something as 'otherworldly' as hell?

Knowing that all our knowledge is partial, we make listening to Jesus, being attentive to Him, our priority. When the voice came to the disciples on the mountain, the command to listen to Jesus was in the context of Peter suggesting that he make three dwellings, one for Moses, one for Elijah and one for Jesus. Mark explains that Peter was not sure what to say. It seems that he was frightened, thought he needed to say something, and came out with this suggestion. Peter himself was probably not sure exactly what he meant by these 'dwellings' and neither are we.

What Peter said does show, however, is that in his mind, Moses, Elijah and Jesus were all of the same 'level'. Moses, Elijah and Jesus should be honoured equally, together in some way but also each distinctively. This suggestion honours all three. It seems like a worthy, even good, religious response to the revelation they have been given. Great Old Testament figures had marked places in a similar way.

Jacob marked the place where he dreamt of a ladder reaching up to heaven with angels ascending and descending and had called it Bethel, the house of God.[4] Years later, God called Jacob to meet with Him there particularly, at Bethel.[5] Peter wanted to honour and record what happened on this mountain in a similar way. He made what seemed like a good, scriptural, suggestion. But it was this very honourable suggestion which provoked God

[2] Rev. 22:5 (NRSV).
[3] 1 Cor. 13:12 (NRSV).
[4] Gen. 28:19 (NRSV).
[5] Gen. 35:1 (NRSV).

himself to draw near in a cloud and speak to Peter, James and John directly.

The voice from heaven urgently needed to correct what Peter was saying and thinking. What seemed a very proper thing to say and to think was, to God, so wrong that He needed to correct Peter himself. We don't know the tone of the voice from the cloud. It could have been calm and even, majestic and untroubled as we normally think of the voice of God. It could have been sharp and urgent: 'Pay attention! Don't keep thinking that way. Jesus is my Son, quite different from Moses and Elijah. Listen to Him!' Peter, in his letter, writes with urgency, not suggesting but urging his readers to be attentive to the voice which came from heaven. It is likely that Peter is reflecting the urgency with which the voice spoke. Thinking of Moses, Elijah and Jesus as 'on the same level' is dangerous. Wanting to return somehow to listen to each of them equally is not right. 'This is my Son, the Beloved. Listen to Him!'

Peter was used to listening to Moses and Elijah. Moses was the writer of the Torah, the first five books of the Old Testament. Moses was the conveyer of God's Law, firstly for the people of Israel, and then for the whole of humanity. Elijah was the great and first prophet of the Old Testament, the father of all the prophets. Peter and the others were used to listening to the words of Moses and of Elijah and the prophets in Synagogue every Saturday. They knew that in listening to Moses and Elijah they were listening to God's messengers, God's message. Peter and the others had often listened in Synagogue with Jesus. Luke tells us that it was Jesus' habit to go to Synagogue on the Sabbath.[6] Luke describes this as Jesus' custom, not necessarily the custom of the disciples. Peter knew that Jesus placed a high priority on listening to Moses and Elijah. Peter naturally thought that Jesus wanted him to continue to listen to Moses and Elijah alongside Jesus. Peter expressed this in his suggestion of marking that place. The voice from heaven responded: 'This is my Son, the Beloved. Listen to Him!'

Treating Jesus and His words in the same way as the words of Moses and Elijah is against what God wants. Listening to Moses and Elijah alongside Jesus is not what Jesus' followers are to do.

[6] Luke 4:16 (NRSV).

This was, no doubt, a surprise and a puzzle to Peter and it is, often, a surprise and a puzzle to Christians today. Many of us are used to the idea that the Bible as a whole is God's Word to us and that we should pay equal attention to all of it. Many Christians, and others, will ask 'What does the Bible say?' We know that 'All scripture is inspired by God and is useful for teaching, for reproof, for correction, and for training in righteousness,' as Paul wrote.[7] We respect the whole Bible as having the authority of God. We listen to Moses in the Bible, to Elijah in the Bible, and to Jesus in the Bible, as though they have equal authority. Asking 'What does the Bible say?' leads people often to start with Genesis and work through the Bible as a whole. But the voice from heaven says: 'This is my Son, the Beloved. Listen to Him!' It is to Jesus alone that we pay attention as to a lamp shining in a dark place, not to Moses, Elijah and Jesus, all three equally.

'Listen to Him!' Be attentive to Him. If we want to know or understand anything, and especially something as 'dark' as hell, we have first and foremost to hear, read, mark, learn and inwardly digest the words of Jesus.[8] We need to separate out the words of Jesus, as recorded for us in the Bible, and pay attention to them uniquely. This is the beginning and the foundation of all Christian doctrine. We ask 'What does Jesus say?' We start with His words, in the Gospels and when He is quoted in the rest of the New Testament, and build from there.

Jesus spoke in other ways about our need to pay attention first and foremost to Him and not to the whole of the Bible:

I am the vine, you are the branches. Those who abide in me and I in them bear much fruit, because apart from me you can do nothing. Whoever does not abide in me is thrown away like a branch and withers; such branches are gathered, thrown into the fire, and burned. If you abide in me, and my words abide in you, ask for whatever you wish, and it will be done for you.

John 15:5-7 (NRSV)

The vine was a common metaphor for the nation of Israel, the heritage of the nation, including the Scriptures. Jesus calls His disciples to abide solely in Him, not to abide in the teaching of

[7] 2 Timothy 3:16 (NRSV).

[8] *Book of Common Prayer*, Collect for the Second Sunday in Advent.

Moses and Elijah. Jesus says that part of this abiding in Him is that His words abide in us. It is not the words of the Bible that are to abide in us, but the words of Jesus. This is the way that we abide in the true vine and bear much fruit, including the fruit of producing good understanding, teaching, and doctrine.

Jesus himself called people to listen to Him with His often repeated call:

Let anyone with ears listen!

Matthew 11:15, 13:9, 13:43, Mark 4:9, 4:23, 7:16, Luke 8:8, 14:35 (NRSV)

Not only is Jesus urging people to listen to Him, but He is declaring that all that is needed is ears. Anyone who has ears, can listen. No-one needs anyone else to explain Jesus' words to them. No-one needs to understand anything else first. No particular background information is needed to understand Jesus' words. No key is needed to unlock the mysteries hidden within Jesus' words. All that is needed is ears to register the words and take them in.

Listening to Jesus is meant to be a straightforward business. The plain and obvious meaning, such as any ordinary person would think of, is the correct meaning. Although Jesus is the Son of God, the beloved, a category of person whom our finite minds struggle fully to understand, all that is needed is to listen to Him. Jesus, the Son of God, is able to speak in such a way that all people can understand Him directly. Humans struggle to make themselves understood and need other people to explain and commentate on their words. The greatest human philosophers are like this. Jesus, the beloved Son of God, is different. He can communicate the deepest, most complex truths, within human language, without any need for outside explanation or commentary. We humans only need our ears. 'This is my Son, the Beloved. Listen to Him!'

Sometimes people claim that, in order properly to understand Jesus, what is needed is particular background information, or even a special key to understanding. For instance, in understanding what Jesus said about hell, it is sometimes said we need to understand how people in His day understood hell. This knowledge is usually useful, although our understanding of what people at the time thought changes and is a subject of debate. But this knowledge is not necessary. It is going too far to claim that without this knowledge we cannot understand what Jesus said. All of us, with ears to hear, can listen to Jesus. We first pay attention to His words, then look at the background.

Some people have gone even further in stating that there is a 'key' which can unlock the mysteries of what Jesus said. The Gnostics were a diverse group of religious people, some of whom respected and incorporated the teaching of Jesus into their understanding. In this way they seemed to be 'Christian'. But they also held to other teachings which they claimed were needed to understand Jesus properly. Usually this was a secret knowledge (*gnosis* in Greek) which only they and their group knew. This is why they were called Gnostics and why the Church deemed them heretics. The extreme example of the Gnostics helps us to understand how inappropriate it is to deem any other knowledge an essential prerequisite for understanding Jesus. Christians listen to Jesus, seeking to understand Him without any other prior knowledge or key.

Paul understood the priority of listening to Jesus and wrote:

He himself is before all things, and in him all things hold together. He is the head of the body, the church; he is the beginning, the firstborn from the dead, so that he might come to have first place in everything.

Colossians 1:17, 18 (NRSV)

Jesus is the head of the Church. Listening to Him has the first place, over listening to Moses, Elijah, or any other authority in Scripture or beyond.

For no one can lay any foundation other than the one that has been laid; that foundation is Jesus Christ.

1 Corinthians 3:11 (NRSV)

For Paul, Jesus is the one and only foundation. We begin all our building, including our building of understanding and doctrine, with Him. This echoes what Jesus said about building wisely and foolishly:

Everyone then who hears these words of mine and acts on them will be like a wise man who built his house on rock. The rain fell, the floods came, and the winds blew and beat on that house, but it did not fall, because it had been founded on rock. And everyone who hears these words of mine and does not act on them will be like a foolish man who built his house on sand. The rain fell, and the floods came, and the winds blew and beat against that house, and it fell - and great was its fall!

Matthew 7:24-27 (NRSV)

The wise foundation, the foundation of wisdom, is to hear the words of Jesus and to act upon them. The first appropriate action is simply to listen, making an effort to take in what Jesus has said. 'This is my Son, the Beloved. Listen to Him!'

Although, in a historical sense, Jesus built on the words of the Old Testament, words which were already there before He began speaking, we are not to start with these Old words, but to start with the words of Jesus.

Paul expressed the same understanding in a slightly different picture:

So then you are no longer strangers and aliens, but you are citizens with the saints and also members of the household of God, built upon the foundation of the apostles and prophets, with Christ Jesus himself as the cornerstone.

Ephesians 2:19,20 (NRSV)

A foundation is the first task that a builder addresses; a cornerstone is meant to be the first stone in a builder's mind. The cornerstone is used to join walls and makes sure the building grows 'true' and in correct alignment. The builder has to see the cornerstone in his mind first, and then work out how the other stones fit so that they are lined up with the cornerstone.

Peter also uses the same picture:

For it stands in scripture: 'See, I am laying in Zion a stone, a cornerstone chosen and precious; and whoever believes in him will not be put to shame.'
To you then who believe, he is precious; but for those who do not believe, 'The stone that the builders rejected has become the very head of the corner',

1 Peter 2:6,7 (NRSV)

The cornerstone is an odd-shaped stone, different from other 'regular' stones. This oddity can be half rejected by the builder, not knowing what to do with it. The builder puts the odd-shaped stone to one side and carries on without it. The odd-shaped stone is still there, tripping the builder up from time to time. The builder needs to take full notice of the cornerstone, making it uppermost in his thinking. He works out how the rest of the building fits around the cornerstone, to give it its prominent, key position. For Christians the cornerstone is Jesus. For building Christian doctrine, the cornerstone is Jesus, His life and teaching. 'This is my Son, the Beloved. Listen to Him!'

Listen to Scripture

Once the foundation has been laid, or the cornerstone is clearly in mind, building can then proceed, with every material that is 'useful'.

All scripture is inspired by God and is useful for teaching, for reproof, for correction, and for training in righteousness,

2 Timothy 3:16 (NRSV)

Paul does not write that all Scripture is foundational to our teaching. It is Jesus alone who gives us that foundation. The rest of Scripture is not to be rejected but to be welcomed as useful in the building. Elsewhere Paul writes about people building on the foundation of Jesus with different materials, gold, silver, precious stones, wood, hay, straw.[9] Some of these are more useful than others. In building Christian teaching or doctrine, the words of the Bible, the words of Moses and Elijah are all useful, helpful. They are not to be dismissed as of no use. They are not foundational, but they are valuable.

The voice from the cloud did not say, 'This is my Son. Listen to Him – and pay no attention to those other two.' Peter, James and John, as we have seen, came up the mountain with their strong understanding, partly fostered by Jesus himself, that the words of the Torah and the Prophets, as well as the other Writings in Scripture, were to be listened to. The voice did not tell them to put aside that understanding altogether, only to make sure that they listened to Jesus first and foremost as He is the Son of God

[9] 1 Cor. 3:12 (NRSV).

Jesus also underlined that His followers are to continue to listen to Moses and Elijah:

Do not think that I have come to abolish the law or the prophets; I have come not to abolish but to fulfil. For truly I tell you, until heaven and earth pass away, not one letter, not one stroke of a letter, will pass from the law until all is accomplished.

Matthew 5:17,18

The Old Testament is not obsolete. It continues to be useful in building doctrine on Jesus the foundation. Rather than begin with Genesis or any other part of the Old Testament, we are to note and incorporate the teaching of Genesis after we have set out the teaching of Jesus. Only then will we have as full an understanding as we can hope for in this life.

What is true for the Old Testament is also true for those Scriptures which the Church deems inspired, as Paul hints at in writing about 'all scripture that is inspired ('God-breathed')' or 'all inspired scripture',[10] Once we have laid down the foundation of our doctrine with Jesus, we can build from there not only with Moses and Elijah, but also with Peter, Paul, John and the other New Testament writers. These writers were the closest to Jesus, their words are the closest to the foundation. Therefore it is best that they are brought in and used first, before the Old Testament.

The approach of this book is to begin with the words of Jesus in the Gospels and the rest of the New Testament. The words of the other New Testament writers are considered next, before the words of the Old Testament. The 'building', the understanding of hell, which emerges is then detailed.

The Holy Spirit Guides the Building

As well as telling His disciples not to make the Old Testament obsolete, Jesus told them to listen also to the Holy Spirit.

I still have many things to say to you, but you cannot bear them now. When the Spirit of truth comes, he will guide you into all the truth; for he will not speak on his own, but will speak whatever he hears, and he will declare to you the things that are

[10] The translators are divided as to which is the better translation of Paul's phrase.

to come. He will glorify me, because he will take what is mine and declare it to you.

John 16:12-14 (NRSV)

Listening to Jesus includes listening to the Holy Spirit, the Spirit of truth. The truth conveyed by the Holy Spirit is also the truth that Jesus wants to convey. The Holy Spirit is our guide in building, the direct representative of the architect, working alongside us. He takes what Jesus has said, brings it to our attention, confirms it, and builds on it for us and with us. He is the one who inspired the Gospel writers to take the words and the life of Jesus and record them for us. He is the one who inspired all those who wrote Holy Scripture. He is the one who still today inspires people in building on the foundation of listening to Jesus.

This Spirit is the Spirit of truth: plain, simple truth. The Holy Spirit helps us to see what is true and works through our applying the tools of logical truth. We are given the foundation or the cornerstone by Jesus. We then cooperate with the Holy Spirit by working out what are the true consequences, the best-fitting next stages in building. Once the foundation is in place, building can proceed according to and within the limits set by this foundation. Within these limits we are free to think and build understanding, logically and faithfully elaborating on the foundation, the cornerstone. We are not only free to build, to elaborate, we are encouraged to do so, as guided by the Spirit of truth. We are not to be limited only to what the Bible tells us. We are to expect that there will be more truth, more understanding, beyond what is in the Bible, but building on the words of Jesus. This truth will emerge through the guidance of the Holy Spirit in and through our truthful, logical minds. Some of this truth will follow necessarily from what Jesus said. Some of this truth will follow from what Jesus said but in different ways in different contexts. As well as asking 'What has Jesus said?' we also ask 'What follows from that?'

What Jesus said about the Spirit of truth echoes closely the 'wisdom tradition' of the Old Testament and beyond. 'The fear of the Lord is the beginning of wisdom.'[11] First we need to respect and honour God, and His Son, and what they have said. Wisdom can then grow and develop; wisdom in every area of life. Studying

[11] Psalm 111:10 (NRSV).

the law is also described in the Old Testament as the way to wisdom. As we make the words of Jesus and the rest of Scripture foundational, our thinking can then develop from there. Such thinking is wisdom, guided by the Spirit of truth.

We can see the Holy Spirit helping people to develop understanding, leading them into more truth, in Mark's Gospel.

He said to them, 'Then do you also fail to understand? Do you not see that whatever goes into a person from outside cannot defile, since it enters, not the heart but the stomach, and goes out into the sewer?' (Thus he declared all foods clean.)

Mark 7:18,19 (NRSV)

Jesus did not himself declare that all foods were clean, that His followers were free from the centuries-old regulation, announced and supported by the Old Testament, that certain foods were unclean and not to be eaten. If Jesus had said that clearly, it would no doubt have caused intense controversy and would have been very hard for the disciples to take in. But when people later reflected on His words about the things going into the stomach not being able to defile a person, the logical consequence was seen to be that all foods were indeed clean. Mark simply says 'thus'. Jesus did not need to spell it out; His followers later understood the logical consequence of his words. The Spirit of truth took what was of Jesus, declared it to the disciples and guided them into a truth which earlier, they could not have borne. We are to expect the same Spirit of truth to guide us, logically, into truth about hell, building on, elaborating, the words of Jesus.

Logic was not the only way that the Holy Spirit guided people to see that all foods are clean. The same message came to Peter in a non-logical, even supernatural, way:

Peter went up on the roof to pray. He became hungry and wanted something to eat; and while it was being prepared, he fell into a trance.
He saw the heaven opened and something like a large sheet coming down, being lowered to the ground by its four corners. In it were all kinds of four-footed creatures and reptiles and birds of the air. Then he heard a voice saying, 'Get up, Peter; kill and eat.' But Peter said, 'By no means, Lord; for I have never eaten anything that is profane or unclean.' The voice said

to him again, a second time, 'What God has made clean, you must not call profane.'

Acts 10:9-15 (NRSV)

This vision with its message is so important that it is repeated twice in the book of Acts. For the early Christians this kind of vision was a normal way that the Holy Spirit spoke, leading them into all truth. For us, especially in the West, the idea of the Holy Spirit guiding our logic fits much more with our perception of what is normal. For those early Christians, this vision was a clear and important communication from the Holy Spirit to be welcomed and heeded. If we hold only to the leading of the Holy Spirit through logical elaboration of the words of Jesus, we will be stopping our ears to much that the Holy Spirit wants to say, we will struggle to be led fully into the truth that Jesus has for us. Instead we are to embrace the truth that the Holy Spirit today is the same Spirit who gave Peter his vision, the Spirit who came at Pentecost, giving young men visions, and old men dreams, speaking in supernatural ways to and through women and slaves.[12]

The vision came in the context of Peter being invited to the house of a gentile, where he would be offered food unclean to Jews. The vision came with a remarkable coincidence, which was part of the discernment that it was from the Holy Spirit and not simply Peter's hunger speaking in desperation. The gentiles with whom Peter spent time and shared a table then received the Holy Spirit in just the same way that the disciples had received the Spirit at Pentecost. It was very clear to Peter that what was happening to the gentiles was indeed from the Holy Spirit. This also confirmed that the vision had been from the same Holy Spirit. Today too we need discernment to test whether a vision, dream or prophecy is from the Holy Spirit or not. Today too we look for other indications that the Holy Spirit is working all things together to give His message, the message of Jesus.

The vision was also given to the man whom Jesus had identified as the rock on which He would build His Church. Peter was the recognised leader. Although Peter himself said that visions, dreams and prophecy come to everyone, when the message was

[12] Acts 2:17,18 (NRSV).

for the whole Church, it was right that it came to the recognised leader of the church. Luke describes Peter explaining in person in different contexts exactly what he had seen and understood, and his listeners respected what he had to say partly because of the evidence that this was indeed from the Holy Spirit, and partly because of Peter's standing and position in the Church. Today too, we pay particular attention to dreams, visions and prophecy coming to and through recognised Church leaders in good standing.

The truth about clean food into which the Holy Spirit guided the Church was not the final truth. Once it had been established that all foods are indeed clean for the followers of Jesus, the whole status of the Jewish Law was questioned. The next development, elaborating on the words and the life of Jesus, was that the followers of Jesus who had not previously been Jews did not need to keep the Jewish Law. This was a highly controversial new truth, difficult to accept. Many Jewish people at the time would have followed the development of this new truth, accepted that it was a logical elaboration of the words of Jesus, confirmed supernaturally by the Holy Spirit, but still found the conclusion hard to accept. It went against much of what they had believed all their lives and what had been believed for generations before them. Hence the intense debate across the Church which led to Paul writing his letters, especially the letters to the Galatians and the Romans.

The intense debate across the Church about clean food and the rest of the Jewish Law was also part of the process of the Holy Spirit leading into all truth, the process of building Christian doctrine. Eventually the Church, through a Council representing all congregations from all areas, proclaimed what seemed good to them and to the Holy Spirit.[13] The whole Church confirmed that the teaching was indeed from the Holy Spirit. This confirmation has often been referred to as the process of 'reception.' A teaching is received by the wider Church as valid, a true expression of the leading of the Holy Spirit. This reception, confirmation, is needed. Without it the Church can be led in many different directions at once by people claiming to have been inspired by the Holy Spirit.

[13] Acts 15:28 (NRSV).

Every spirit, every teaching, has to be tested by the Church and its leadership.[14]

The process of reception appears messy – a process of debate and argument, sometimes fierce. Paul's letters and Luke's description of how he was treated in various churches show how fierce the argument can be. For Paul and others the law about clean and unclean food was a matter of the utmost importance and for several years there was no agreed ruling. Such debate and argument has continued in the life of the Church. No Church or Christian wants to have this argument; it feels divisive.[15] The example of Scripture, especially the book of Acts, shows that we have to continue arguing, hoping and trusting that, eventually, there will be agreement. Even when the great majority of the Church has come to agreement, there will always be some people, some Christians, who cannot go along with this agreement. They will, with reluctance, be deemed 'heretics'. Eventually the Holy Spirit will lead the Church into further truth, and this truth is of such importance that the Church has to hold to its agreed understanding even if not all members can accept this understanding. The process of reception needs honesty and integrity, for everyone to debate clearly and respectfully. It also needs a mechanism for the whole Church to come to a considered view, and plenty of time.

Jesus had warned His disciples that they would find the 'more' revealed to them by the Holy Spirit difficult to bear. So it proved to be in Acts, and so it can prove to be today. The most difficult truths to bear are truths which seem to be revealed by the Holy Spirit but which are also contrary to at least some of the teaching of the Bible. The truth that all foods are clean, and that God's people do not need to keep to the whole of God's Law as revealed to Moses, was perhaps the most major such truth. The truth that slavery is against the will of God was similar. For most of Scripture, slavery is part of life as God has established it. The Holy Spirit led people to understand that it is impossible for anyone to love their neighbour as themselves while their neighbour is their

[14] 1 John 4:1 (NRSV).

[15] Maybe the Church, in this as in other ways, needs to learn from the Jews, who have a strong tradition of arguing fiercely among themselves. Jews are proud to say 'Wherever you have three Jews, you find four opinions.'

slave. The Holy Spirit showed and inspired certain leading Christians, in particular Quakers, that slavery was against the will of God, despite not being against most of Scripture.

The Biblical example and precedent of the doctrine that all foods are clean, with its consequences, and the historical example of the doctrine that slavery is against the will of God, show the benefit of reading the Bible with the words of Jesus as the foundation and cornerstone. This narrow focus firstly on the words of Jesus has not been promoted widely. Evangelicals, instead, have focused on the whole of the Bible without distinction. Roman Catholics have focused on the teaching of the Church as it has been developed and received from the time of the writing of the New Testament onwards. Both these more common approaches to building Christian doctrine make sure that we include the breadth of doctrine-building material available. Both these approaches, however, fail to do full justice to the voice from heaven saying 'Listen to Him', to Jesus' authoritative statements about His own foundation words, confirmed by Peter and Paul, and to the precedent of the forming of doctrine in the book of Acts. If the Church, guided by the Holy Spirit, had not made the words of Jesus the most important part of their thinking, they would not have accepted that all foods are clean and that slavery is against God's will.

Truths revealed by the words of Jesus and the Holy Spirit, but contrary to much of Scripture, are few and far between. The process outlined in this chapter is helpful whenever we find ourselves with significant questions about a doctrine, as we do with the doctrine of hell. We return to the words of Jesus, hold to the whole of Scripture as 'useful' in building Christian understanding, and hold to the revelation of the Holy Spirit, the Spirit of truth, taking what is of Jesus, declaring it to us and leading us into a truth which, before, we could not bear. We will expect this Spirit of truth to lead us both logically and supernaturally. When the logical and the supernatural cohere, as they did concerning clean foods, we will pay particular attention to the message.

Insights From Beyond the Bible

Christians are divided on the degree of usefulness of insights and teaching from beyond the Bible for Christian doctrine. One approach is to say that, for instance, the insights of modern science, of historical and literary criticism, are valuable and to be read alongside the insights of Jesus and the Bible. A few would go so far as to take these modern, widely accepted, insights, hold them in mind first and then read the Bible with them in mind or 'through' them. The insights of other religions and cultures can also be used in the same way, alongside or even interpreting the words of the Bible.

The opposite approach is to say that the insights of modern science or of other religions are worthless, when compared to the Bible, in building Christian doctrine. Some people consider these insights dangerous and contrary to true Christianity.

The approach outlined already, the approach that builds on the voice from the cloud telling us to listen to Jesus, is closer to the second approach but can incorporate some elements of the first. We are first and foremost to listen to Jesus. All other insights, from whatever source, are secondary. We do not read Moses and Elijah alongside Jesus, nor do we read Einstein or the Buddha alongside Jesus. Once we have established what Jesus has said and have the foundation for our understanding and doctrine, we then turn to the rest of the Bible, for we have been assured that it is useful for the first parts of the building after the foundation. We look for the Holy Spirit to lead us into further truth, logically and supernaturally. Then we can turn to other sources, including modern or ancient scientists or philosophers. If what we learn from these sources fits in with the foundation, the first parts of the building, and truth shown us by the Holy Spirit, these insights can also be incorporated. Just as the voice from the cloud did not tell the disciples to ignore Moses and Elijah, so we are not necessarily to ignore Einstein and the Buddha.

We will, however, be more wary of Einstein and the Buddha, than of Moses and Elijah, in matters of Christian doctrine, especially concerning salvation. Neither Jesus, nor the rest of our Bible, tells us to pay attention to scientists and philosophers for our Church doctrine. Indeed there are warnings to the contrary:

I appeal to you therefore, brothers and sisters, by the mercies of God, to present your bodies as a living sacrifice, holy and acceptable to God, which is your spiritual worship. Do not be conformed to this world, but be transformed by the renewing of your minds, so that you may discern what is the will of God - what is good and acceptable and perfect.

Romans 12:1,2 (NRSV)

See to it that no one takes you captive through philosophy and empty deceit, according to human tradition, according to the elemental spirits of the universe, and not according to Christ.

Colossians 2:8 (NRSV)

Paul in these letters is continuing the Old Testament tradition of paying no heed to idols and the teaching of idols. Pagan understanding, even widespread understanding, such as the existence of several gods (maybe or maybe not under or within the one high god) is not to be incorporated into the understanding of God's people, neither the people of Israel, nor the followers of Jesus. This is clear from the first of the Ten Commandments:

I am the Lord your God, who brought you out of the land of Egypt, out of the house of slavery; you shall have no other gods before me.

Exodus 20:2,3 (NRSV)

As we look at our understanding of the ultimate fate of the wicked, we can eventually turn to the teaching of other religions and cultures, but we Christians have to be careful that these understandings do not take the place of our foundation and the first developments of our doctrine. If Buddhist, Pagan, Greek or Moslem understanding does not fit in with what we learn from Jesus and the rest of the Bible, it is to be rejected.

If, on the other hand, the insights of any other sources accord with what we know from Jesus, the Holy Spirit, and the rest of the Bible, they are to be welcomed and valued.

Finally, beloved, whatever is true, whatever is honourable, whatever is just, whatever is pure, whatever is pleasing, whatever is commendable, if there is any excellence and if there is anything worthy of praise, think about these things.

Philippians 4:8 (NRSV)

Paul here, writing to people of a very cosmopolitan city, is encouraging them to be widely inclusive. Knowing the Gospel, secure on the foundation, they can rejoice in whatever this Gospel and this foundation shows to be good, from whatever source. They, and we, are to listen to Jesus, the beloved Son, to expect to be guided by the Holy Spirit, to listen to Moses and Elijah, and then also to Einstein and the Buddha.

The Words of the Gospel Writers and the Words of Jesus

One of the insights of modern historical and literary criticism is a scepticism about whether the words of Jesus as recorded in the New Testament are accurately recorded or not. There is much scholarly debate about which recorded words are truly those of Jesus. A more popular similar scepticism is the view that a lot of 'Chinese whispers' were involved in the creation of the Gospels, with one person telling another, who told another, who told another, until it was all written down hundreds of years later.

It is not possible in this context to give a full response to this scepticism. Recognising the scepticism, though, we can present good reasons that it can be set aside for our current purposes.

Firstly, not all scholars are sceptical. Richard Bauckham, author of *Jesus and the Eyewitnesses*,[16] is one of several modern scholars who argue that the Gospels are a reliable record of what Jesus said and did. In scholarly theology and history, there is a generally agreed understanding of the date of the writing of the Gospels, with Mark the first at about 65 AD, Luke and Matthew at between 75 and 85 AD and John at about 90 AD. This means that the Gospels were written between 30 and 60 years after Jesus died, certainly not the 'hundreds of years' of popular scepticism. It is also generally accepted that the Gospels were not the first written records of the deeds and words of Jesus. Matthew and Luke record the teaching of Jesus using very similar wording, indicating that they were copying a previously written record. Christians, meeting in houses to remember Jesus as He told them to, probably treasured and recorded people's memories of Jesus, especially as

[16] *Jesus and the Eyewitnesses: The Gospels as Eyewitness Testimony* (Eerdmans, 2006).

the eyewitness generation was dying. The Gospel writers then collected these existing records of first- and second-hand memories of Jesus, checked them for consistency and reliability, and put them in order. This commonly accepted scholarly view is in line with what Luke writes about the background to his Gospel:

> Since many have undertaken to set down an orderly account of the events that have been fulfilled among us, just as they were handed on to us by those who from the beginning were eyewitnesses and servants of the word, I too decided, after investigating everything carefully from the very first, to write an orderly account for you, most excellent Theophilus, so that you may know the truth concerning the things about which you have been instructed.
>
> *Luke 1:1-4 (NRSV)*

Some scepticism may continue about particular stories and sayings of Jesus, but it is reasonable to consider that the recorded words are, generally, accurate.

Secondly, there is no agreed understanding among the most sceptical scholars as to which words of Jesus are authentic and which are not. Some scholars argue that particular words show 'clear evidence' of having originated from the very early Christians rather than from Jesus, whereas other scholars argue that the same words show 'clear evidence' of having originated from Jesus himself. Back in 1929, writing about hell, Percy Dearmer criticised the great Biblical scholar Albert Schweitzer: 'Schweitzer . . . has made a somewhat reckless use of the results of New Testament criticism, preferring Matthew to the earlier sources whenever it suits his argument, and rejecting as "unhistorical" every adverse passage, as so many others have done.'[17]

Dearmer himself prefers to treat Matthew's record of Jesus' words, especially those which have been taken to refer to hell, as 'unhistorical', that is as originating not from Jesus but from the community of which Matthew was a part. In the years since 1929 there has been no more convergence of scholarly opinion. (If anything scholarly reasons for the reliability of the Gospels in

[17] Dearmer, *The Legend of Hell* (Cassell, 1929), p. 194.

recording Jesus have strengthened, for instance with the recent work of N. T. Wright and Richard Bauckham.)

Scepticism about the sceptics is therefore reasonable. Since the sceptical scholars cannot agree, there are no reliable objective grounds to accept one and reject the other. Trusting authors writing between 30 and 60 years from the event, as opposed to scholars writing 1970 years from the event, is also reasonable.

Thirdly, as Christians, we believe, to varying degrees, with Paul, that the writers of the Gospels were 'inspired', guided in their writing by the Holy Spirit. They were guided in retaining some stories and sayings and rejecting others. They were guided in recording, as faithfully as possible, people's memories of Jesus.

The existence of the Holy Spirit and His role in the creation of the New Testament is a subject too large to be argued extensively here. For the purposes of building Christian doctrine, however, it is reasonable to believe that God has not left His Church entirely on its own, but that He works with the Church, both in forming Scripture and in continuing to help us to understand what is recorded of Jesus, Moses and Elijah in Scripture. Followers of Jesus indeed believe that the Spirit leads us into all truth, including leading the New Testament writers in recording the truth about what Jesus said and did.

Human reason on its own cannot be sure which are the authentic words of Jesus, Christians can reasonably take the words of Jesus as recorded in the Bible and use them as the foundation of our doctrine. Those who believe that Jesus is indeed the beloved only Son of God are confident in paying close attention to His words as recorded for us, and all the other words of the Bible which He commended.

CHAPTER TWO

BUILDING BEGINS ON JESUS, THE FOUNDATION AND CORNERSTONE

The stone which the builders rejected has become the very head of the corner.

1 Peter 2:7 (NRSV)

Hades and *Gehenna*

Jesus, His life and teaching, is the foundation on which we build all our understanding. As soon as we look at the Gospel record of Jesus speaking about Hell, in the original Greek, we are immediately struck by a fact hidden by English translators. This fact, like all of Jesus' teaching on Hell, is a cornerstone. In a way common with cornerstones, this fact has been ignored, put aside as odd, but it is impossible to remove it altogether. The fact is that Jesus used two different words which have long been translated by the one English word 'Hell'.

Jesus talked of *Gehenna* and He talked of *Hades.* In the Greek text of the Gospels this distinction is plain and obvious. The distinction was preserved in the Latin. In nearly every English text of the Gospels, from William Tyndale's 1525 translation onwards, the distinction is overridden by translators using the one word 'Hell'. Most English Bible readers are unaware that Jesus used two words. Those who do know about the two words do not refer to them much. The two words are often treated as an oddity. Little thought is given to why Jesus used two words. It is assumed that these are two words to describe the same place. Jesus' two words certainly do not form the foundation of most people's thinking about Hell. Yet all that Jesus said is meant to be the foundation and cornerstone of all our understanding and teaching, of all our doctrine.

We need to take the words of Jesus, as recorded, in the Gospels, with the two different words for Hell, and, first of all, listen carefully to them. The following are all the verses where Jesus speaks of 'Hell' with the different words in the original Greek.

But I say to you that if you are angry with a brother or sister, you will be liable to judgement; and if you insult a brother or sister, you will be liable to the council; and if you say, "You fool", you will be liable to the *Gehenna* of fire.

Matthew 5:22 (NRSV alt.)

If your right eye causes you to sin, tear it out and throw it away; it is better for you to lose one of your members than for your whole body to be thrown into *Gehenna*.
And if your right hand causes you to sin, cut it off and throw it away; it is better for you to lose one of your members than for your whole body to go into *Gehenna*.

Matthew 5:29,30 (NRSV alt.)

And if your eye causes you to stumble, tear it out and throw it away; it is better for you to enter life with one eye than to have two eyes and to be thrown into the *Gehenna* of fire.

Matthew 18:9 (NRSV alt.)

If your hand causes you to stumble, cut it off; it is better for you to enter life maimed than to have two hands and to go to *Gehenna*, to the unquenchable fire.
[where their worm never dies, and the fire is never quenched.]
And if your foot causes you to stumble, cut it off; it is better for you to enter life lame than to have two feet and to be thrown into *Gehenna*,
[where their worm never dies, and the fire is never quenched.]
And if your eye causes you to stumble, tear it out; it is better for you to enter the kingdom of God with one eye than to have two eyes and to be thrown into *Gehenna*,
where their worm never dies, and the fire is never quenched.

Mark 9:43-48 (NRSV alt.)

Do not fear those who kill the body but cannot kill the soul; rather fear him who can destroy both soul and body in *Gehenna*.

Matthew 10:28 (NRSV alt.)

But I will warn you whom to fear: fear him who, after he has killed, has authority to cast into *Gehenna*. Yes, I tell you, fear him!

Luke 12:5 (NRSV alt.)

Woe to you, scribes and Pharisees, hypocrites! For you cross sea and land to make a single convert, and you make the new convert twice as much a child of *Gehenna* as yourselves.

Matthew 23:15 (NRSV alt.)

You snakes, you brood of vipers! How can you escape being sentenced to *Gehenna*?

Matthew 23:33 (NRSV alt.)

And you, Capernaum, will you be exalted to heaven? No, you will be brought down to *Hades*. For if the deeds of power done in you had been done in Sodom, it would have remained until this day.

Matthew 11:23 (NRSV)

And you, Capernaum, will you be exalted to heaven? No, you will be brought down to *Hades*.

Luke 10:15 (NRSV)

And I tell you, you are Peter, and on this rock I will build my church, and the gates of *Hades* will not prevail against it.

Matthew 16:18 (NRSV)

In *Hades*, where he was being tormented, he looked up and saw Abraham far away with Lazarus by his side.
He called out, "Father Abraham, have mercy on me, and send Lazarus to dip the tip of his finger in water and cool my tongue; for I am in agony in these flames."
But Abraham said, "Child, remember that during your lifetime you received your good things, and Lazarus in like manner evil things; but now he is comforted here, and you are in agony. Besides all this, between you and us a great chasm has been fixed, so that those who might want to pass from here to you cannot do so, and no one can cross from there to us."

Luke 16:23-26 (NRSV)

These verses form the cornerstone, or the first foundation, of our understanding of what happens to the unrepentant wicked after death. Traditional teaching has been that these people, who have injured others, broken laws, and refuse to admit their wrongdoing, burn forever in Hell. We need to examine Jesus' words carefully and make sure that we have understood them fully before considering anything else, even traditional teaching. We try to look at these verses with no preconceptions. If someone who had never heard of *Gehenna*, *Hades*, or Hell, was reading these verses, what would they conclude?

Gehenna

- is a place of fire (Matthew) or is itself an unquenchable fire (Mark and Luke);
- is the opposite of life, of the Kingdom of God;
- is a place of destruction for both body and soul; the destructive power, described as fire and worm, never ceases;
- is a place where people go after being sentenced for sin, sent by the one whom we are to fear;
- is the likely ultimate destination for those who do not listen to Jesus' teaching, and those who oppose Him vehemently and repeatedly.

Hades

- is a low place, people are brought down there; it is far lower than the place where Abraham is; there is a great chasm between *Hades* and the higher place;
- has gates, but the Church is more powerful than these gates;
- is a place where a whole town which ignores Jesus and makes light of His miracles may be taken;
- is a place of torment, of agony, in flames, a place where people can talk, can remember;
- even though there is a chasm between *Hades* and the higher place, there can be communication across that chasm.

Looking at Jesus' words we see that there are some similarities between *Gehenna* and *Hades*, but also significant differences. People go to both *Gehenna* and *Hades* as a consequence of their sin, but whereas *Gehenna* is a place of destruction for body and soul, *Hades* is a place where people can feel, think and talk. *Gehenna* is a place of fire, or is itself a fire. *Hades* has flames and gates. If read without preconceptions, *Gehenna* and *Hades* look like two similar but different 'places'. (Various English words, for instance 'spheres' or 'existences', could be used to describe the category of *Gehenna* and *Hades*. We will use the general word 'place' as the simplest.) Although this is not how *Gehenna* and *Hades* have generally been understood, there are good reasons for seeing them as two different places.

The first and obvious reason for seeing *Gehenna* and *Hades* as separate and different is that Jesus gave them different names.

The two names cannot be confused; they sound very different. *Gehenna* is not a Greek name, but a Hebrew / Aramaic name transliterated into Greek (the word is Hebrew, but spelt with Greek letters) *Hades* is a Greek name, a translation of the Hebrew or Aramaic. The Hebrew or Aramaic which Jesus would have used is '*Sheol*' (usually pronounced shay-oll.)

Whichever language is used, the two names sound markedly different. The simple meaning of hearing any two different place names is that they refer to two different places. Bethany and Emmaus are two places named in the Gospels, said to be near Jerusalem. There has been debate about where exactly these places were, but we rightly assume that they are two distinct places. Similarly with *Gehenna* and *Hades / Sheol*. There has been debate about what these places are like, but, from what Jesus said, there is no reason to believe that they are the same place.

To say that two different place names refer to the same place is to argue that the speaker did not really know what they were talking about, or was muddled, or was speaking in some kind of code. Jesus knew what He was talking about and was not muddled. Nor did He speak in code, in which a separate key, known only to the initiated, is needed to understand what is said.

Jesus used metaphors and parables whose meanings were not always obvious. He said that understanding would come 'to those who had ears to hear'. This means that all we need to understand Jesus is our own ears and, probably, some time and mental effort to draw out the meaning. Jesus did not say that understanding would come to those who had been given a key - quite the opposite. If a key was needed, Jesus would have said so. He said, instead, that all we need is our ears.

The claim that *Gehenna* and *Hades* are the same place, with no evidence for this in the text itself, relies on an understanding from outside the text. It may have been the general Greek or Hebrew understanding at the time that there was only one place for the unrepentant wicked after death (or it may not have been), but this is not mentioned by Jesus. The assertion that there is only one place for the unrepentant wicked after death is not found anywhere in the Gospels. The claim, in other words, is that here, uniquely, Jesus expected people to know something which He had not told them, in order to understand what He was saying. Those who only had ears to hear could not have come to understand that He was using two different names for the same place. There is nothing in the New Testament to indicate that, in talking of the fate of the unrepentant wicked, Jesus made such a significant exception to His normal way of speaking. Those who hear the Gospels afresh will assume that Jesus used two different names because He was talking about two different places.

Looking in more detail at what Jesus said, we can see more reason to believe that *Gehenna* and *Hades* are separate and different, not only in name but in nature. One is a place of destruction, the other a place of agony. *Gehenna* is a place of the opposite of life, of death; *Hades* is a place where people are still living in some way, although not as in this life. *Gehenna* is a place to which people are specifically sentenced by one person in particular; *Hades* is a place to which people are brought down more impersonally, anonymously. *Hades* has gates, like a city or a house; *Gehenna* is a fire. (Nowhere else in the Bible is a fire described as having gates. Gates in the Bible are for dwelling places, mostly for people, sometimes for animals.)

Gehenna is categorically permanent, the fire is unquenchable, the worm never dies. Note that Jesus did not say that the people never die. It is the destructive power, the worm that eats bodies, the fire that consumes, which is permanent. Jesus does not say that the people never die, but that 'their' worm never dies. It is 'their' worm in the sense that it is there for them, not that it is part of them. (This would be a very strange reference to humans, meaning that we all have a 'worm' part of us. The Bible does not refer to humans in such animal-like derogatory terms.) Jesus means that the power which reduces dead bodies to nothing never dies, likening poetically this power to a worm and a fire. The worm and the fire never die, but the people most assuredly do. *Hades* is not described as permanent in the same way. Moreover the gates of *Hades* will not prevail against Jesus' Church, implying some change when the gates finally give way.

From examining what Jesus said, we come to an important cornerstone conclusion – that Jesus talked of two similar but distinct places for the unrepentant wicked after this life. That this conclusion does not fit with the traditional view of Hell is not our first concern. Instead of putting Jesus' words to one side and holding to the traditional view, we need to put the traditional view to one side and carry on focusing on what Jesus said.

More Relevant Sayings

Jesus spoke at other times about the fate of the wicked without using the words *Gehenna* or *Hades*. These verses are examined next, grouped according to similarity with each other, to see if they confirm or correct the conclusions so far.

I tell you, many will come from east and west and will eat with Abraham and Isaac and Jacob in the kingdom of heaven, while the heirs of the kingdom will be thrown into the outer darkness, where there will be weeping and gnashing of teeth.

Matthew 8:11,12 (The Faithful Centurion; NRSV)

There will be weeping and gnashing of teeth when you see Abraham and Isaac and Jacob and all the prophets in the kingdom of God, and you yourselves thrown out.

Luke 13:28 (NRSV)

Just as the weeds are collected and burned up with fire, so will it be at the end of the age. The Son of Man will send his angels, and they will collect out of his kingdom all causes of sin and all evildoers, and they will throw them into the furnace of fire, where there will be weeping and gnashing of teeth.

Matthew 13:40-42 (the explanation of the parable of the Weeds and Wheat Growing Together; NRSV)

Then the king said to the attendants, "Bind him hand and foot, and throw him into the outer darkness, where there will be weeping and gnashing of teeth."

Matthew 22:13 (the parable of the Guests Invited to the Wedding; NRSV)

But if that wicked slave says to himself, "My master is delayed", and he begins to beat his fellow-slaves, and eats and drinks with drunkards, the master of that slave will come on a day when he does not expect him and at an hour that he does not know. He will cut him in pieces and put him with the hypocrites, where there will be weeping and gnashing of teeth.

Matthew 24:48-51 (NRSV)

As for this worthless slave, throw him into the outer darkness, where there will be weeping and gnashing of teeth.

Matthew 25:30 (the Parable of the Talents; NRSV)

Then he will say to those at his left hand, "You that are accursed, depart from me into the eternal fire prepared for the devil and his angels . . .
And these will go away into eternal punishment, but the righteous into eternal life.

Matthew 25:41,46 (the parable of the Sheep and the Goats; NRSV)

'The outer darkness' is an expression of Jesus which only Matthew has recorded. Three times we read of 'the outer darkness where there will be weeping and gnashing of teeth'. Once we read of 'the eternal fire prepared for the devil and his angels'. These two phrases have no words, nor concepts, in common. The fire is not described as a place of weeping and gnashing of teeth, the outer darkness is not described as prepared for the devil and his angels. In addition we read once of 'the furnace of fire where there will be weeping and gnashing of teeth'. This phrase uniquely brings the two concepts together.

The conclusion so far, from eleven verses, is that *Gehenna* and *Hades* are different places. This is echoed by an apparent distinction in three verses between 'the eternal fire' and 'the outer darkness'. One verse, however, Matthew 13:42, brings together the 'furnace of fire' with 'weeping and gnashing of teeth', maybe indicating one place rather than two. The rich man in *Hades* is also in flames, although these flames do not destroy him, as the fire of *Gehenna* is described as doing.

The fire which Jesus named in other places *Gehenna*, a fire into which people are consigned after a specific judgement, is now shown to be a fire 'prepared for the devil and his angels'. The original purpose of *Gehenna* was therefore not to destroy people but to burn the devil and his angels. We will draw out more of this in Chapter Five. This fire is the place of 'eternal punishment', presumably in contrast to a place of punishment which is not eternal, not of the age to come, but is temporary, of the age before the Final Judgement.

The people who are consigned to the eternal fire prepared for the devil and his angels are clearly the callous, those who have seen the suffering of others and not responded with compassion. The judgement is a judgement against hearts hardened to human suffering, evidenced in doing nothing to relieve suffering. This

Final Judgement is similar to the judgement of the rich man in *Hades* in the parable of the beggar Lazarus, for this rich man's fate was determined by his callousness to the suffering Lazarus. We will also draw out more of this in Chapter Five. But we note that the foundation and cornerstone, as far as we have examined it, shows that judgement is on the basis of response to human suffering.

If the eternal fire prepared for the devil and his angels is *Gehenna* and is distinct from the outer darkness, it is logical to see the outer darkness as *Hades*. As mentioned in Chapter One, if we take the plain meaning of Jesus' words, it is unlikely that a fire will be a place of darkness, certainly not outer darkness. Fire of its nature is bright and light. If Jesus had wanted to convey that the place of weeping and wailing was a fire He would not have called it a place of outer darkness; that would only have caused confusion. If, on the other hand, Jesus wanted to convey or indicate, for those who had ears to hear, that He was talking about two distinct places, it would be natural to describe one as darkness and one as fire, knowing that, in the lives of His hearers, darkness and fire may occur close to each other but are separate.[1]

'The outer darkness where there will be weeping and gnashing of teeth' echoes closely what we know already know about *Hades*. There is no sense that people in this darkness are destroyed, no more than the rich man had been destroyed in *Hades*. But in the darkness people are in anguish, as the rich man was in anguish in *Hades*. The darkness is 'outer', far removed, similar to the rich man being far removed, beyond a great chasm from Abraham. The place where there is weeping and gnashing of teeth is a place where people will see Abraham, Isaac and Jacob, as the rich man in *Hades* saw Abraham. The place which Jesus named *Hades* / *Sheol* is now shown to be a place where people weep and gnash their teeth.

Matthew also records Jesus talking of the unfaithful servant weeping and gnashing teeth in company with the hypocrites, after having been 'cut in pieces'. It is hard to know exactly what to make of this unique phrase other than this man suffers some human physical capital punishment which ensures his place in *Hades*.

[1] 'fire and darkness exclude each other', John Stott, *Essentials*, p. 314.

Matthew, as we have already noted, also once records Jesus talking of his angels throwing the wicked into 'the furnace of fire where there will be weeping and gnashing of teeth'. This one verse seems to contradict what we have concluded so far about the distinct separate places of *Hades* and *Gehenna*. But this is the only verse pointing to the conjunction of *Gehenna* and *Hades*, in contrast to the many verses which point to their distinction. We generally base our understanding on the message of the majority of the Gospel verses, from which we are led to believe that *Hades* and *Gehenna* are not two different names for the same place but two similar, but different, places.

It could also be that the weeping and gnashing of teeth in the furnace of fire is very short-lived. In the time that people are conscious before they are destroyed by the eternal fire of *Gehenna*, they weep and gnash their teeth as people do in *Hades*. This verse may be used to argue that *Hades and Gehenna* are the same place, but may also be explained as consistent with the other verses which describe *Hades* and *Gehenna* as different places.

Destruction

As well as talking of *Gehenna* and *Hades,* the eternal fire and the outer darkness, Jesus used other words referring to the fate beyond death of the unrepentant wicked. Jesus warned about possible destruction:

'Enter through the narrow gate; for the gate is wide and the road is easy that leads to destruction, and there are many who take it. For the gate is narrow and the road is hard that leads to life, and there are few who find it.

Matthew 7:13,14 (NRSV)

We know already that *Gehenna* is the place of destruction. To this is added the sobering thought that 'many' may end in that place prepared not for them, but for the devil and his angels. However we must beware of reading too much into this saying. Jesus says that many are on the road that leads to destruction. He does not specifically say that many follow that road to the very end, to the destruction.

Jesus also used the picture of a tree being destroyed:

A good tree cannot bear bad fruit, nor can a bad tree bear good fruit. Every tree that does not bear good fruit is cut down and thrown into the fire.

Matthew 7:18,19 (similar to Luke 13:6-9; NRSV)

Even now the axe is lying at the root of the trees; every tree therefore that does not bear good fruit is cut down and thrown into the fire. I baptize you with water for repentance, but one who is more powerful than I is coming after me; I am not worthy to carry his sandals. He will baptize you with the Holy Spirit and fire. His winnowing-fork is in his hand, and he will clear his threshing-floor and will gather his wheat into the granary; but the chaff he will burn with unquenchable fire.

Matthew 3:10,12 (NRSV)

If there is any doubt about whether the tree is destroyed or whether it continues to smoulder, this doubt is removed by the parallel picture of chaff. Chaff does not smoulder. It is quickly burnt up leaving no remains.

Jesus also spoke in terms of a building being destroyed:

Not everyone who says to me, "Lord, Lord", will enter the kingdom of heaven, but only one who does the will of my Father in heaven. On that day many will say to me, "Lord, Lord, did we not prophesy in your name, and cast out demons in your name, and do many deeds of power in your name?" Then I will declare to them, "I never knew you; go away from me, you evildoers." Everyone then who hears these words of mine and acts on them will be like a wise man who built his house on rock. The rain fell, the floods came, and the winds blew and beat on that house, but it did not fall, because it had been founded on rock. And everyone who hears these words of mine and does not act on them will be like a foolish man who built his house on sand. The rain fell, and the floods came, and the winds blew and beat against that house, and it fell - and great was its fall!

Matthew 7:21-27 (NRSV)

The fall of the house is not a minor, repairable, event, but specifically a 'great' fall. In the parallel passage in Luke the house is described as fallen in 'great ruin'.[2] The house in not merely

[2] Luke 6:49 (NRSV).

ruined, never to serve as a house again, but is in 'great ruin' indicating even more thorough destruction.

The Fate of the Wicked

In Matthew 7, Jesus also makes clear that what causes the house to fall is not acting on His words. The foolish man, it seems, believes in Jesus enough to hear His words. It is not his belief or otherwise which determines the fall of his house. His behaviour, not putting into practice the teaching of Jesus, rather than his unbelief, causes his house to fall. The people Jesus talks of immediately before are similar. They believe in Jesus enough to prophesy, cast out demons and do many works of power in Jesus' name. Jesus sends them away from him, not as unbelievers, but as evildoers. It is possible to have a strong belief in Jesus, but still to be an 'evildoer'. In the end it is the doing of evil, or not doing the will of Jesus' Father, rather than believing in Jesus, that is more important.

The same message comes from the parable of the talents.[3] All the servants who have been given money believe their master to be real and alive, and they all believe that this master will return. Their belief is correct. But the one who is judged is the one who, believing correctly in the return, hid the money and did nothing with it. His fault, again, was in his behaviour, not his belief.

The parable of the wicked tenants has a similar message.[4] The wicked tenants believe that their landlord is real and alive. They believe that the son, whom the landlord eventually sends, is indeed the son. This is specifically their reason for killing him. Their belief is correct, but their actions are clearly evil.

Jesus states starkly that human behaviour, not human belief is what is reckoned at the Final Judgement:

'For the Son of Man is to come with his angels in the glory of his Father, and then he will repay everyone for what has been done.

Matthew 16:27 (NRSV)

The deeds on which we are to be judged include the words we say:

[3] Matthew 25:14–30 and Luke 19:12–27 (NRSV).

[4] Mark 12:1–11, Matthew 25:14–30, Luke 20:9–18 (NRSV).

I tell you, on the day of judgement you will have to give an account for every careless word you utter; for by your words you will be justified, and by your words you will be condemned.

Matthew 12:36 (NRSV)

Careless words are the same as careless deeds. Careless, hurtful, words spoken to other people matter for eternity, as much as careless religious words.

Jesus described judgement coming on people as at the flood and as on Sodom and Gomorrah. In Genesis it is clear that what caused God to send the flood was not the unbelief of the people but their wickedness.[5] Jesus also explained more about the outcome of judgement for those whose deeds have been wicked.

Just as it was in the days of Noah, so too it will be in the days of the Son of Man. They were eating and drinking, and marrying and being given in marriage, until the day Noah entered the ark, and the flood came and destroyed all of them.
Likewise, just as it was in the days of Lot: they were eating and drinking, buying and selling, planting and building, but on the day that Lot left Sodom, it rained fire and sulphur from heaven and destroyed all of them. It will be like that on the day that the Son of Man is revealed.

Luke 17:26-30 (parallel: Matthew 24:38,39; NRSV)

The destruction of the wicked which Jesus talked of is of the same order as the destruction of the flood or of Sodom and Gomorrah. This was a total destruction, a death which left not a trace behind. The people before the flood and in Sodom and Gomorrah were annihilated – reduced to nothing, leaving no evidence that they had ever existed. In Jesus' time and today no-one knows where Sodom and Gomorrah were.

Appolumi

The Greek word translated 'destroy' is *appolumi.* The same word is translated in other places 'perish'. From what we have seen, for Jesus destruction/perishing is akin to what happened in the flood and to Sodom and Gomorrah – annihilation. The people who were drowned in the flood or burnt in the fire from heaven did not continue to live in some way or in some part. The traditional

[5] Genesis 6:5 (NRSV).

understanding of Hell is based in the idea that people's souls do continue to live eternally. It has therefore been argued that *appolumi* does not mean to be annihilated but to be punished without ceasing to exist. This debate is to be kept in mind as we continue to examine how the Gospels show Jesus using the word *appolumi.* The English word translating *appolumi* is in italics.

For God so loved the world that he gave his only Son, so that everyone who believes in him may not *perish* but may have eternal life.
Indeed, God did not send the Son into the world to condemn the world, but in order that the world might be saved through him. Those who believe in him are not condemned; but those who do not believe are condemned already, because they have not believed in the name of the only Son of God.
And this is the judgement, that the light has come into the world, and people loved darkness rather than light because their deeds were evil. For all who do evil hate the light and do not come to the light, so that their deeds may not be exposed. But those who do what is true come to the light, so that it may be clearly seen that their deeds have been done in God.

John 3:16-21 (NRSV)

This is the most well known statement of Jesus about the fate of the wicked being that they 'perish'. 'Perishing' is in opposition to 'having eternal life'. The usual opposite of life is death, or destruction. The warning is the same as that given in Matthew 10:28 about body and soul being 'destroyed' in *Gehenna.* Here too the judgement which determines whether someone lives eternally or is destroyed is on the basis of 'evil deeds'. Jesus is less specific here, but it is clear that the reason for 'perishing' is wicked, callous, hard-hearted behaviour.

To this understanding is added the teaching that believing in Jesus saves people from being condemned on account of their evil deeds. People who can welcome the light in Jesus for what it is (John has described it earlier as 'the glory of the only Son from the Father, full of grace and truth'; John 1:14; NRSV) are delivered from condemnation. They are willing for their deeds to be shown openly in order to see where exactly they need forgiveness. They trust that the light is a kind light. Those who refuse to welcome that light of truth, showing the evil of their deeds, are condemned.

Their opportunity to escape the consequences of their evil deeds is lost because they do not believe that the light of truth is also and primarily the light of grace, the light of a Son more than the light of a judge. Judgement is shown to be more complex. The basis is still evil deeds, but belief or unbelief in Jesus as God's Son either nullifies or confirms that judgement.

The same truth is conveyed later in John's Gospel:

Again he said to them, 'I am going away, and you will search for me, but you will die in your sin. Where I am going, you cannot come.'
Then the Jews said, 'Is he going to kill himself? Is that what he means by saying, "Where I am going, you cannot come"?'
He said to them, 'You are from below, I am from above; you are of this world, I am not of this world. I told you that you would die in your sins, for you will die in your sins unless you believe that I am he.

John 8:21-24 (NRSV)

Very truly, I tell you, the hour is coming, and is now here, when the dead will hear the voice of the Son of God, and those who hear will live. For just as the Father has life in himself, so he has granted the Son also to have life in himself; and he has given him authority to execute judgement, because he is the Son of Man. Do not be astonished at this; for the hour is coming when all who are in their graves will hear his voice and will come out - those who have done good, to the resurrection of life, and those who have done evil, to the resurrection of condemnation.

John 5:25-29 (NRSV)

Here too Jesus is very clear that the Final Judgement by the Son of Man is on the basis of whether people have done good or done evil. But there is an opportunity, through the grace of the Father, not to die in our sins, but to have our sins forgiven by Jesus before death. For this to happen we have to believe that He truly is the Son of God, coming from heaven with the offer of grace and forgiveness. The teaching is the same as in John 3, although the word to describe what happens after judgement is different - people 'die' rather than 'perish'. Dying and perishing (*appolumi*) are shown to be the same.

These words in John's Gospel elaborate what is hinted at in Matthew and Luke where Jesus talks of the people of His time having an opportunity for repentance and forgiveness which will apply to the Final Judgement:

The people of Nineveh will rise up at the judgement with this generation and condemn it, because they repented at the proclamation of Jonah, and see, something greater than Jonah is here! The queen of the South will rise up at the judgement with this generation and condemn it, because she came from the ends of the earth to listen to the wisdom of Solomon, and see, something greater than Solomon is here!

Matthew 12:41,42 (also in Luke 11:31, 32 NRSV)

Those who fail to take the opportunity to repent in this life will have to face judgement with calls for their condemnation. In these verses there is no description of what happens after condemnation: destruction / perishing / death.

Jesus' use of *appolumi* bears further exploration.

Then Jesus said to him, 'Put your sword back into its place; for all who take the sword *will perish* by the sword.

Matthew 26:52 (NRSV)

To perish is to suffer the fate of those dealt with by a sword: death.

At that very time there were some present who told him about the Galileans whose blood Pilate had mingled with their sacrifices. He asked them, 'Do you think that because these Galileans suffered in this way they were worse sinners than all other Galileans? No, I tell you; but unless you repent, you will all *perish* as they did.
Or those eighteen who were killed when the tower of Siloam fell on them - do you think that they were worse offenders than all the others living in Jerusalem? No, I tell you; but unless you repent, you will all *perish* just as they did.'

Luke 13:1-5 (NRSV)

Again perishing is equivalent to death.

You will be betrayed even by parents and brothers, by relatives and friends; and they will put some of you to death. You will be hated by all because of my name. But not a hair of your head will *perish*. By your endurance you will gain your souls.

Luke 21:16-19 (NRSV)

Perishing here is contrasted with death. Some of those faithful to Jesus will be put to death but not even one hair will perish. Death will come, but not the destruction of body and soul in *Gehenna.*

My sheep hear my voice. I know them, and they follow me. I give them eternal life, and they will never *perish*. No one will snatch them out of my hand.

John 10:27 (NRSV)

Perishing seems to be 'eternal death', as opposed to eternal life, held in Jesus' hand.

In other verses in John's Gospel Jesus also speaks about the 'eternal life' which is available through him, in contrast to 'death'.[6] There is no difference between Jesus' talk of 'perishing/destruction' and 'death'.

Very truly, I tell you, anyone who hears my word and believes him who sent me has eternal life, and does not come under judgement, but has passed from death to life.

John 5:24 (NRSV)

This is the bread that comes down from heaven, so that one may eat of it and not die.

John 6:50 (NRSV)

In Luke's Gospel also we read of Jesus promising life to a rich young man who lives according to what Jesus has said:

And he said to him, 'You have given the right answer; do this, and you will live.'

Luke 10:28 (NRSV)

The implication, as in John's Gospel, is that, if the man does not do what he has said, he will die. This cannot be the death of the body. The life that Jesus promises is not the life that he has already, for the man is clearly currently alive. The life that Jesus promises is called in John's Gospel 'eternal life', as opposed to eternal, irrevocable, death.

The examination so far of the use of the word *appolumi* in the Gospels shows that it is equivalent to dying, a death so thorough that there is no trace left. The same word is used of Herod searching for the child Jesus to destroy Him (Matthew 2:13), by the hearers of the parable of the vineyard who expect the owner

[6] 'Eternal life' is also promised to those loyal to Jesus in Mark 10:30.

to put those who killed his son to death. (Matthew 21:41, Mark 12:9, Luke 20:16) and by Matthew describing the crowd's request to have Jesus killed (Matthew 22:20). In Mark *appolumi* is used by an unclean spirit asking Jesus if He had come to 'destroy' it (Mark 1:24, Luke 4:34), to describe what an unclean spirit tries to do to a child by pushing him into fire or water (Mark 9:10), and to describe the Pharisees and Herodians conspiring how to destroy or kill Jesus (Mark 3:6, 11:18, Luke 19:47). In John, Jesus describes the thief coming not only to steal and to kill but also to destroy – a*ppolumi.* These uses confirm that *appolumi* means to be destroyed, annihilated. *Appolumi* nowhere means to be punished or tormented.

It has been argued, however, by supporters of the traditional doctrine of Hell, that when Jesus used the word 'perishing' He meant instead 'continuing to exist but in terrible and unending torment'. *Appolumi* is the verb translated as 'lost' with regard to the Lost Sheep, the Lost Coin and the Prodigal Son in Luke 15. The sheep, the coin, and the son continued to exist throughout their respective story. They were lost in that they were separated from their owner or parent. In a similar way, it is argued, those in Hell have cut themselves off from God for ever, while continuing to exist. (This argument is weakened by the parallel the father makes between his son being 'dead' and 'lost': 'he was *lost* and is found, was dead and is alive'; Luke 15:32).

Appolumi is also translated 'lost' elsewhere:

For those who want to save their life will *lose* it, and those who *lose* their life for my sake and for the sake of the gospel will save it.

Mark 8:35 (also in Matthew 10:39, 16:25; Luke 9:24,25, 17:33; John 12:25; NRSV)

For truly I tell you, whoever gives you a cup of water to drink because you bear the name of Christ will by no means *lose* the reward.

Mark 9:41 (as also in Matthew 10:42; NRSV)

And this is the will of him who sent me, that I should *lose* nothing of all he has given me, but raise it up on the last day.

John 6:39 (NRSV)

This was to fulfill the word that he had spoken, 'I did not *lose* a single one of those whom you gave me.

John 18:9 (NRSV)

The 'losing' described here is clearly connected with death, in contrast to the eternal life which begins in the resurrection. This is not a temporary losing of something which can then be recovered. The thing 'lost' could be consigned to an irretrievable place, or it could also be destroyed. Given the other usages of *appolumi,* the latter is more likely. *Appolumi* could, in these instances, also be translated 'destroy': 'For those who want to save their life will have it destroyed, and those who destroy their life for my sake and for the sake of the gospel will save it.'

As we have seen in the parable of the Rich Man and Lazarus, Jesus spoke of people being 'tormented' in Hades. Jesus clearly could have used this word more, but nowhere else does He use it. 'Torment' is only spoken of by unclean spirits:

When he came to the other side, to the country of the Gadarenes, two demoniacs coming out of the tombs met him. They were so fierce that no one could pass that way. Suddenly they shouted, 'What have you to do with us, Son of God? Have you come here to torment us before the time?'

Matthew 8:28,29 (and parallels; NRSV)

The unclean spirits express their understanding that Jesus' role is to torment them at 'the time'. We must be wary of drawing conclusions from what unclean spirits say, for they are the minions of the 'father of lies'[7] and therefore habitually lie. It could be that their referring to Jesus tormenting them is a lie designed to make people afraid that there is a hidden, tormenting, side to Jesus. The unclean spirits do not agree about torment being their destiny, elsewhere saying:

'Let us alone! What have you to do with us, Jesus of Nazareth? Have you come to destroy us? I know who you are, the Holy One of God.'

Luke 4:34 (NRSV)

It could be that each unclean spirit lies in its own way. If the talk of torment, however, is not a lie, it seems that Jesus can and will

[7] John 8:44.

torment unclean spirits, or demons. This, however, says nothing about how Jesus treats humans, who are a different order of creation. Whatever happens to unclean spirits, humans are treated differently.

Elsewhere in the New Testament there is another Greek word translated 'destroy' – *phtheiro*.

If anyone destroys God's temple, God will destroy that person. For God's temple is holy, and you are that temple.

1 Corinthians 3:17 (NRSV)

Some translations translate *phtheiro* in relation to God's temple as 'defile'. It is also translated 'mar or corrupt'. A more thorough version of the same word is *diaphtheiro*, which can be translated 'mar or thoroughly corrupt' (Revelation 8:9, 11:18; Young's Concordance). Here is a word which can mean 'to be become so thoroughly corrupt that it ceases to be what it was, although still existing in some way'. The Gospel writers never use this word to describe Jesus' teaching about the fate of the unrepentant wicked. If they, and the Jesus who inspired them, wanted to convey that the unrepentant wicked continue to exist, painfully, in the fire, this word was available. They chose to use different words, words meaning ceasing to exist, leaving no trace behind, dying and being destroyed, annihilated.

The teaching of Jesus in the Gospels is that the unrepentant wicked who come to the Final Judgement will be destroyed, body and soul, in the fire *Gehenna*. Nowhere does Jesus say that people, souls, continue to exist in this fire. This teaching is in marked contrast with the teaching of the Koran, where Hell is repeatedly described as a fire for the unbelievers who 'shall dwell therein' (Surah 2:39, 81, 162, 217, 257, 275). If Jesus had wanted to convey that people, souls, exist eternally in *Gehenna,* He could easily have done so, but did not. Jesus did convey that people continue to exist, to think, feel and talk in *Hades* but as we have seen, for Jesus *Hades* is not the same place as *Gehenna*.

Eternal Punishment

Gehenna is 'eternal punishment' following judgement.[8] This seems to be contrasted with the 'not eternal' punishment of *Hades.* The Greek word translated 'eternal', *aionios,* can also mean, 'of the age to come'. The age to come is the eternal age, the age beyond the return and judgement of Jesus when there will be no more death. *Gehenna* is the punishment of the age to come, that is, irreversible destruction. *Hades* is the punishment of the age before judgement although beyond death. *Hades* is a remand prison for people awaiting trial. Some people have argued, however, that 'eternal' punishment must mean 'eternal consciousness of punishment', or that the 'punishment of the age to come' must mean 'punishment of which people are conscious throughout the age to come'. But there is no Scriptural basis for the argument. The rest of what Jesus said about *Gehenna* and about the ultimate fate of the unrepentant wicked indicates not an eternal punishment of torment, but an eternal punishment of destruction.

The Real *Hades*

When *Hades* has not been taken as another name for the one place 'Hell', it has sometimes been taken as a purely fictional place. Jesus spoke of *Hades* most graphically in the story of the Rich Man and Lazarus. Because this story is seen as a parable, it has been argued that *Hades* is no more real than the family home in the Parable of the Prodigal Son. We know now that versions of this story were fairly common in the Middle East at the time of Jesus.[9] Perhaps Jesus deliberately chose a fictional story so that people would not think He was teaching that there is a real place called *Hades* beyond death?

The parable of the Rich Man and Lazarus, however, is not the only occasion when Jesus warns of a fate very similar to that of the Rich Man.

[8] Matthew 25:46 (NRSV).

[9] This view has been argued by scholars as diverse as Leroy Froom and Richard Bauckham.

But woe to you who are rich, for you have received your consolation. Woe to you who are full now, for you will be hungry. 'Woe to you who are laughing now, for you will mourn and weep.

Luke 6:24,25 (NRSV)

This saying is not part of a parable, this teaching is not in a fictional form. Here Jesus is warning less graphically of the same fate as the rich man in the story, indicating that this is not a fictional fate.

Someone asked him, 'Lord, will only a few be saved?' He said to them, 'Strive to enter through the narrow door; for many, I tell you, will try to enter and will not be able. When once the owner of the house has got up and shut the door, and you begin to stand outside and to knock at the door, saying, "Lord, open to us", then in reply he will say to you, "I do not know where you come from." Then you will begin to say, "We ate and drank with you, and you taught in our streets."
But he will say, "I do not know where you come from; go away from me, all you evildoers!" There will be weeping and gnashing of teeth when you see Abraham and Isaac and Jacob and all the prophets in the kingdom of God, and you yourselves thrown out. Then people will come from east and west, from north and south, and will eat in the kingdom of God. Indeed, some are last who will be first, and some are first who will be last.'

Luke 13:23-30 (NRSV)

Here too Jesus speaks of His hearers suffering a very similar fate to that of the rich man in the story. These people, seeing Abraham, and others, while they themselves are in great distress are not here fictional characters but the very people to whom Jesus was talking. Their fate described here cannot be a fictional fate, indicating again that the fate of the rich man in the story is not fictional either.

Another argument against drawing conclusions about life beyond death from this parable is that Jesus' 'point' is that we need to care for the poor in this life, or that we need to trust God to right injustice.[10] This argument assumes that in telling this parable Jesus only had one point in mind, and that a complex

[10] This argument has been put forward in their respective commentaries on Luke's Gospel by G. B. Caird and N. Geldenhuys.

point, such as 'care for the poor in this life or you will suffer after this life' is unthinkable as coming from Jesus. The claim that Jesus' parables only had one point is a helpful reaction against the tendency to draw meaning from every tiny detail of every parable, but is also an over-reaction. When Jesus explained the Parable of the Sower, He explained what each type of seed represents in terms of people. He did not explain what His 'main point' was. Was it that we should keep sowing trusting that the harvest we see more than makes up for the lost seed? Or was it that we should take care not to sow on hard, stony or weed-infested soil? Or that we would do well to prepare our ground first? Jesus simply did not say, even when He was explaining His parable. If He had a main point in mind, He would have included it in His explanation. Parables, stories, cannot be reduced to one main point, which is presumably why Jesus told parables. If He had wanted to convey a series of main points He would have only spoken in commands and precepts, which were also part of His teaching.

The parable of the Rich Man and Lazarus can therefore, especially as it was told by the greatest story-teller and most insightful, yet complex, theologian who has ever lived, be understood to shed light on more than one thing. It shows our need to care for the poor and it shows our need to be concerned about how we will fare beyond this life. These concerns are intimately, indeed in the parable inextricably, connected, and we must assume that this was part at least of what Jesus wanted to convey. On other occasions Jesus urged people to maintain both concerns. Jesus' parabolic warning about His hearers suffering the same fate as the rich man cannot have been a fictional, only-for-effect warning. This would not only weaken His main point, but also leave Him open to the accusation of having told a 'white lie'. Jesus did not lie. When He spoke about Hades, including in this parable, He was speaking about truth as He saw it.

First Conclusions

Examining all that Jesus is recorded as saying about the fate of the unrepentant wicked leads to important cornerstone conclusions. Jesus talked of *Gehenna* and of *Hades* referring to two different places. *Gehenna* is the eternal fire of death and destruction for both body and soul following the Final Judgement. *Gehenna* destroys all human life so that there can be no more feeling, thinking or talking. *Hades* is the place of outer darkness, weeping and gnashing of teeth. In *Hades* people continue to feel, think and talk. Jesus nowhere makes explicit the relation of *Gehenna* to *Hades*. Logically, though, it is clear that *Hades* can precede *Gehenna*, but *Gehenna* cannot precede *Hades*. For humans nothing can follow beyond *Gehenna*. It is also clear that people are consigned to *Gehenna* after the Final Judgement by Jesus. It is logical, then, to see *Hades* as preceding the Final Judgement.

The teaching of Jesus about *Hades* and *Gehenna*, described in this chapter, is at odds with traditional teaching about Hell. Given the longevity of the traditional view and the vehemence with which it is supported by some Biblical teachers, we can defer a final conclusion until after we have looked at the rest of the Bible. With the slightly puzzling 'furnace of fire, where there will be weeping and gnashing of teeth' (Matthew 13:42), the argument about *appolumi* meaning 'lost', and some questioning about the meaning of 'eternal', we cannot be categorically certain that we have understood Jesus' teaching correctly. The rest of the Bible should help, as these books are also useful for our instruction (2 Timothy 3:16). Do the Epistles, Revelation, and the Old Testament point us to an understanding of the ultimate fate of the wicked – 'perishing' 'destruction' or 'death' – as being eternal torment or ceasing to exist? And do they point us to a single destination for the unrepentant wicked after death, or to two?

CHAPTER THREE

THE NEW TESTAMENT:

BUILDING UP

For no one can lay any foundation other than the one that has been laid; that foundation is Jesus Christ. Now if anyone builds on the foundation with gold, silver, precious stones, wood, hay, straw - the work of each builder will become visible, for the Day will disclose it, because it will be revealed with fire, and the fire will test what sort of work each has done.

1 Corinthians 3:11-13 (NRSV)

Hades and *Gehenna* in Acts, the Epistles, and Revelation

From Acts to Revelation, the word *Gehenna* is used only once:

So also the tongue is a small member, yet it boasts of great exploits. How great a forest is set ablaze by a small fire! And the tongue is a fire. The tongue is placed among our members as a world of iniquity; it stains the whole body, sets on fire the cycle of nature, and is itself set on fire by *Gehenna.*

James 3:5,6 (NRSV alt.)

For James, *Gehenna* and fire are closely linked. *Gehenna* is a place of fire. As he thinks of fire, he thinks of *Gehenna.* James also implies that the effect of *Gehenna* can be felt in this life, although this implication is not developed. Destruction, rather than torment, is more likely in James' mind, as he gives this warning: the tongue can be destructive, playing with fire. The tongue, and its user, runs the risk of ending in *Gehenna*.

Only James, the brother of Jesus, uses the word *Gehenna.* In the Bible *Gehenna* is a Jesus word, unique to Him. Other New Testament writers did address or refer to the ultimate fate of the unrepentant wicked, as we shall see, but *Gehenna* was not in their vocabulary. Scholars tell us that *Gehenna* was also used by some Jewish writers from about the time of Jesus. *Gehenna* was not a word coined by Jesus, but, for the Christians who wrote the New

Testament, it was an unusual word to use. Tom Wright has argued that a hallmark denoting that a saying attributed to Jesus is authentic is that the words both fit with the general cultural context and are different from the language used by other New Testament writers. Wright calls this the test of double similarity/dissimilarity.[1] *Gehenna* as the actual word spoken by Jesus fits Wright's criteria. *Gehenna* is a Jesus word, part of the foundation and cornerstone that is Jesus. Therefore we Christians need to make sure that the doctrine we construct includes the word *Gehenna* as an integral part of our thinking.

The word *Hades*, also used by Jesus, is also part of our foundation and cornerstone. *Hades* occurs four times in Acts, the Epistles, and Revelation. Firstly early in Acts:

But God raised him up, having freed him from death, because it was impossible for him to be held in its power.
For David says concerning him, "I saw the Lord always before me, for he is at my right hand so that I will not be shaken; therefore my heart was glad, and my tongue rejoiced; moreover, my flesh will live in hope.
For you will not abandon my soul to Hades, or let your Holy One experience corruption. You have made known to me the ways of life; you will make me full of gladness with your presence."
'Fellow Israelites, I may say to you confidently of our ancestor David that he both died and was buried, and his tomb is with us to this day. Since he was a prophet, he knew that God had sworn with an oath to him that he would put one of his descendants on his throne. Foreseeing this, David spoke of the resurrection of the Messiah, saying, "He was not abandoned to Hades, nor did his flesh experience corruption."

Acts 2:24-31 (NRSV)

These words are part of Peter's speech to the crowd on the day of Pentecost. Peter explains that the extraordinary noises they have heard are from God, in fulfilment of a prophecy from Joel, and connected with Jesus, the one who was crucified and raised to life. Peter's understanding, as recorded by Luke, is that Jesus went into death, was captured by death. But God freed Jesus from death, and

[1] N. T. Wright, *Jesus and the Victory of God* (SPCK, 1996), p. 131–133.

raised Jesus to life. Peter equates death with *Hades*, quoting Psalm 16. For Peter death and *Hades* were much the same thing.

In the original Hebrew of Psalm 16, the word used was *Sheol*, the Hebrew word for the place of the dead. In Acts *Hades* is used instead of *Sheol*, indicating clearly that *Hades* is a translation of *Sheol.* We will explore in more detail the use and meaning of *Sheol* in the next chapter. We note for now that Death and *Hades / Sheol* are shown to be inextricably connected. Death is the power that takes people away from life. *Hades / Sheol* is the place of death to which people are taken.

Peter explains that Jesus has been in death, been in *Hades.* Jesus was not held there, He was freed. After a short time in *Hades,* Jesus came out again, soul and, uniquely, body. For Peter, this was the indication that Jesus was indeed the true son of David, Messiah, Jewish King, indicated in the Jewish Scriptures. For us it adds a new element to our understanding of *Hades*: Jesus has been there and come out again. For Jesus at least there was a way out of *Hades.* For Jesus at least, *Hades* was not the end of the story.

The next time we read the word *Hades* is not until Revelation, the last book of the Bible.

When I saw him, I fell at his feet as though dead. But he placed his right hand on me, saying, 'Do not be afraid; I am the first and the last, and the living one. I was dead, and see, I am alive for ever and ever; and I have the keys of Death and of Hades.

Revelation 1:17,18 (NRSV)

John, the writer of Revelation, has described a vision of an unbearably bright human figure, dressed in white and gold, standing among seven golden lampstands, holding seven stars, with a sword coming from his mouth. John calls Him 'one like the Son of Man', using the phrase that Jesus often used in the Gospels to describe Himself. From this, and from what the figure says, it is clear that the figure is Jesus Himself. Not only John, but countless Christians, from that day to this, recognise this figure as Jesus. The words that John records are the words of Jesus. This means that these words also form part of the foundation and cornerstone of our doctrine. The foundation is not 'the words of the Gospels' but 'the words of Jesus'. These words about *Hades*, although not written in the Gospels, are foundational to all our understanding of *Hades*.

Jesus here confirms what Peter has said: He was dead, He is now alive. He has been in the place, the realm, of the dead, and now He has come out. Death and *Hades* are connected; the keys to one are the keys to the other. *Hades* is a place where Jesus has been, as Peter explained at Pentecost. To this is added a striking new insight: Jesus now holds the keys of *Hades.*

Because these words are foundation, cornerstone words we need to hold them high in our thinking, looking to see what other thoughts, concepts fit in with them. A cornerstone idea is an 'odd-shaped' idea, which needs other ideas to fit in with it and make it whole and useful. What we certainly must not do is put this idea to one side and carry on as though it is not there.

Jesus has the keys of *Hades*. Jesus has the authority and the ability to open the gates and doors of *Hades*. Jesus can open the doors and chains which He chooses to open, lock the doors and chains which He chooses to shut, and do this whenever He chooses. Jesus has the authority and ability to go in and out of *Hades.* The way which Jesus took out of *Hades* is not now closed behind Him. It is open whenever He wants it open.

Jesus has already talked about 'the gates of *Hades*' not prevailing against his Church, founded on the rock of Peter and his recognition that Jesus is the Son of God. (Matthew 16:18) Here the picture is of the Church being able to enter *Hades*. The Church is like a besieging army; *Hades* tries to keep the Church out. But the gates of *Hades* will not prevail. Sooner or later those gates will give way and the Church will be able to go in and out of *Hades* at will.

Many commentators have seen this picture of the gates of *Hades* back to front. They talk and write of it as though the powers of *Hades* are besieging the Church, and they will not prevail. They write as though Jesus had talked about the gates of the Church prevailing against the power of the evil one. But this is not what we read in Matthew. The gates are clearly 'the gates of *Hades*'*;* it is the Church which prevails. This means that the Church is trying to gain entry to *Hades. Hades* resists, but the Church prevails. Eventually the Church will have entry and access to *Hades*. It is as though the Christians keep arguing with the gate-keepers of *Hades.* 'You have to let us in.' 'Who says?' asks the gatekeeper. 'Jesus says', proclaim the Christians. 'Who's he to me? What authority does he have here?' 'He's the Son of God. He's the Son of the One who built this place and every place in the first place. He's not just someone with a job to do for a time, even an eternity. He's greater than anyone doing any job. He's The Son. He always has been and always will be. He has authority everywhere. And He says "Open up to us". You have to do it.' To this the gatekeeper of *Hades* can make no further reply. He has to open the gate.

Revelation 1 confirms and explains the picture of Matthew 16. Jesus has the keys of *Hades*. He can give those keys to anyone He trusts, to anyone who sees clearly who He is, what His ministry is, and will cooperate faithfully in that ministry. The gates of *Hades* have not prevailed against Jesus. God, His Father, has brought Him out. The powers of *Hades* wanted to keep Jesus there, but they did not prevail. The gates of *Hades* will never prevail against Jesus. He has the keys. The gates of *Hades* will not prevail against Jesus' 'called-out ones', His Church. They know that Jesus has the keys. He has told them. They can use this knowledge as Jesus directs. They can use His keys with Him and for Him. The gates of *Hades* are powerless, useless against Jesus and His Church. The ability to keep people in *Hades* or to free people from *Hades* now rests with Jesus and His Church. We will explore more of this later, in chapters Five and Eight, building on this foundation. So far we have taken the foundation, the cornerstone, that comes from Jesus, examined it, and begun to set it in place.

The third place where we read the word *Hades* is a little later in Revelation:

> When He opened the fourth seal, I heard the voice of the fourth living creature call out, 'Come!'
> I looked and there was a pale green horse! Its rider's name was Death, and *Hades* followed with him; they were given authority over a fourth of the earth, to kill with sword, famine, and pestilence, and by the wild animals of the earth.
>
> *Revelation 6:7,8 (NRSV)*

Within Revelation we read descriptions of several series of visionary events, each one numbered. Chapter 6 describes the opening of six seals out of a total of seven seals which the Lamb has been declared worthy to open. The opening of each seal brings a different kind of disaster upon the earth. After the opening of the sixth seal, we read that the great day of wrath, of judgement, has come. The fourth seal, therefore, is before that final wrath, Final Judgement. The opening of the fourth seal releases *Hades* to accompany Death in killing a fourth of the earth.

Revelation 6 confirms that *Hades* and Death are inextricably linked. As Death takes away life from people in this life, *Hades* follows close behind. The influence of the place of Death is felt in the midst of this life. Death and *Hades* are twin realities of life as we know it, life in this age. *Hades* is active before the Final Judgement.

The power of Death and *Hades* is, however, limited and controlled by the Lamb, by Jesus. Death and *Hades* cannot come fully out onto the earth until the Lamb breaks the seal and the order is given: 'Come!' Death and *Hades* are given limited authority by the Lamb. Three-quarters of humanity are safe from their influence. They have to operate within the bounds set by Jesus.

Jesus not only has the keys of *Hades,* He has authority over the whole of *Hades.* Jesus limits the number of people whom *Hades* can capture. That captivity is itself limited because Jesus and His Church have the right of entry and exit. Jesus allows *Hades* to capture a quarter of the people of earth, knowing that He has the keys. People will be captured by *Hades,* but there is and there will be a way out for them through Jesus. The 'victory' of Death and *Hades* is terrible and painful, but it has indeed lost its ultimate sting.

Hades is named for the fourth and final time near the end of Revelation.

Then I saw a great white throne and the one who sat on it; the earth and the heaven fled from his presence, and no place was found for them. And I saw the dead, great and small, standing before the throne, and books were opened. Also another book was opened, the book of life. And the dead were judged according to their works, as recorded in the books. And the sea gave up the dead that were in it, Death and Hades gave up the dead that were in them, and all were judged according to what they had done.
Then Death and Hades were thrown into the lake of fire. This is the second death, the lake of fire; and anyone whose name was

not found written in the book of life was thrown into the lake of fire.

Revelation 20:11-15 (NRSV)

Here we have a picture of the Final Judgement. Everyone who has been in *Hades* now comes out to be judged according to what they have done. *Hades* is confirmed as being the great remand prison, a holding place prior to trial and judgement. In the end, everyone comes out of *Hades*. *Hades* is emptied of all its human occupants. The remand prison has served its purpose and now all the prisoners are transferred to the court, for judgement.

Hades, along with Death, is then thrown into the lake of fire. The remand prison has fulfilled its horrific purpose and has no more use. *Hades* itself comes to a complete and final end. *Hades* is contaminated irrevocably by all the uncleanness of its inhabitants, and by the willingness with which it fulfilled its gruesome task. It is guilty through its association with Death, the great enemy of Life and of the author of life. *Hades* is consigned to the fire. Whether *Hades* continues to exist in the fire we do not know. Whether *Hades* is ultimately purified in the fire or whether *Hades* is consumed by the fire, we are not told. The impression given is that this is the end of *Hades*. It has outlived its purpose. Like a flea-ridden, blood-stained, concentration camp barracks shack, is only fit for the fire.

Hades is not eternal in the sense that it exists and will exist for ever. *Hades* is not of this age, this era, and it remains in existence immeasurably longer than any human life. But, in the end, *Hades* will be emptied and consigned to the lake of fire. Life will carry on but without *Hades*.

What, then, is the lake of fire? From all that we know already, we recognise here a picture of the eternal fire or furnace to which Jesus gave the name *Gehenna*. *Hades* comes to an end, the fire remains. *Hades* has served its purpose, *Gehenna* is now coming into its purpose. *Hades* and *Gehenna* are not two names for the same place; they cannot possibly be. *Hades* and *Gehenna* are two very distinct places.

Jesus said that *Gehenna* was prepared for the devil and his angels. The purpose of *Gehenna* is to deal with the evil one and all that is associated with him, including Death and *Hades*. Revelation gives us a glimpse of *Gehenna* serving this purpose, burning as a lake of fire, ready for when Jesus has decided that the time has come to consign the devil, all his angels and his works, to this fire.

The verse immediately preceding Revelation 20:11 confirms that the lake of fire is primarily for the devil.

And the devil who had deceived them was thrown into the lake of fire and sulphur, where the beast and the false prophet were, and they will be tormented day and night for ever and ever.

Revelation 20:10 (NRSV)

First the devil, the false prophet and the beast are thrown into the fire. This is the primary purpose of the fire: to be the final defeat of the devil. The devil, the false prophet, and the beast are tormented in the fire for ever and ever, or, literally, 'to the ages of ages', 'to the eras of eras'. The fire, we are specifically told, torments the devil and his accomplices. They burn for ever. But this burning, this torment, is not for humans. No humans have been thrown into the fire at this stage. The Final Judgement has not taken place. Humans are dealt with quite differently from the devil and his associates. From elsewhere in Revelation and the Bible, it is clear that the devil and his angels are supernatural beings of a different order to humans. Jesus specifically stated that angels are immortal innately and humans only become immortal like angels if, after the resurrection, 'they are considered worthy of a place in that age.'[2]

The lake of fire, *Gehenna,* is also named here 'the second death'. The first death is the death that we know, the end of human life as we know it, but one that our souls survive while our bodies await resurrection. The second death, beyond the Final Judgement, is the complete and final end of human life, body and soul destroyed in *Gehenna*, as Jesus indicated. The ultimate end of humans who fail the Final Judgement is death, a death more thorough than the death that we know about already. Judgement leads to death, death in the lake of fire prepared for the devil and his angels.

The most sobering message of Revelation 20 is that, after the Final Judgement, some people will also be thrown into the fire of *Gehenna.* Although the purpose of *Gehenna* is not to burn up humans, there will be some people for whom this is their end. These people will be those who have been tried on their deeds

[2] Luke 20:35 (NRSV).

and found guilty. They will have refused every offer of forgiveness. Their names, we are told, will not be found written in the book of life. We cannot be certain exactly what this book of life means. It seems to be a record of the living. All who have lived have their names recorded in this book. But there will be some who have so lived that their names are no longer found there. They have rejected life, rejected the giver of life, and rejected the redeemer of life. What they have done has caused their names to be deleted from the book of life.

What people have done is the great, indeed the only, criterion, at the Final Judgement. 'The dead were judged according to their works' (v.12), 'All were judged according to what they had done' (v.13). The repetition drives the point home. Final Judgement is according to what we have done. Final Judgement is not according to what we have believed. We will not be judged according to which religion we have followed, but according to what we have done.

Revelation 20 here confirms what we have read already in the Gospels. The sheep and the goats are separated according to what they have done for the poor, the naked, the imprisoned. It is not those who say to Jesus, 'Lord, Lord' who have eternal life, but those who do in practice what His Father wants. The light of Jesus, the light which is Jesus, shows up people's deeds. If they avoid that light, they do not want their deeds to be seen openly. By fleeing from the light they show that their deeds are evil and that they are not facing them nor asking for forgiveness; they are 'condemned already' (John 3:17–21). Beginning with Jesus, and throughout the New Testament, the message is clear: all people will be judged according to what they have done.

This does not mean that believing or not believing in Jesus is irrelevant. Those who recognise in Jesus the judge, the light, and the forgiving Son, who welcome Him showing them where they have gone wrong, and who trust that, through His death on the cross, they can and will be forgiven, these people are saved from the Final Judgement. They have already faced the judge. They have already been declared forgiven. The Final Judgement, if they face it at all, will only be a formality. Jesus the judge will say, 'I know you! And you know that you have been forgiven'. We may then say 'and I'm also sorry that I . . . , and that I . . .', for there may be bad deeds which we have not, up until that point, recognised. But we go to meet our maker and judge knowing that we are forgiven and forgivable. We go, having put on the white robes of forgiveness and righteousness which have been given to us. Those who believe in Jesus, who know Jesus, have no fear at all in meeting Him as judge.

Those who do not believe in Jesus, who do not know Him, will have to go through His all-revealing review of their lives, their deeds. They will be judged according to their works. Some will then be thrown into the lake of fire. We do not know who these people will be. In Revelation 20 we are given no clue as to the identity of those whose names were not found written in the book of life. All we know is that this fate, for them, is the consequence of having been finally judged according to their deeds. We are not told how many will be thrown into the lake of fire. Despite John, the writer of Revelation, being a man who provides numbers at every opportunity, the number of those who are thrown into the fire is known only by Jesus. The wording of v.15 gives some impression that those thrown into the lake of fire are not a great number: 'anyone whose name was not found written in the book of life'. Elsewhere in Revelation we read of multitudes and great hosts of people. Here it is 'anyone'. 'Anyone' could be as few as two or three, or could be considerably greater. If this meant a great number, we would expect John to have described them also as a multitude.

This detailed examination of all the specific mentions of *Hades* and *Gehenna* by name from Acts to Revelation has confirmed what we have read in the Gospels:

- *Hades* and *Gehenna* are different, distinct places. *Hades,* in the end, is thrown into *Gehenna*. This is a definite indication that *Hades* and *Gehenna* are not different names for the same place.
- *Hades* serves its purpose before the Final Judgement, *Gehenna* serves its purpose after the Final Judgement. Many people go into *Hades* awaiting Final Judgement. The number of people who go into *Gehenna* is not revealed but is unlikely to be great.
- *Hades,* the place of torment for the rich man who ignored Lazarus, is shown to be not eternal, but a remand prison with an extensive but limited duration. Before the Final Judgement, even now, Jesus has the keys of *Hades,* and limits the power

and scope of *Hades. Gehenna,* the place prepared for the devil and his angels, but also the place of destruction of body and soul, continues beyond the Final Judgement, indeed only comes into its own after the Final Judgement. *Gehenna* is eternal, of the age beyond all ages, the era beyond all eras. *Gehenna* is the place of eternal, irrevocable punishment.

The Fate of the Wicked in Revelation

There is still more that we can learn. The verses where *Hades* and *Gehenna* are specifically named are not the only verses which speak of the fate of the unrepentant wicked. As in the Gospels, from Acts to Revelation we read in other places of judgement and the outcome of that judgement. We turn now to these verses.

Immediately following the throne, the Judgement, the throwing of Death and *Hades* and some people into the lake of fire, all in Revelation 20, we read of a new heaven and a new earth, the holy city, the new Jerusalem, where God is with His people, Death being no more.

And the one who was seated on the throne said, 'See, I am making all things new'. Also he said, 'Write this, for these words are trustworthy and true.'
Then he said to me, 'It is done! I am the Alpha and the Omega, the beginning and the end. To the thirsty I will give water as a gift from the spring of the water of life. Those who conquer will inherit these things, and I will be their God and they will be my children.
But as for the cowardly, the faithless, the polluted, the murderers, the fornicators, the sorcerers, the idolaters, and all liars, their place will be in the lake that burns with fire and sulphur, which is the second death.'

Revelation 21:5-8 (NRSV)

The one seated on the throne, who is the Alpha and Omega, giving the water of life to the thirsty, is clearly Jesus. The words that are spoken are the words of Jesus. Once again, we have here another part of the foundation and cornerstone. Words which are known to be the words of Jesus are as much part of the foundation and cornerstone as the words of Jesus recorded in the Gospels.

The fact that some people will end up in the lake of fire, the second death, is a word of Jesus, a warning of Jesus. Jesus confirms the picture which John has described shortly before, with a little more detail as to who will suffer this fate. Those who are too afraid to face their Final Judgement, who flee from the searching light of Jesus, those who have no faith at all in the God and Father of Jesus and His forgiveness, those who have been made unclean and refuse any notion of being cleaned up, those who have deliberately taken other people's lives, those who have mistreated others as sex objects, those who have tried to manipulate spiritual powers for their own ends, those who have turned away from the true God to give their allegiance elsewhere, those who hold to lies rather than to the truth – all of these who also, even after the Final Judgement, refuse to look for any forgiveness, these people will end up in the lake of fire.

Again, we know the categories of people but we do not know the total number. It could be as few as two in each category, sixteen in all. It could be considerably more. We are not told. Nor are we told here exactly what happens to these people in the lake of fire. We are not told that they will be tormented. When the devil and his accomplices are thrown into this fire, we are told that they will be tormented for ever. If humans will be tormented, like the devil, for ever, we would expect to be told of this, as we are told of the devil. No torment of humans is mentioned. The implication is that humans will not be tormented. They will instead be destroyed, body and soul, as Jesus said in Matthew 12:8.

Reading on in Revelation we see more detail of the holy city Jerusalem. Chapter 21 concludes:

I saw no temple in the city, for its temple is the Lord God the Almighty and the Lamb. And the city has no need of sun or moon to shine on it, for the glory of God is its light, and its lamp is the Lamb. The nations will walk by its light, and the kings of the earth will bring their glory into it. Its gates will never be shut by day - and there will be no night there. People will bring into it the glory and the honour of the nations. But nothing unclean will enter it, nor anyone who practises abomination or falsehood, but only those who are written in the Lamb's book of life.

Revelation 21:22-27 (NRSV)

Again we read that there is to be a final separation of humans. The righteous, the forgiven, the faithful, will be in the city with Jesus.

They will enjoy the light, the presence of Jesus, for ever. The unrighteous, those whose behaviour is abominable, those who persist in lying, will be outside, separated from the light, the presence of Jesus.

This separation is confirmed in Chapter 22:

Then the angel showed me the river of the water of life, bright as crystal, flowing from the throne of God and of the Lamb through the middle of the street of the city. On either side of the river is the tree of life with its twelve kinds of fruit, producing its fruit each month; and the leaves of the tree are for the healing of the nations.
Nothing accursed will be found there any more. But the throne of God and of the Lamb will be in it, and his servants will worship him; they will see his face, and his name will be on their foreheads. And there will be no more night; they need no light of lamp or sun, for the Lord God will be their light, and they will reign for ever and ever.

Revelation 22:1-5 (NRSV)

Blessed are those who wash their robes, so that they will have the right to the tree of life and may enter the city by the gates.
Outside are the dogs and sorcerers and fornicators and murderers and idolaters, and everyone who loves and practises falsehood.
It is I, Jesus, who sent my angel to you with this testimony for the churches. I am the root and the descendant of David, the bright morning star.

Revelation 22:14-16 (NRSV)

The final place of the unrepentant wicked, those who have refused, by their choice, to wash themselves of uncleanness, will be 'outside'. As well as having been thrown into the fire, they are described as being outside the place of eternal life, separated from the life-giver, Jesus. Where Jesus is, they are not.

We have examined Revelation 20 to 22 in detail following on naturally from the last place where *Hades* is specifically named. We now turn to an earlier passage in Revelation which also describes the plight of the unrepentant wicked:

Then another angel, a third, followed them, crying with a loud voice, 'Those who worship the beast and its image, and receive a mark on their foreheads or on their hands, they will also drink

the wine of God's wrath, poured unmixed into the cup of his anger, and they will be tormented with fire and sulphur in the presence of the holy angels and in the presence of the Lamb. And the smoke of their torment goes up for ever and ever. There is no rest day or night for those who worship the beast and its image and for anyone who receives the mark of its name.
Here is a call for the endurance of the saints, those who keep the commandments of God and hold fast to the faith of Jesus. And I heard a voice from heaven saying, 'Write this: Blessed are the dead who from now on die in the Lord'. 'Yes', says the Spirit, 'they will rest from their labours, for their deeds follow them.'

Revelation 14:9-13 (NRSV)

At first glance this passage seems to show people being tormented for ever, and these words have been used as the proof text for the doctrine of hell as eternal torment.[3] A close examination is needed.

In Revelation 14 we read of a series of six angels. The passage we are considering concerns the third angel. Immediately after the third angel we read:

Then I looked, and there was a white cloud, and seated on the cloud was one like the Son of Man, with a golden crown on his head, and a sharp sickle in his hand!
Another angel came out of the temple, calling with a loud voice to the one who sat on the cloud, 'Use your sickle and reap, for the hour to reap has come, because the harvest of the earth is fully ripe'. So the one who sat on the cloud swung his sickle over the earth, and the earth was reaped.

Revelation 14:14-16 (NRSV)

After the third angel comes Jesus and the time of the Final Judgement. The fourth, fifth and sixth angels are part of that judgement process. The third angel comes before the Final Judgement. What happens to people following the cry of the third angel is also before the Final Judgement. The torment described is not the torment of those who have been judged, but the torment of those yet to be judged. The fire and sulphur described is not the

3 'Traditional apologists regularly contend that the plain sense of the text clinches the argument for eternal conscious punishment. Indeed John Wenham concedes that this is 'the most difficult passage that the conditionalist has to deal with': ACUTE, *The Nature of Hell*, p. 82.

fire and sulphur into which those who have been judged are thrown, but a different, if similar, experience.

As well as suffering torment by fire and sulphur, the people described following the third angel are 'in the presence of the holy angels and in the presence of the Lamb' (v.10). The wicked who have gone through the Final Judgement are separated from the presence of Jesus. This separation from Jesus, we have seen, is of the essence of their final fate. Those described as being in Jesus' presence cannot therefore have gone through the Final Judgement. The torment they are in cannot be their final fate for it is a torment which Jesus shares with them.

The smoke of the torment described in Revelation 14:9–13 continues 'for ever and ever', or, literally 'to ages of ages', 'to eras of eras'. The wording here is slightly unique. Everywhere else in the New Testament the Greek used is literally 'to *the* ages of ages'. Here the wording is 'to ages of ages'. This is a slight difference and not one on which a whole case can be based. But it is notable that the expression of the duration of the smoke of the torment is different. It is also notable that it is the smoke which is described as continuing. Smoke can continue to exist for some time after a fire has been put out. The torment itself is not described as continuing 'to ages of ages.'

Those in torment are described as having 'no rest day or night' (v.11). After the Final Judgement, for those in the city, there is no night. It seems that night and day, part of the old heaven and earth, do not continue into the new heaven and earth. Torment which continues day and night is therefore torment which is before the Final Judgement, not after, torment which is not fully eternal.

The revelation of this torment is described in verses 12 and 13 as intended for the endurance of the saints. The purpose of this revelation is not to warn or challenge the wicked, but to encourage the saints. They are to endure through the hard times knowing that the end is not yet here, that their final relief and new beginning are still to come. Again the message is given that all that is described in Revelation 14:9–13 is before the Final Judgement, in the time when *Hades* still exists, when people, especially the wicked, are still in *Hades.*

From all indications, the whole picture described in Revelation 14:9–13 is therefore a picture of *Hades*, not *Gehenna.* This is the same place that Jesus described as the place of the Rich Man who had ignored Jesus, where he was in torment in flames (Luke 16:24). The Greek word used for torment in Revelation 14 is the same word used in Luke 16. Jesus named the place of the Rich Man *Hades.*

Revelation 14:9–13 is not a picture of eternal torment, but of the 'ages long' torment of the wicked in the remand prison of *Hades* as they await the Final Judgement. It appears that in *Hades* the wicked experience a foretaste of the fire of *Gehenna.* This is presumably a warning to them, that they are more than uncomfortably close to this fire. In the flames of *Hades* the Rich Man is made aware that his torment is due to his callousness in life. He responds with concern for his brothers, wanting them to be warned. But he also reveals his continuing lack of sympathy for Lazarus, wanting Lazarus to leave the comfort of Abraham's bosom to serve the Rich Man's desire.[4]

Revelation 14:9–13 gives us a remarkable new insight: those in torment in *Hades* are 'in the presence of the holy angels and of the Lamb'. The Rich Man looked to see Abraham, and saw Lazarus by his side. The Rich Man thought of his brothers who had not yet died. The Rich Man looked to Abraham and was given the insight into why he was being tormented. Looking to his Jewish ancestry, Jewish tradition, he was shown where he had gone wrong. This is the function of the Jewish tradition of the Law. But knowing where we have gone wrong is of limited use for those for whom it is too late, as is made plain to the Rich Man.

Since Jesus' death and resurrection, we have a new insight into *Hades,* a new development in *Hades,* as described in Revelation 14 – the presence of the Lamb. Those who look to the Lamb do not just gain insight into where they have gone wrong, they see someone with them who can put things right. The Lamb, the Lamb of God who takes away the sins of the world, is with those suffering torment in *Hades.* Until they go through the Final Judgement, Jesus can be with them. It is not too late for them to

[4] See Rob Bell, *Love Wins,* p. 75.

see Him, as the Rich Man saw Abraham, to recognise Him, not a great distance away as Abraham was, but with them.

The Lamb is with those in *Hades* as the one who has the keys of *Hades.* The same one can take their sins away from them and take them out of *Hades.* The truth is all one and the same. The Lamb has angels with Him, indeed it seems that it is the angels who are more noticeable than the Lamb for they are mentioned first. Angels are defined as 'spirits in the divine service, sent to serve for the sake of those who are to inherit salvation' (Hebrews 1:14). The angels serve God's purpose of bringing people to salvation. They are sent to the earth and they are sent also to *Hades.* Where the Lamb has access and goes, where the Lamb is present, the angels go also, serving His purpose of releasing souls from *Hades,* saving from the Final Judgement, and, ultimately, from *Gehenna.*

Revelation does not describe the Lamb saving people from *Hades.* This is a possibility that we can see and deduce from other parts of the Bible. But it remains only a possibility. All we know and can say for certain is that the Lamb and the holy angels are with those in *Hades* or can be with those in *Hades.* Whether those people recognise Him or not, we are not told. Whether they look to Him for help or not, we are not told. Those in torment may see His deathly wounds and innocent blood stains and respond in sympathy towards Him as did one thief on the cross. They may dismiss and deride 'that bloody lamb', like the other thief on the cross. However they respond, He is still with them. They are indeed in torment but 'in the presence of the holy angels and of the Lamb.'

The whole picture of *Hades* in Revelation is remarkable and wonderful and contrary to what has traditionally been taught about hell.

The Fate of the Wicked in the Epistles

Peter

Turning to the rest of the New Testament, we find one place where 'hell' is specifically mentioned in English versions, although the Greek word used is neither *Hades* nor *Gehenna*:

For if God did not spare the angels when they sinned, but cast them into *Tartaros* and committed them to chains of deepest darkness to be kept until the judgement;

2 Peter 2:4 (NRSV)

This *Tartaros* is a place like *Hades*, a remand prison for those awaiting the Final Judgement, but it is for angels, not humans. Perhaps it is a separate place, perhaps it is a specific section of *Hades* for angels. We cannot say. We do know that *Tartaros* is for angels rather than humans, so it will concern us no more.

Peter does write about the fate of humans beyond death:

then the Lord knows how to rescue the godly from trial, and to keep the unrighteous under punishment until the day of judgement - especially those who indulge their flesh in depraved lust, and who despise authority. Bold and wilful, they are not afraid to slander the glorious ones.

2 Peter 2:9,10 (NRSV)

Here too we read of punishment before the day of judgement. clearly the punishment, the torment, of *Hades*. Peter goes on to write of the unrighteous in darkness:

These are waterless springs and mists driven by a storm; for them the deepest darkness has been reserved.

2 Peter 2:17 (NRSV)

In the Gospels, Jesus describes darkness as a chief characteristic of *Hades*. Peter also sees the place of punishment until the day of judgement as a place of deepest darkness.

Peter also writes of the wicked being destroyed:

But false prophets also arose among the people, just as there will be false teachers among you, who will secretly bring in destructive opinions. They will even deny the Master who bought them - bringing swift destruction on themselves.
Even so, many will follow their licentious ways, and because of these teachers the way of truth will be maligned. And in their greed they will exploit you with deceptive words. Their condemnation, pronounced against them long ago, has not been idle, and their destruction is not asleep.

2 Peter 2:1-3 (NRSV)

and if he did not spare the ancient world, even though he saved Noah, a herald of righteousness, with seven others, when he brought a flood on a world of the ungodly;
and if by turning the cities of Sodom and Gomorrah to ashes he condemned them to extinction and made them an example of what is coming to the ungodly;

2 Peter 2:5,6 (NRSV)

These people, however, are like irrational animals, mere creatures of instinct, born to be caught and killed. They slander what they do not understand, and when those creatures are destroyed, they also will be destroyed, suffering the penalty for doing wrong.

2 Peter 2:12,13 (NRSV)

Peter writes of the fate of the wicked in two ways – being kept in punishment and darkness until judgement, and being destroyed, made extinct. These two ways correspond closely to what we already know of the two places *Hades* and *Gehenna*. If Peter is writing about one place for the wicked, he is confused and contradictory. If he is writing with a distinction in his mind between *Hades* before the Final Judgement and *Gehenna* after it, he is clear and understandable. Peter also, following Jesus, states that the flood and the fate of Sodom and Gomorrah are examples of the judgement of God, judgement that leads to obliteration.

Peter also writes of people in prison:

For Christ also suffered for sins once for all, the righteous for the unrighteous, in order to bring you to God. He was put to death in the flesh, but made alive in the spirit, in which also he went and made a proclamation to the spirits in prison, who in former times did not obey, when God waited patiently in the days of Noah, during the building of the ark, in which a few, that is, eight people, were saved through water.

1 Peter 3:18-20 (NRSV)

This echoes Peter's speech in Acts 2, where Luke records him talking of Jesus who had not been abandoned to *Hades* but made alive again by God. The 'prison' is the prison of *Hades* where Jesus, writes Peter, made a proclamation to the human spirits. It seems that here Peter is specifically referring to the spirits of those who died in the flood in Genesis 7. Yet a little further on, Peter widens his scope:

You have already spent enough time in doing what the Gentiles like to do, living in licentiousness, passions, drunkenness, revels, carousing, and lawless idolatry.
They are surprised that you no longer join them in the same excesses of dissipation, and so they blaspheme.
But they will have to give an account to him who stands ready to judge the living and the dead. For this is the reason the gospel was proclaimed even to the dead, so that, though they had been judged in the flesh as everyone is judged, they might live in the spirit as God does.

1 Peter 4:3-6 (NRSV)

Peter describes the gospel as having been proclaimed to the dead, presumably by Jesus when He was in *Hades* before He was raised. Here there is no restriction on which section of the dead this is. What Peter writes is not as extensive as what we read in Revelation about Jesus continuing to hold the keys of *Hades* and continuing to be with those in *Hades,* but there is a strong similarity. In neither Peter's letter, nor in Revelation, do we encounter the concept that those who have died are beyond the reach of Jesus and of the gospel. Quite the opposite: we are told that, in *Hades,* Jesus has the right of access to them, and is present with them.

Hebrews

The concept that those who have died are beyond the redemptive action of Jesus is usually understood to have come from the book of Hebrews:

And just as it is appointed for mortals to die once, and after that the judgement, so Christ, having been offered once to bear the sins of many, will appear a second time, not to deal with sin, but to save those who are eagerly waiting for him.

Hebrews 9:27,28 (NRSV)

These words are often taken to mean that judgement and hell follow immediately after death, but that is adding to their straightforward meaning. What the writer to the Hebrews does affirm is that after dying once, people come to judgement. There is no indication of how immediately or otherwise judgement follows death.[5] Hebrews affirms that the judgement will be the second appearing of Christ, and that those who have been eagerly waiting for Him will be saved. From what we have learnt already from Jesus and the New Testament, we see that between death and the Final Judgement is *Hades* in which people who have died are waiting for Jesus. At this judgement, Jesus confirms and realises the salvation of those who have been eagerly waiting for Him, and confirms and realises the verdict of destruction in the second death for those who have been avoiding Him, refusing to admit their bad deeds. Hebrews 9:27,28 is consistent with this understanding.

The rest of Hebrews is also consistent with the understanding to which we have been led so far:

For if the message declared through angels was valid, and every transgression or disobedience received a just penalty, how can we escape if we neglect so great a salvation? It was declared at first through the Lord, and it was attested to us by those who heard him,

Hebrews 2:2 (NRSV)

We receive a just penalty for all our transgressions and acts of disobedience – for our deeds, not for our right or wrong beliefs in themselves – but we can be saved from this penalty.

Therefore let us go on towards perfection, leaving behind the basic teaching about Christ, and not laying again the foundation: repentance from dead works and faith towards God, instruction about baptisms, laying on of hands, resurrection of the dead, and eternal judgement.

Hebrews 6:1,2 (NRSV)

The fact of judgement which has eternal consequences[6] is a basic part of Christian understanding.

For if we wilfully persist in sin after having received the knowledge of the truth, there no longer remains a sacrifice for

[5] 'While this verse certainly rules out reincarnation, it does not rule out the possibility of intermediate events between death and judgment': Gregory Boyd, *Across the Spectrum: Understanding Issues in Evangelical Theology* (Baker Academic, 2002), p. 188.
[6] A phrase used much by John Stott.

sins, but a fearful prospect of judgement, and a fury of fire that will consume the adversaries.

Hebrews 10:26,27 (NRSV)

The eternal consequence of judgement for the unrepentant wicked is destruction, being consumed in the fire of *Gehenna*. The writer sees the same fire as destroying even the devil.

Since, therefore, the children share flesh and blood, he himself likewise shared the same things, so that through death he might destroy the one who has the power of death, that is, the devil, and free those who all their lives were held in slavery by the fear of death.

Hebrews 2:14,15 (NRSV)

For the writer to the Hebrews, the devil is certainly not the eternal ruler of his hellish domain. The power of the devil to trap people in death, and the fear of death, is forever broken.

Jude

The ultimate destruction of the unrepentant wicked is also taught in the book of Jude:

Now I desire to remind you, though you are fully informed, that the Lord, who once for all saved a people out of the land of Egypt, afterwards destroyed those who did not believe. And the angels who did not keep their own position, but left their proper dwelling, he has kept in eternal chains in deepest darkness for the judgement of the great day.
Likewise, Sodom and Gomorrah and the surrounding cities, which, in the same manner as they, indulged in sexual immorality and pursued unnatural lust, serve as an example by undergoing a punishment of eternal fire.

Jude 1:5-7 (NRSV)

According to Jude, the judgement of Sodom and Gomorrah shows us clearly what the outcome of the Final Judgement for the unrepentant wicked will be like – destruction by eternal fire. As Sodom and Gomorrah were so completely destroyed that no trace of them remained, and no one could say exactly where they had existed, so the wicked will also be destroyed. Jude uses the word *appolumi* in a way similar to Jesus in the Gospels, describing a destructive punishment similar to that brought to Sodom and Gomorrrah.

Jude also writes of the judgement in the same terms as other New Testament writers:

It was also about these that Enoch, in the seventh generation from Adam, prophesied, saying, 'See, the Lord is coming with tens of thousands of his holy ones, to execute judgement on all, and to convict everyone of all the deeds of ungodliness that they have committed in such an ungodly way, and of all the harsh things that ungodly sinners have spoken against him.

Jude 1:14,15 (NRSV)

The Final Judgement is to be by Jesus, at His coming again. Jesus will judge all people on the basis of their deeds, not their beliefs, although these deeds include harsh words spoken against Jesus.

The Gospels and the New Testament writers we have looked at so far present the same picture. The wicked who remain unrepentant through the Final Judgement will be destroyed in the fire which Jesus named *Gehenna.* Before being judged, the wicked will be in *Hades*, a place of torment, of weeping and wailing and gnashing of teeth.

Paul

Paul, in his letters, writes of the same ultimate realities. Here we will summarise his teaching under the various terms he uses. The words highlighted are not unique to Paul, but they are characteristic of him. No other New Testament writer uses quite the same language, language that is consistent through all the letters attributed to Paul.

Jesus will judge all people:

For we will all stand before the judgement seat of God. For it is written, 'As I live, says the Lord, every knee shall bow to me, and every tongue shall give praise to God'. So then, each of us will be accountable to God.

Romans 14:10-12 (NRSV)
See also 1 Corinthians 4:5,2; Corinthians 5:10;
1 Timothy 5:24 (and Acts 17:31 and Acts 24:15)

The unrepentant wicked will experience the wrath of God:

For he will repay according to each one's deeds: to those who by patiently doing good seek for glory and honour and immortality, he will give eternal life; while for those who are self-seeking and who obey not the truth but wickedness, there will be wrath and fury. There will be anguish and distress for everyone who does evil, the Jew first and also the Greek, but glory and honour and peace for everyone who does good, the Jew first and also the Greek. For God shows no partiality.

Romans 2:6-11 (NRSV)
See also Romans 1:18; Ephesians 2:3; Ephesians 5:6; Colossians 3:5,6.

The unrepentant wicked will experience condemnation:

For the judgement following one trespass brought condemnation, but the free gift following many trespasses brings justification.

Romans 5:16 (NRSV)
See also Romans 3:8; Romans 8:1; 1 Corinthians 11:32; 2 Corinthians 3:9

God's wrath against sin, condemnation of sin, leads to death; sin itself brings on death:

just as sin came into the world through one man, and death came through sin, and so death spread to all because all have sinned

Romans 5:12 (NRSV)
See also Romans 1:32; Romans 6:23; Romans 7:5; 1 Corinthians 15:22-26; 1 Corinthians 15:56; 2 Corinthians 3:7-8; 2 Corinthians 7:10; Ephesians 2:1-4; Colossians 2:13

Those who are condemned will be destroyed (Paul uses the word *appolumi* and words associated with it):

when the Lord Jesus is revealed from heaven with his mighty angels in flaming fire, inflicting vengeance on those who do not know God and on those who do not obey the gospel of our Lord Jesus. These will suffer the punishment of eternal destruction, separated from the presence of the Lord and from the glory of his might,

2 Thessalonians 1:7-9 (NRSV)
See also Romans 2:12; Romans 9:22; 1 Corinthians 1:18; 1 Corinthians 10:9,10; Philippians 3:18,19; 2 Thessalonians 2:3, 8-12

In these verses, Paul's focus throughout is on the ultimate fate of the wicked, from which those who have faith in Jesus are saved.

Not once in all his writing does Paul write of torment as the ultimate result of sin. Instead Paul writes consistently using the same interchangeable terms as Jesus in the Gospels: death and destruction.

In these verses too Paul is clear that judging wrath comes to those whose deeds, not beliefs, have been wicked, the death which follows condemnation is caused by sin, not by unbelief or wrong belief. Those who do not believe in Jesus will be judged according to their deeds. He holds out no hope for anyone standing before the judgement seat of Jesus, since all have sinned and fall short of the glory of God.[7] All who have sinned need forgiveness and forgiveness only comes from Jesus. We do nothing to deserve or pay for this forgiveness, we only trust and believe that we are forgiven. We place our faith in the One who has been shown to be Saviour. This dual message, that judgement will be according to deeds not beliefs, and that all need to have faith in Jesus for forgiveness and salvation, is the same message, as we have seen, spoken by Jesus in John's Gospel in slightly different terminology.

Paul also writes of death not being a barrier to the love of God:

For I am convinced that neither death, nor life, nor angels, nor rulers, nor things present, nor things to come, nor powers, norheight, nor depth, nor anything else in all creation, will be able to separate us from the love of God in Christ Jesus our Lord.

Romans 8:38,39 (NRSV)

These verses are a hint that Paul believes that those in *Hades* are still able to be reached by the love of God. If judgement, condemnation, and destruction of the wicked follow on immediately after death, it is hard to understand how death cannot be a barrier to God's love. But if the judgement is preceded by a considerable time when people will still have the opportunity to respond to God's love in Jesus, Paul's words make more sense.

Paul also writes of Jesus having descended to the dead:

Therefore it is said, 'When he ascended on high he made captivity itself a captive; he gave gifts to his people'. (When it

[7] Romans 3:23.

says, 'He ascended', what does it mean but that he had also descended into the lower parts of the earth?)

Ephesians 4:8,9 (NRSV)

The 'lower parts of the earth' cannot refer to areas such as round the Dead Sea which are lower than sea level, nor to the earth below the sea. There is no mention anywhere of Jesus ever having gone to these places. The 'lower parts of the earth' refer instead to the grave, into which people were lowered. These parts of 'the earth', as opposed to 'the heavens', were where people were understood to have gone when they die: *Hades / Sheol.* Paul is referring to the common understanding, voiced by Peter at Pentecost, that Jesus has been in *Hades*.

Paul also seems to link 'the lower parts of the earth' with 'captivity'. This too is consistent with the general Biblical understanding of *Hades* as a place of captivity, captivity to death and sin. But now, writes Paul, through the descent of Jesus, this captivity is now captive. *Hades* is now captive to Jesus. This echoes Jesus' proclamation that He now has the keys of *Hades*: Jesus has locked up the power of *Hades* and made it serve His purposes. From this capturing by Jesus, people receive gifts, Jesus is shown as the gift-giver.

Hades is not the main subject of Paul's writing here, more the subject of a slight digression. But from these verses we can see that Paul's understanding of *Hades,* and the understanding of the people in Ephesus, was consistent with *Hades* being the low place, the place of death, to which Jesus now has the keys.

John the Baptist

If there is any lingering doubt that the ultimate fate of the unrepentant wicked as taught by Jesus and the writers of the New Testament is not annihilation, but a terrible tormented survival, this doubt should be dispelled by the words of John the Baptist, recorded by Matthew and Luke. Although not himself a writer, John the Baptist had and was a significant voice which needs to be heard in this context:

Even now the axe is lying at the root of the trees; every tree therefore that does not bear good fruit is cut down and thrown into the fire.

I baptize you with water for repentance, but one who is more powerful than I is coming after me; I am not worthy to carry his sandals. He will baptize you with the Holy Spirit and fire. His winnowing-fork is in his hand, and he will clear his threshing-floor and will gather his wheat into the granary; but the chaff he will burn with unquenchable fire.

Matthew 3:10-12 (NRSV, parallel to Luke 3:16,17)

John uses the picture of a grain harvest to describe Jesus executing the Final Judgement. The wicked will be burnt like chaff in a fire. Of all the pictures that could be used of the fate of the unrepentant wicked, chaff thrown into the fire is the most vivid picture of annihilation. Coals, candles, smoking tallow, oil wicks, logs, could all be used to express the sense that what is burnt continues to exist in some way. Chaff thrown into a fire flares and disappears completely. So it will be with the wicked in the fire to which Jesus gave the name *Gehenna*.

CHAPTER FOUR

THE OLD TESTAMENT: FURTHER BUILDING

. . . they welcomed the message very eagerly and examined the scriptures every day to see whether these things were so.

Acts 17:11 (NRSV)

We continue looking through the Bible to see if the separate natures of Gehenna and Hades are confirmed, strengthened, developed. We turn to the Old Testament.

Gehenna: Consuming Fire

John the Baptist's picture of the wicked as chaff in the fire of the judgement of Jesus was not an original picture. The wicked as chaff, straw, or stubble is a common picture in the Old Testament. Sometimes the chaff is blown away by God's judgement. Chaff blown away has gone, disappeared, and cannot be found again by the most diligent of human searches. It could, however, be argued that an all-powerful God could gather the chaff again. But in the Old Testament the chaff is also sometimes described as thrown into, consumed by the fire. In the fire the chaff or stubble is completely destroyed and there is absolutely no possibility of it surviving.

In Exodus 15 we hear Moses celebrating God's victory over the Egyptians:

In the greatness of your majesty you overthrew your adversaries; you sent out your fury, it consumed them like stubble.

Exodus 15:7 (NRSV)

In Isaiah it is made plain that the fire of God's judgement against the wicked is all-consuming.

Therefore, as the tongue of fire devours the stubble, and as dry grass sinks down in the flame, so their root will become rotten, and their blossom go up like dust; for they have rejected the instruction of the Lord of hosts, and have despised the word of the Holy One of Israel.

Isaiah 5:24 (NRSV)

See, they are like stubble, the fire consumes them; they cannot deliver themselves from the power of the flame. No coal for warming oneself is this, no fire to sit before!

Isaiah 47:14 (NRSV)

In the last chapter of the Old Testament the picture is confirmed:

See, the day is coming, burning like an oven, when all the arrogant and all evildoers will be stubble; the day that comes shall burn them up, says the Lord of hosts, so that it will leave them neither root nor branch.

Malachi 4:1 (NRSV)

The day which Malachi foresaw is the same day which John the Baptist saw. John saw a little more than Malachi, seeing one who would carry out the threshing and the burning, but the essential picture is the same in the Old Testament as in the New Testament: the ultimate fate of the unrepentant wicked will be that they are burnt up completely in the fire which Jesus named Gehenna.

Many commentators and scholars have failed to make this connection between the consuming fire of *Gehenna* and the fire of judgement in the Old Testament, precisely because the fire of Old Testament judgement is a consuming and not a tormenting fire. A search for Old Testament references to Hell, the tormenting fire, yields nothing. A search for the consuming, annihilating fire yields many references. A search for Old Testament teaching about wicked souls living on in torment is fruitless. A search for the wicked dying a final irrevocable death yields extensive results.

Genesis

The first warning of God's judgement in the Old Testament is very early in Genesis:

And the Lord God commanded the man, 'You may freely eat of every tree of the garden; but of the tree of the knowledge of good and evil you shall not eat, for in the day that you eat of it you shall die.'

Genesis 2:16 (NRSV)

This well-known verse introduces several themes of God's judgement which are later confirmed and expanded.

God does not say specifically here that He will kill Adam and Eve for their disobedience. God actively causing their death could be included in what is warned, but it reads most normally that the death will come as a natural consequence of what Adam and Eve do. The constructor of a nuclear power plant may say to the people who work there, 'If you do not wear protective clothing in this area, you will die'. It is not that the constructor is allowing himself a temper tantrum about his rules being disobeyed, but that there is a very real, lethally dangerous, consequence of not doing what he has said. Although it may be hard to see the similarity between a nuclear reactor and a garden with a particular fruit tree (assumed to be an apple although this is not specified) we are told that there is indeed a mortal danger here which will come as a result of Adam and Eve not doing what God says.

The responsibility, however, for placing such a dangerous tree in front of Adam and Eve is clearly God's. Even if the consequence of the people going their own way is lethal, the judgement can still be described as God's because He set up the consequence. This dual way of looking at judgement, as a consequence of our own actions and as God's doing, continues through the Old Testament.

In Genesis 2 also the consequence of disobedience, the effect of God's judgement is set out: 'You shall die'. In the light of our exploration of the concept of Hell, it is notable that God does not say 'You shall be tormented'. The idea that Adam and Eve will somehow live but in terrible pain, either for ever or for some remedial period, does not appear here. The warning here is that they will forfeit the life that God has given them. The God who has so recently created them is now warning that this life may not continue if they do not follow what He has said. The distinction is clear in Genesis: life created through God's word having been heard and acted upon, and life destroyed through God's word having been heard and disregarded. God wants to give life. He is the life-giver. But people can instead choose death, ceasing to exist. This too is a serious choice, which recurs through the Old Testament: life as opposed to death, not life-in-bliss as opposed to life-in-torment.

Immediately, in Genesis, however, the veracity of the warning of death is questioned. Surely that can't be? Surely God won't simply destroy what He has created!

But the serpent said to the woman, 'You will not die!

Genesis 3:4 (NRSV)

The idea that people will truly die, cease to exist, is challenged as unthinkable. This challenge comes from the creature understood to be a picture of the devil, Satan, the enemy. From the beginning of Genesis we read God explaining that the consequence of disobedience is death, and the devil maintaining that there will be no such consequence.

The idea that human beings, human souls, do not, indeed cannot, die is common in human culture and religion. Most peoples, from the Aztecs to the Egyptians, the Greeks to the Vikings, have believed that humans continue to live in some way after death. It was commonly accepted that these souls of the departed could be cared for by what was placed in their tombs and that they continue to have some influence on this life. The Old Testament is unique in the complete absence of such thinking. In the Old Testament and historic Jewish culture there is no assumption that people live on in some way after they die. Sometimes in the Old Testament there is simply ignorance about the fate of the dead. Sometimes the assumption is that after this life, there is no more. Sometimes, as we shall see, a gloomy half existence is glimpsed beyond death. The Jews have been the only people to live without the common assumption that people will not, cannot, die.

The message of the serpent and the message of the traditional religions of the world is similar: people live on for ever after death in some way. The Old Testament, which has little or no interest in the content of other religions, never makes this connection, but it is a connection which can reasonably be made. As Christians, followers of the Jewish Jesus, we are called to read and respect the Old Testament in its entirety,[1] paying more heed to these

[1] 'Do not think that I have come to abolish the law or the prophets; I have come not to abolish but to fulfill. For truly I tell you, until heaven and earth pass away, not one letter, not one stroke of a letter, will pass from the law until all is accomplished.' Matthew 5:17,18 (NRSV).

Scriptures than to any other human religious texts. It is these Scriptures which bring us God's warning 'You shall die.'

The possibility that Adam and Eve could live on in perpetual rebellion against God is seen by God:

Then the Lord God said, 'See, the man has become like one of us, knowing good and evil; and now, he might reach out his hand and take also from the tree of life, and eat, and live for ever' – therefore the Lord God sent him forth from the garden of Eden, to till the ground from which he was taken.

Genesis 3:22, 23 (NRSV)

This underlines that death is the consequence fully intended by God. If there was a possibility that people could in some way live eternally in disobedience, God has ensured that this possibility is ruled out. There is absolutely no access to the tree of life for Adam, Eve, and all humanity. The warning is carried out and physical death comes into humanity. The serpent is shown to be a liar. Death comes very soon, firstly to the innocent Abel. Adam, Eve and their children eventually die. Whether this is limited to the death of their bodies and not their 'souls' is a question that is not asked. The distinction between body and soul in this way is not an Old Testament distinction.

The death of Abel also shows that whereas death comes through the disobedience of certain people, all people are now vulnerable to death. Death, the consequence of those who disobey God, comes even, and strangely especially, to those who, like Abel, please God. The judgement of death is not affected by a good life or by good worship. Through one man's disobedience all were made mortal. There is now no immortality in the whole of humanity.

Primarily, however, death is seen as God's judgement against the wicked and God's judgement against the wicked is seen to be death.

The Lord saw that the wickedness of humankind was great in the earth, and that every inclination of the thoughts of their hearts was only evil continually. And the Lord was sorry that he had made humankind on the earth, and it grieved him to his heart. So the Lord said, 'I will blot out from the earth the human beings I have created – people together with animals and creeping things and birds of the air, for I am sorry that I have made them.'

Genesis 6:5-7 (NRSV)

These words introduce the story of the great flood and Noah's Ark. The flood destroyed all life, including human life. Humans did not survive in some way in the water. The water did not teach the humans a salutary lesson, it removed them from the face of the earth. They were killed, destroyed, blotted out. The water of judgement, sent as a consequence of the wickedness of humans, was not a tormenting water but an annihilating water.

Noah, the righteous man, and his family did not die in the flood, but as we read on, it is clear that even Noah eventually died. (In the end he too was not entirely blameless.)

The next great picture of God's destroying judgement is the fate of Sodom and Gomorrah.

Then the Lord rained on Sodom and Gomorrah sulphur and fire from the Lord out of heaven; and he overthrew those cities, and all the Plain, and all the inhabitants of the cities, and what grew on the ground.
Abraham went early in the morning to the place where he had stood before the Lord; and he looked down towards Sodom and Gomorrah and towards all the land of the Plain, and saw the smoke of the land going up like the smoke of a furnace.

Genesis 19:24,25,27,28 (NRSV)

Here again there is a clear judgement against wicked people, against whom there has been a vehement and widespread outcry. (Genesis 18:20,21) Not even ten righteous people were found there. God shows surprising willingness to spare the wicked their judgement, going as far as Abraham chooses to push him to avert judgement, and, it seems, He would have gone further if pushed further. But in the end, the wickedness of the people is so deep and widespread that judgement has to come. These people cannot be turned, in the end, into righteous people. The judgement of God brings fire and death; the people are destroyed, the cities are destroyed. For the rest of the Old Testament and even today no-one knows where Sodom and Gomorrah were, so complete was their annihilation.

The flood and the outcome of Sodom and Gomorrah show clearly the fate of the unrepentant wicked: they are not tormented but destroyed. The fire which rained down on Sodom and Gomorrah prefigures the destroying fire of *Gehenna* which Jesus talked of.

> . . . he did not spare the ancient world, even though he saved Noah, a herald of righteousness, with seven others, when he brought a flood on a world of the ungodly; by turning the cities of Sodom and Gomorrah to ashes he condemned them to extinction and made them an example of what is coming to the ungodly;
>
> *2 Peter 2:5,6 (NRSV)*

What we know so far of *Gehenna* is confirmed clearly by Genesis.

Exodus

The wicked in the book of Exodus are firstly the Egyptians, particularly Pharaoh and his soldiers. Their ultimate fate too is to be destroyed, drowned in the sea, a judgement which, as we have seen, Moses likens to their having been burnt up like stubble. Once again, God goes to great lengths to avert judgement, firstly pleading through Moses, then showing the Egyptians His power through a succession of plagues which make their life uncomfortable. Eventually God is pushed to show more clearly what the full consequence of Pharaoh refusing to pay heed to Him is: death. Only one member of each family dies. This is the final plague after which Pharaoh finally accepts God's word. But even then, having let God's people go, Pharaoh sends his army to recapture God's people. His army is destroyed, by God, in the sea.

Throughout all this central drama of the Old Testament there is no hint that God's judgement on the wicked means that they will live in torment. The judgement on the wicked that is described vividly leaves them dead, lifeless, 'not one of them remained' (Exodus 14:28).

Another people who serve in Exodus, and elsewhere, as the epitome of evil are the Amalekites. Their refusal to afford any hospitality to God's people, indeed their attacks on God's people, show that they are implacable enemies. In rejecting the people who carry God's word (literally carrying the stone tablets with the Ten Commandments in the ark of the covenant) they are rejecting the life-giving word and choosing the path of death. In embracing violence as their response to God's people, shedding innocent blood, they show that they are wicked. Of all the other nations among whom the people of Israel travel in Exodus, the Amalekites are the fiercest enemies. What then is to be their fate? Are they to be consigned to a place of torment to suffer for their wickedness? Maybe such torment will eventually purge them of their hatred of God's people?

Then the Lord said to Moses, 'Write this as a reminder in a book and recite it in the hearing of Joshua: I will utterly blot out the remembrance of Amalek from under heaven.'

Exodus 17:14 (NRSV)

The judgment on Amalek is the same as on the wicked world in the time of Noah – being 'blotted out'. This annihilation is so all-encompassing, so complete, that people will not even remember them. It will be as though they had never existed. Such is the God of Israel's judgement on the wicked.

The Law

See, I have set before you today life and prosperity, death and adversity.

If you obey the commandments of the Lord your God that I am commanding you today, by loving the Lord your God, walking in his ways, and observing his commandments, decrees, and ordinances, then you shall live and become numerous, and the Lord your God will bless you in the land that you are entering to possess.

But if your heart turns away and you do not hear, but are led astray to bow down to other gods and serve them, I declare to you today that you shall perish; you shall not live long in the land that you are crossing the Jordan to enter and possess.

I call heaven and earth to witness against you today that I have set before you life and death, blessings and curses. Choose life so that you and your descendants may live, loving the Lord your God, obeying him, and holding fast to him; for that means life to you and length of days, so that you may live in the land that the Lord swore to give to your ancestors, to Abraham, to Isaac, and to Jacob.

Deuteronomy 30:15-20 (NRSV)

Moses here is summing up for the people the importance of the Law, which he has detailed extensively. These are his final words about the Law, the climax of his presentation, the call which, above all else, he wants to leave ringing in the people's ears. 'You have a choice: life or death'. Not 'life in prosperity or life in misery', not 'life in the Promised Land or life in slavery'. The choice is life following what God says, or no life at all. God's judgement on those who choose to ignore His word is death. This applies to the people of Israel and then to all people. Ultimately all who stubbornly, repeatedly, and determinedly ignore God's word for them will cease to exist. The whole Law is summed up in this warning.

The Law pertaining to sacrifices points to the same choice. Forgiveness and life can come to people through the death of the animals. The death which the people have brought on themselves can be transferred to the animals. L. E. Froom writes: 'Indeed, in the entire system of sacrifices, patriarchal and Mosaic, both of which were ordained by God, the substitute victim was never subject to prolonged torture, or imprisonment for life, but was put to death.'[2]

Occupying the Land

The Lord your God himself will cross over before you. He will destroy these nations before you, and you shall dispossess them. Joshua also will cross over before you, as the Lord promised. The Lord will do to them as he did to Sihon and Og, the kings of the Amorites, and to their land, when he destroyed them.

Deuteronomy 31:3,4 (NRSV)

God's judgement is shown, again, to bring death and destruction. God's judgement does not lead to torment, either ongoing, or temporary and purging. This time the judgement is against nations who stood vehemently against the people of Israel as they passed through Sinai, and against nations in Canaan also setting themselves against the newcomers sent from God.

This judgement is seen firstly as solely God's doing, like the destruction of Pharaoh's army, in which the people have no hand. Then, with Joshua, the judgement is further seen as God's doing

[2] L. E. Froom, *The Conditionalist Faith of our Fathers*, vol. 1, p.98.

which He inflicts through His people, through Joshua and his soldiers. People taking the destroying judgement of God into their own hands is probably the most controversial part of the Old Testament. To us today it seems cruel, vindictive, heartless, a far cry from the Jesus who told His followers to love enemies, even from the God who a chapter later says 'vengeance is mine' (Deuteronomy 32:35).

It is not possible now to explore all the implications of the military campaign of Joshua. For our purposes, the important implication is, again, that judgement issues in death and destruction, not slavery and torment. For the peoples of that era, one of the purposes of war was to gain slaves. Slavery was normal, and the chief way a nation acquired slaves was as booty in war. The people of Israel were told that they were not to copy the other nations, especially in this. If the people did take judgement into their own hands, they were to do it in a way similar to their God, the God who never consigns people to a life of endless slavery and torment.

Psalms, Proverbs, and Prophets

The historical books (Judges to Esther) do not so directly address the fate of the wicked. In Psalms, Proverbs and the Prophets there is a clear answer to the question: 'What is the ultimate fate of the unrepentant wicked?' They are destroyed. The following verses are a selection from these books, showing that the judgement of the God of Israel against the wicked means their annihilation.

Wait for the Lord, and keep to his way, and he will exalt you to inherit the land; you will look on the destruction of the wicked.
I have seen the wicked oppressing, and towering like a cedar of Lebanon.
Again I passed by, and they were no more; though I sought them, they could not be found.
Mark the blameless, and behold the upright, for there is posterity for the peaceable. But transgressors shall be altogether destroyed; the posterity of the wicked shall be cut off.

Psalm 37:34-38 (NRSV)

The dullard cannot know, the stupid cannot understand this:
though the wicked sprout like grass and all evildoers flourish,
they are doomed to destruction for ever,

Psalm 92:6,7 (NRSV)

Those who despise the word bring destruction on themselves, but those who respect the commandment will be rewarded.

Proverbs 13:13 (NRSV)

Do not fret because of evildoers. Do not envy the wicked;
for the evil have no future; the lamp of the wicked will go out.

Proverbs 24:19,20 (NRSV)

Wail, for the day of the Lord is near; it will come like destruction from the Almighty!

Isaiah 13:6 (NRSV)

The dead do not live; shades do not rise – because you have punished and destroyed them, and wiped out all memory of them.

Isaiah 26:14 (NRSV)

When you finish reading this scroll, tie a stone to it, and throw it into the middle of the Euphrates, and say, "Thus shall Babylon sink, to rise no more, because of the disasters that I am bringing on her."

Jeremiah 51:63,64 (NRSV)

By the multitude of your iniquities, in the unrighteousness of your trade, you profaned your sanctuaries. So I brought out fire from within you; it consumed you, and I turned you to ashes on the earth in the sight of all who saw you.
All who know you among the peoples are appalled at you; you have come to a dreadful end and shall be no more for ever.

Ezekiel 28:18,19 (NRSV)

Then the iron, the clay, the bronze, the silver, and the gold, were all broken in pieces and became like the chaff of the summer threshing-floors; and the wind carried them away, so that not a trace of them could be found. But the stone that struck the statue became a great mountain and filled the whole earth.

Daniel 2:35 (NRSV)

Alas for the day! For the day of the Lord is near, and as destruction from the Almighty it comes.

Joel 1:15 (NRSV)

The house of Jacob shall be a fire, the house of Joseph a flame, and the house of Esau stubble; they shall burn them and consume them, and there shall be no survivor of the house of Esau; for the Lord has spoken.

Obadiah 1:18 (NRSV)

Why do you plot against the Lord? He will make an end; no adversary will rise up twice. Like thorns they are entangled, like drunkards they are drunk; they are consumed like dry straw.

Nahum 1:9 (NRSV)

Gather together, gather, O shameless nation, before you are driven away like the drifting chaff, before there comes upon you the fierce anger of the Lord, before there comes upon you the day of the Lord's wrath.

Zephaniah 2:1,2 (NRSV)

See, the day is coming, burning like an oven, when all the arrogant and all evildoers will be stubble; the day that comes shall burn them up, says the Lord of hosts, so that it will leave them neither root nor branch.

Malachi 4:1 (also quoted above NRSV)

More verses could be quoted showing that the wrath of the God of Israel is a destroying, not a tormenting wrath. The ultimate fate of the wicked is to be no more, burnt up like straw in a furnace.

Hints of Eternal Torment?

The clear witness of the Old Testament to the ultimate destruction of the wicked has often been ignored by Bible teachers. For instance, Daniel I. Block, Professor of Old Testament Interpretation and Associate Dean at the Southern Baptist Theological Seminary, Louisville, Kentucky, writes, 'What does the Old Testament teach about Hell? The simple answer to this question is, "Very little".'[3] In a book setting out to expound the traditional doctrine of Hell, Block looks in the Old Testament for teaching about the eternal torment of the wicked and finds very little. He pays no attention to the widespread teaching about the ultimate destruction of the wicked.

[3] 'The Old Testament on Hell', in Morgan and Peterson (eds), *Hell under Fire* (Zondervan, 2004), p. 44.

Block then details the 'very little' in the Old Testament pointing to eternal torment:

And they shall go out and look at the dead bodies of the people who have rebelled against me; for their worm shall not die, their fire shall not be quenched, and they shall be an abhorrence to all flesh.

Isaiah 66:24 (NRSV)

Many of those who sleep in the dust of the earth shall awake, some to everlasting life, and some to shame and everlasting contempt.

Daniel 12:2 (NRSV)

According to this Old Testament professor, writing to confirm Hell as eternal torment, these two verses are the only hints of that torment in the entire Old Testament.

Isaiah 66:24 is referred to by Jesus and we have looked at it already in examining His teaching. This verse states that the power of destruction shall not itself ever die. The worm, which eats until there is nothing left, will never die. The fire, which consumes the chaff, the stubble, will never go out. This verse is unusual in describing something that remains after or even in the worm and the fire, but what remains are dead bodies, not living souls. The dead bodies here cannot walk, talk, or feel. There are no cries of anguish, as in the traditional picture of Hell. There is no pain. They are simply dead bodies. There is no hope that they will return to life for the destructive power of the worm and the fire will never cease. In Isaiah 66:24 there is no torment, no eternal life for the wicked. Only the destructive power 'shall not die.'

Daniel 12:2 says that at the resurrection the wicked will enter 'shame and everlasting contempt'. Shame and contempt are the attitudes of others towards the wicked. The wicked will be looked on with shame and contempt which will never end. Nothing is said about what the wicked themselves will be experiencing. There is no indication whether the wicked will or will not be conscious of the contempt that others have for them, and certainly no teaching that the wicked will live in eternal torment.

The Old Testament as a whole gives no support at all to the concept of eternal torment. From beginning to end, from Genesis to the last chapter of Malachi, the last book of the Old Testament, the God of Abraham, Isaac and Jacob is nowhere shown to be a torturing, tormenting God. His judgement is expressed in utter destruction, of body and soul, in the place which Jesus named *Gehenna.*

Hades

We have seen that in Acts 2 Luke records Peter, on the day of Pentecost, quoting Psalm 16, using the Greek word *Hades* for the Hebrew *Sheol.*

For you do not give me up to Sheol, or let your faithful one see the Pit.

Psalms 16:10 (NRSV)

Sheol is shown to be the Old Testament name for the place the New Testament calls *Hades.* Another name for the same place is the Pit.

Jacob is the first person in the Old Testament to use the word *Sheol*:

Then Jacob tore his garments, and put sackcloth on his loins, and mourned for his son for many days. All his sons and all his daughters sought to comfort him; but he refused to be comforted, and said, 'No, I shall go down to Sheol to my son, mourning.'

Genesis 37:34,35 (NRSV)

Here *Sheol* is simply the place of the dead. Jacob believes Joseph to be dead and, grief-stricken, says that he will follow him into death. Neither Joseph nor Jacob can be counted among the wicked. There is no sense here that Sheol is a place of punishment. Sheol, like the grave or the Pit, is a low place; people go down to *Sheol,* as the rich man in the parable of Jesus went down to *Hades.*

David later speaks of *Sheol* in the same way:

the cords of Sheol entangled me, the snares of death confronted me.

2 Samuel 22:6 (also Psalm 116:3 NRSV)

Sheol is the place and the power of death for the righteous and for the wicked.

This understanding of *Sheol* as the place of all the dead continues through the Old Testament.

Job, for instance, laments that the wicked have an easy life

They spend their days in prosperity, and in peace they go down to Sheol.

Job 21:13 (NRSV)

Sheol is a dark place, where people live a muted life, a half-life:

Whatever your hand finds to do, do with your might; for there is no work or thought or knowledge or wisdom in Sheol, to which you are going.

Ecclesiastes 9:10 (NRSV)

For Sheol cannot thank you, death cannot praise you; those who go down to the Pit cannot hope for your faithfulness.

Isaiah 38:18 (NRSV)

Sometimes *Sheol* is seen particularly as a place for the wicked:

Such is the fate of the foolhardy, the end of those who are pleased with their lot.
Like sheep they are appointed for Sheol; Death shall be their shepherd; straight to the grave they descend, and their form shall waste away; Sheol shall be their home.

Psalms 49:13,14 (NRSV)

The book of Proverbs, particularly, teaches that the wicked go to *Sheol* while the wise avoid it:

For the wise the path of life leads upwards, in order to avoid Sheol below.

Proverbs 15:24 (NRSV)

We also read that God can hear people who cry to Him from *Sheol*:

Then Jonah prayed to the Lord his God from the belly of the fish, saying, 'I called to the Lord out of my distress, and he answered me; out of the belly of Sheol I cried, and you heard my voice.

Jonah 2:1,2 (NRSV)

Sheol and Abaddon lie open before the Lord.

Proverbs 15:11 (NRSV)

One verse talks of God being present in *Sheol*:

If I ascend to heaven, you are there; if I make my bed in Sheol, you are there.

Psalms 139:8 (NRSV)

We read also of the hope of being delivered from *Sheol*. This can be through healing which delivers people from imminent death:

For great is your steadfast love towards me; you have delivered my soul from the depths of Sheol.

Psalms 86:13 (NRSV)

Bless the Lord, O my soul, and do not forget all his benefits - who forgives all your iniquity, who heals all your diseases, who redeems your life from the Pit, who crowns you with steadfast love and mercy,

Psalms 103:2-4 (NRSV)

Deliverance from *Sheol* is also glimpsed as those in *Sheol* being raised by God:

Your dead shall live, their corpses shall rise. O dwellers in the dust, awake and sing for joy! For your dew is a radiant dew, and the earth will give birth to those long dead.

Isaiah 26:19 (NRSV)

The Lord kills and brings to life; he brings down to Sheol and raises up.

1 Samuel 2:6 (NRSV)

Philip S. Johnston has written a whole book about *Sheol:*

> the underworld was not a particularly important concept for the Israelite writers . . . Descriptive details are very sparse, but suggest a somnolent, gloomy existence without meaningful activity or social distinction . . . There is certainly no elaborate journey through the gates or stages of the underworld, in Mesopotamian or Egyptian style.
>
> Indeed in the majority of instances *Sheol* is used to describe human fate. Sometimes this is a destiny which the righteous wish to avoid, or which in desperate circumstances they see as divine punishment on themselves. More often it is a destiny wished on the ungodly. The occasional synonyms of *Sheol* portray the same picture. So the underworld in Israel's canonical literature can be summarized as an infrequent theme and an unwelcome fate.[4]

The UK Evangelical Alliance Report, *The Nature of Hell,* makes a similar summary about *Sheol*:

> it is important for current debates about hell to note that the underworld (sic) is never explicitly portrayed in the Old

[4] P. S. Johnston, *Shades of Sheol – Death and Afterlife in the Old Testament* (Apollos IVP, 2002), p. 85.

> Testament as a place of judgment, punishment or torture. While psalmists often want the wicked to go there, the fate they have in mind is death itself, rather than any specific form of afterlife . . . The Old Testament largely implies a common fate of death and the gloomy underworld for all.[5]

The teaching of Jesus and of the New Testament is that *Hades* is a place of darkness and distress for the dead, including and especially the wicked, a temporary place from which people will be resurrected to face the Final Judgement. Jesus describes *Hades* as more anguished than does the Old Testament, giving detail about weeping, wailing, gnashing of teeth and painful heat. Jesus also asserts that He has the keys to *Hades*, building on the Old Testament description of *Sheol* open to God. Jesus, the Lamb, is described in Revelation as present with the wicked in *Hades*, building on the Old Testament description of God being present in *Sheol*. Revelation also describes *Hades* as eventually giving up all the people it contains, building on the Old Testament reference to people being raised from *Sheol*. There are enough connections to assert confidently that the Old Testament *Sheol* and Jesus' *Hades* are the same place, as Luke described Peter explaining in Acts 2.

Learning From Judaism

There is one longstanding indication that the traditional picture of Hell is not found in the Old Testament, and that is that Judaism has, mostly, not believed in Hell.

Rabbi Dan Cohn-Sherbrook has written that in the Torah or Old Testament 'there is no indication of a clearly defined concept of Hell; it is only later in the Graeco-Roman world that such a concept began to take shape.'[6]

Rabbi Naftali Brawer confirms this:

> The term Gehinom as a place of damnation for souls first occurs in the Talmud and Midrash.
>
> There is a key argument in the Talmud regarding the length of sentence in Gehinom for sinners and the widely accepted view

[5] *The Nature of Hell*, pp. 39, 51.

[6] Dan Cohn-Sherbrook, 'The Jewish Doctrine of Hell', in *idem.*, *Beyond Death* (St Martin's Press, 1995), p. 56.

is that with rare exception the longest sentence does not exceed twelve months.[7]

The Talmud and Midrash are writings of rabbis from the Middle Ages. Before then there was no Jewish concept of a place of damnation / torment for souls. Even in and with the development of the concept of *Gehinom* (almost the same word as Jesus' *Gehenna*) there is no sense of eternal torment, only of a purifying and very temporary experience which enables the person to cope with the glorious light of God's closer presence. This 'damnation' is properly a cleansing, with no attendant devils, full of hope for a glorious future soon to come.

Gehinom, as expounded in Judaism well after the time of Jesus, does not fit closely with His teaching, nor, as we have seen, with the teaching of the Old Testament. But, more importantly for Christians, this *Gehinom* is very far from the traditional concept of Hell. Some people wrongly assume that the God of the Old Testament must be more fierce than the God of Jesus and that Hell must therefore be an Old Testament doctrine. Both the text of the Old Testament and the history of Jewish understanding of the fate of the wicked show this to be untrue.

Conclusion

When we look in the Old Testament for Hell as eternal torment, all that can be found are two inconclusive references. When we look in the Old Testament for the ultimate complete destruction of the wicked, we find numerous passages and a strong theme running from the beginning of Genesis to the end of Malachi. When we look in the Old Testament for a place of waiting before Final Judgement, we find numerous passages showing a distinctive view that immediately after death all people, but especially the wicked, go to the gloomy waiting place called *Sheol.*

The Old Testament teaches clearly that the ultimate fate of the wicked is to be destroyed. Jesus added to this teaching by confirming that the method of destruction is fire, that the place is called *Gehenna,* and that it was prepared not for people but for the devil and his angels. The Old Testament also teaches that the

[7] *Jewish Chronicle*, 25 August 2011.

immediate fate of both the wicked and the righteous is *Sheol*, for which the Greek writers of the New Testament used the word *Hades.* Jesus added to this teaching by describing people in *Hades* as 'weeping, wailing and gnashing teeth' in 'outer darkness'. Jesus taught about *Hades* and *Gehenna* using two different words for two different places. The Old Testament confirms this teaching.

CHAPTER FIVE

BIBLICAL CONCLUSIONS: THE TRUTH OF *HADES* AND *GEHENNA*

Then Death and Hades were thrown into the lake of fire.

Revelation 20:14 (NRSV)

We started by listening to Jesus. We have taken His words as foundation, cornerstone, words on which we can build, with the help of the Holy Spirit. We have begun to see what follows logically from what Jesus said. We have listened also to the people who knew Jesus and followed closely after Him. We have listened to Moses and Elijah. We are now able to draw conclusions.

The ultimate fate of the unrepentant wicked is to be destroyed in the place that Jesus called *Gehenna* and which the book of Revelation describes as the lake of fire. The Old Testament, clearly and repeatedly, from start to finish, teaches that the wicked shall die, shall be destroyed. This destruction happens in *Gehenna.*

The lake of fire, which destroys wicked people, also torments the devil and his angels, who are of a different order of creation. This torment for the devil is the original purpose of *Gehenna*, the lake of fire. *Gehenna* was created to deal with the devil, to be the ultimate fate of the devil. God never intended that humans should end up in *Gehenna.* But humans who are resolutely attached to the devil and his ways will also be thrown with the devil into the lake of fire. The devil will survive in torment. Humans will not. Like chaff, straw, or weeds thrown into a furnace, the unrepentant wicked will burn very briefly, suffer intensely but briefly, and then will be annihilated. There will be no way out of the fire. There will be no trace of the wicked left.

Jesus himself will determine who exactly is thrown into *Gehenna* to accompany the devil and his angels. No one else has both the authority and the understanding to make this decision. He alone is worthy to judge. Even people who say to the end that they do not believe in heaven and do not want to go there, preferring anywhere else instead, will not necessarily go to *Gehenna.* Jesus has the final say.

Jesus will judge according to the good that people have done in their lives, looking at what is most in their heart. What matters in the Final Judgement is how people have responded to those in need around them, how they have cared for the poor, the naked, the thirsty, those in prison. Those who have injured others and show no remorse will be liable to the eternal fire. The injuries inflicted may be great: torture and anguish caused to other people. The injuries inflicted may be slight: calling someone 'you fool', looking lustfully at a woman. All such injuries count. It is supremely important that we love our neighbour as we love ourselves. If we do not, and do not repent, the Final Judgement will not be in our favour.

If anyone recognises their need for forgiveness, that may be enough for Jesus to draw them into heaven despite their own reservations. But those who insist that there was nothing wrong in how they acted towards their neighbour, while holding orthodox Christian belief, may find themselves unexpectedly heading for the lake of fire.

The Final Judgement will not be made according to people's beliefs. There will be some people who call Jesus 'Lord', and who have done remarkable things in His name but to whom Jesus will say that He has never known them. God is not looking for humans only to believe in Him and worship Him. He is looking for humans to practice true religion by caring for widows and orphans and breaking unjust yokes. People of all religions, cultures, backgrounds will be judged in the same way, according to what they have done or not done in love for their neighbour.

As people come to meet Jesus the Judge they will at the same time meet Jesus the Saviour. The name 'Jesus' means 'God saves' or 'God saving', 'God rescuing'. The name Jesus shows what His nature is: He is always God saving. In meeting Jesus everyone will meet God saving – God saving all people, God rescuing each one personally. It is impossible to meet Jesus the Judge without also meeting Jesus the Saviour. Jesus saves and recues people primarily by forgiving their sins. Jesus intervenes so that we do not suffer the consequences of our actions. Jesus the Saviour saves people from the eternal fire prepared for the devil and his angels. Jesus has the power and authority to rescue people from being destroyed. Jesus takes on responsibility for putting right our sins and mistakes. Jesus the healer can heal all the injury that we have caused, great and small, so that we are free from its consequences, we are forgiven.

Jesus continually offers the forgiveness, the rescue, which we all need. Saving, rescuing, is in His name, in His nature. He cannot stop saving, rescuing, forgiving. But Jesus never forces Himself, His forgiveness, His rescue, on anyone. We have to want to be forgiven, to be rescued. We have to confess, to recognise and say out loud the wrong that we have done. Everyone has to come to the point where we give up blaming other people or claiming that we had to do everything we did. All of us need to recognise and admit how badly we have treated other people, loving ourselves far more than our neighbour. Then we can be forgiven, saved, rescued.

Without this recognition and admission, we are heading for *Gehenna,* the eternal fire, with the devil. We need to come into the light where the truth about the way we have lived is made clear. But we can choose darkness instead, hiding from the truth. If, in the end, we reject Jesus and His light, we cannot be saved. No-one, ultimately, can turn their back on 'God Saving' and survive. Despite God's best efforts, in the end there will be such unrepentant wicked people. Not everyone will admit their wrongdoing, turn to Jesus, and so be saved.

Hades is the remand prison before the Final Judgement. Jesus does not specifically send people to *Hades* as He does to *Gehenna,* but people's actions in this life determine their going to *Hades.* Most people who do not know Jesus, go to one part or another of *Hades. Hades* is a low place, similar to the grave, far removed from the light, a place from which people are to be raised. Before this resurrection, *Hades* is a place of darkness, of distress or torment, of weeping, wailing, and gnashing of teeth. Teeth are gnashed mostly in resentment. In the darkness of *Hades* people weep bitter tears, wail loudly over their misfortune, resenting anyone who is better off than them and the God who has put them in this horrendous place. In *Hades* people can continually think, talk and feel. For some in *Hades* there are flames of unbearable heat causing great thirst. There can also be awareness that other humans are not suffering the same fate, but, instead, are in blissful peace.

Like any prison, *Hades* has different areas for different people. Some areas are simply gloomy waiting rooms. The worst area is the outer darkness, the place nearest to the eternal fire of *Gehenna. Hades* is an unbearably horrible place. No one in their right mind would want to spend even half an hour there.

Jesus has the keys of *Hades.* Jesus has the right of access to *Hades.* Jesus can and does share these keys, this right of access with His people, His Church, those who recognise Him as the Messiah, the Son of God. Jesus can be and is also present in *Hades* with His angels. Jesus, the Lamb, is present in the outer darkness with the worst criminals. Jesus is the Lamb who looks as though slain, a lamb lifeless, wounded, bloodied, but still the one who takes away the sins of the world.

Jesus in *Hades* is the same Jesus as the Judge at the Final Judgement, He is still God Saving, God rescuing. Jesus in *Hades* offers to those in gloom, deep darkness and torment a rescue: His forgiveness and the forgiveness of His Father. Jesus the Lamb invites those in *Hades* to respond to Him with pity, with compassion, as one thief on the cross recognised that Jesus should not have been there alongside him. Those who respond to Jesus will be offered an immediate escape. 'Today you will be with me in paradise.'[1] The angels with Jesus can and will carry out His desire to see people lifted out of *Hades.* As soon as Jesus says it, it is done.

The offer of Jesus remains an offer. People in *Hades* can and will reject the presence of Jesus, the Lamb, alongside them, as did the other thief on the cross. If they continue to reject God Saving, they will eventually meet God Judging and, in the end, go with the unclean spirits and the lord of the unclean, the devil,[2] into the fire of *Gehenna.*

Those lifted out of *Hades* are taken to Paradise. As *Hades* is the place of waiting for the unrepentant wicked, Paradise is the place of waiting for the righteous, the forgiven. After the Final Judgement the righteous, the forgiven, will be welcomed into the Wedding Feast of the Lamb, into the Father's House, the Heavenly City, the Kingdom prepared for them from before the foundation of the world. As they wait for the Final Judgement, the righteous,

[1] Luke 23:43 (NRSV).

[2] Beelzebul means Lord of Flies. The unclean spirits are like infecting flies, with the devil as their lord.

the forgiven, are in the Garden leading up to the House, a place of waiting in delight and anticipation, in light and love, a place where they are fully with Jesus and Jesus is fully with them.

The unrepentant wicked go first to *Hades*, the place of darkness and torment, and then to *Gehenna*, the fire in which body and soul are destroyed. This is the truth of which Jesus talked and to which the rest of the Bible bears consistent witness. This truth is different from the traditional understanding of Hell in several important respects.

People do not suffer for eternity. In *Hades* people suffer and are in torment or distress. But *Hades* will give up everyone inside so that they can be judged, and *Hades* will then itself be thrown into the lake of fire. The people who suffer most are those who have been most callous in this life, but even their suffering will come to an end eventually. In the meantime even they are not excluded from the saving presence of Jesus, His angels, and His Church, should they decide to embrace that presence.

People do not suffer judgement the moment they die. All people, for an 'age' or 'ages' after they die, wait for the Final Judgement. The unrepentant wicked wait in *Hades*, to which Jesus has the keys and in which Jesus can be and is present. Nothing is final until the Final Judgement.

The righteous in Paradise do not rejoice in the suffering of others in *Hades*, but share the compassion and mission of Jesus and His Father. The Church has been given the keys of the kingdom of heaven. Along with Jesus the keyholder for *Hades*, the Church can force open the gates of *Hades*. However hard the gates of *Hades* resist, the Church will prevail, Jesus' people will enter *Hades*, sharing in God's rescue. The Church in this life takes part in the mission of God to rescue and redeem. The Church beyond this life still has a role to play in this mission.

People end up in the fire because they have been wicked, callous, unloving, not because they have believed in the wrong God. Believing in the name of Jesus, in the Lamb as God Saving, is necessary to be rescued from Judgement and *Gehenna*. This is very different from saying that the basis of judgement is people's response to Jesus in this life. All will be judged according to their deeds – deeds of love or deeds of evil.

The wicked will be destroyed. All those who continually and determinedly refuse to accept God's offer of forgiveness and salvation will go with the devil and his angels into the eternal fire prepared for the devil and his angels. God will not, in the end, stand in the way of anyone who chooses to embrace the devil's future rather than the future with God. The future without God, for human beings, is no future at all. It is complete and irreversible annihilation in the consuming fire, extremely painful for a short while, before all feeling, thought, memory, is lost forever.

The devil is not in charge, but is trapped; he is not the chief torturer but is tortured. Ultimately the devil will be in the fire of *Gehenna*, not as the ruler of his own realm, but as the victim of his rebellion against God and of his crime in killing the innocent Jesus. In *Gehenna* the devil suffers judgement. He does not torture others but is himself tortured for eternity. There is no place, no realm, over which the devil exercises more authority than he does in this world, the kingdom of darkness. Even in *Hades* the power of the devil and his agents is limited by Jesus and can be undone by Jesus, His angels and His Church.

These differences from the traditional understanding of Hell are major, not minor. The true understanding of the fate of the unrepentant wicked is very different from the traditional understanding of Hell. Some of these differences are extreme, the truth of the Bible diametrically opposed to the traditional doctrine of Hell. Teaching in extreme opposition to the truth can only be a lie. The traditional doctrine of Hell is indeed a lie.

CHAPTER SIX

REVIEW OF OTHER BOOKS: ANNIHILATIONIST, UNIVERSALIST, TRADITIONALIST, ESCAPIST, EXPERIENCE

Writers have explored the understanding of hell in many ways and many books, especially in recent years. For much of the 20th century, hell was not a topic of debate and discussion. As the last century drew to an end, by contrast, and continuing into this century, considerable numbers of books on hell have been published.

Four understandings of hell have been promoted: the final annihilation of the unrepentant wicked, the eventual universal repentance of all the wicked, the eternal torment of the unrepentant wicked, and, more rarely and hesitantly, the opportunity, which may or may not be taken, for the wicked, who do not repent in this life, to repent beyond this life.

Annihilationist

Writers have explained at length the truth of *Gehenna.* With this as their main focus, they have, generally, not explained *Hades* as well.

John Stott and David Edwards, *Essentials* (Hodder and Stoughton, 1988)

Essentials is subtitled 'a liberal-evangelical dialogue' between David Edwards, a leading Anglican Liberal, and John Stott, the leading Anglican Evangelical and probably the foremost Evangelical teacher, globally, of the 20th century. Edwards sets out his liberal understanding of key points of Christian doctrine, stating where and why he disagrees with Stott's published Evangelical writings. Stott responds with further clarification. As part of this dialogue, Edwards challenges the notion of hell. 'I would rather be an atheist than believe in a God who accepts it as inevitable that hell (however conceived) is the inescapable destiny of many, or of any, of his children' (p. 295).

'It is with great reluctance and with a heavy heart that I now approach this subject' of Judgement and Hell, writes Stott (p. 312). Part of Stott's reluctance was, as he later explained, that he did not want to fracture Evangelical unity. Stott had been instrumental in wording some key Evangelical statements so that they could refer to hell as eternal torment but could also refer to eternal annihilation. The Lausanne Covenant of 1974, 'the most authoritative statement of Evangelical belief in recent years', according to Edwards (p. 287), states 'those who reject Christ repudiate the joy of salvation and condemn themselves to eternal separation from God.'[1] Elsewhere in his writings, Stott ensured the wording of the unrepentant wicked suffering 'eternal consequences' rather than eternal torment.

> But will the final destiny of the impenitent be eternal conscious torment, 'for ever and ever', or will it be a total annihilation of their being? The former has to be described as traditional orthodoxy, for most of the church fathers, the medieval theologians and the Reformers held it. And probably most Evangelical leaders hold it today. Do I hold it however? Well, emotionally I find the concept intolerable and do not understand how people can live with it without either cauterising their feelings or cracking under the strain. But our emotions are a fluctuating, unreliable guide to truth and must not be exalted to the place of supreme authority in determining it. As a committed Evangelical, my question must be – and is – not what does my heart tell me, but what does God's word say? (*Essentials*, p. 314f.)

Stott then goes on to outline four arguments pointing to the annihilation of the impenitent. Firstly he refers to many New Testament verses which describe destruction.

> It would seem strange, therefore, if people who are said to suffer destruction are in fact not destroyed, and, as you put it, it is 'difficult to imagine a perpetually inconclusive process of perishing.' It cannot, I think, be replied that it is impossible to destroy human beings because they are immortal, for the immortality – and therefore indestructibility – of the soul is a Greek not a biblical concept. According to Scripture only God possesses immortality in himself (1 Timothy 1:17, 6:16); he

[1] *Explaining the Lausanne Covenant* (Scripture Union, 1975), p. 9.

> reveals and gives it to us through the gospel (2 Timothy 1:10). (p. 316)

Secondly Stott argues that fire, the chief image in Scripture of hell, points to destruction. '[T]he main function of fire is not to cause pain, but to secure destruction, as all the world's incinerators bear witness . . . The fire itself is termed "eternal" and "unquenchable", but it would be very odd if what is thrown into it proves indestructible' (p. 316).

Thirdly Stott argues according to the biblical vision of justice.

> Fundamental to it is the belief that God will judge people 'according to what they [have] done' (e.g. Revelation 20:12) which implies that the penalty inflicted will be commensurate with the evil done . . . Would there not, then, be a serious disproportion between sins committed in time and torment consciously experienced throughout eternity? (p. 318)

Fourthly Stott argues that 'the eternal existence of the impenitent in hell would be hard to reconcile with the promises of God's final victory over evil' (p. 319).

> I do not dogmatise about the position to which I have come. I hold it tentatively on the basis of Scripture. I also believe that the ultimate annihilation of the wicked should at least be accepted as a legitimate, biblically founded alternative to their eternal torment. (p. 320)

Edwards had also raised the likelihood that people in *Hades* could be saved:

> if this blend of hope and fear is what the New Testament taken as a whole affirms – it seems necessary to believe that an opportunity will be given after death, in the condition pictured in the Bible as *Sheol* or *Hades.* This so-called 'Hades Gospel' has usually been rejected by Evangelicals, often because of abuse in the medieval Church (surviving despite some reforms into Roman Catholicism in our own time). (p. 302)

Stott did not respond in detail about *Hades,* but made some observations.

'I myself believe that this will be the time (if indeed we shall be aware of the passage of time) when the lost will come to the unimaginably painful realisation of their fate' (p. 317). 'Although the guess that people will be given in the next world an opportunity to believe is an attractive one, it remains a guess and lacks biblical warrant' (p. 326). 'I cherish the hope that the majority of the human race will be saved. And I have a solid biblical basis for this belief . . . even while I remain agnostic about how God will bring it to pass' (p. 327f).

Stott was aware that his clear statement of belief in annihilation, and his tentative support for people being saved after death, would ignite controversy among Evangelicals. So it did. After a decade or so of debate, the UK Evangelical Alliance in 1995 established the Alliance Commission on Unity and Truth among Evangelicals, or ACUTE, which in 2000 published its report *The Nature of Hell*.

Alliance Commission on Unity and Truth among Evangelicals (ACUTE), *The Nature of Hell* (Paternoster Press, 2000).
Group Convenor and Report Editor: David Hilborn.

The Nature of Hell fulfilled Stott's hope that hell as annihilation could be seen as an acceptable Evangelical alternative to hell as eternal torment. Those who teach that hell is annihilation are described as 'conditionalists' because they believe that human immortality is not innate but is conditional on forgiveness by and faith in Jesus.

After describing in detail the arguments, with extensive references and quotes, *The Nature of Hell* concluded: 'We recognise that the interpretation of hell in terms of conditional immortality is a significant minority evangelical view. Furthermore, we believe that the traditionalist-conditionalist debate on hell should be regarded as a secondary rather than a primary issue for evangelical theology' (p. 134).

E. W. Fudge, The Fire that Consumes: A Biblical and Historical Study of the Doctrine of Final Punishment (Paternoster Press, 1994)
This is the most detailed and most quoted case for the annihilation of the unrepentant wicked. A new edition was published by Wipf and Stock in 2011. Fudge has the unique distinction among theologians of having had a movie made of him and his work during his lifetime: *Hell and Mr. Fudge*.[2]

[2] Released 2012. See www.hellandmrfudge.com.

Fudge begins by describing his dispassionate, objective, study of the nature of hell:

> The prospect of someone suffering endless torment did not make me glad, but neither did it trouble me to a noticeable extent. Mostly I thought about something else . . . When my research began to uncover biblical and historical data challenging the traditional view, I was not eager to accept the conclusions to which the information seemed to lead. . . . I wrote *The Fire that Consumes* with a desire to be biblical reverent and fair, and to state objectively and comprehensively what my own research had found. (p. xi)

Fudge details how the Old Testament describes the fate of the wicked as destruction. He quotes *The Interpreter's Dictionary of the Bible*:[3] 'Nowhere in the OT is the abode of the dead regarded as a place of punishment or torment.' Fudge concludes: 'The wicked, however proud their boasts today, will one day not be found. Their place will be empty. They will vanish like a slug as it moves along. They will disappear like smoke. Those who search for them will not find them. Even their memory will perish.' (p. 66)

Fudge highlights the importance of listening to Jesus: 'It is easy to hear Jesus against such background noise that we confuse what he is saying with sounds of our own surroundings. We must not only listen to Christ reverently – we must also listen carefully' (p. 2). Fudge's listening to Jesus leads him to the conclusion that the unrepentant wicked will be utterly consumed, not tormented, in eternal fire.

When Jesus quotes Isaiah 66 about the undying worm and unquenchable fire, Fudge explains: 'Scripture supplies no basis for making the worm a metaphor for remorse, an interpretation now almost universal and documented as early as Origen. This is a devouring worm, and what it eats . . . is already dead' (p. 114).

Fudge also quotes others:

> 'The expressions of . . . "unquenchable fire," may mean merely that there is to be no deliverance, - no revival, - no restoration, - of the condemned. "Death," simply, does not cut out the hope of being brought to life again: "eternal death" does. "Fire" may be quenched before it has entirely consumed what it is

[3] T. H. Gaster, *The Interpreter's Dictionary of the Bible* (Abingdon Press, 1962), 1:788.

> burning: "unquenchable fire" would seem most naturally to mean that which destroys utterly.' Richard Whately, *View of the Scripture Revelations concerning a Future State*, 1873. (p. 183)

Fudge demonstrates that the *Gehenna* described by Jesus is the consuming fire which can and will destroy body and soul. This fire was never intended for humans, but for the devil and his angels. But people who are resolutely attached to the devil can and will go into the fire with the devil: 'God formed the human creatures for glory with himself, a destiny wholly of grace. Those who align themselves instead with the rebel creatures of a higher and previous order must finally share their fate' (p. 113). Fudge further demonstrates that the same concept of the ultimate destruction of the unrepentant wicked is in Paul's writings:

> certain intertestamental writers took the Old Testament language and added everlasting conscious torment. Paul takes the Old Testament language and adds Jesus Christ. (p. 56)

> For Paul, immortality is always God's gift to the faithful, to be awarded in the resurrection. He never views it as an inherent characteristic, nor does he ever attribute it to the wicked. (p. 162)

> Paul never gives us reason to suppose that eternal death is anything other than what it sounds like. Rather, he strengthens these connotations by such words as 'perish,' 'destruction' and 'corruption.' (p. 165)

Similarly in the letter to the Hebrews: for 'land that produces thorns and thistles is worthless and in danger of being cursed. In the end it will be burned' (Hebrews 6:8):

> Thorns and thistles are directly related to sin, as is the 'curse' (Gen. 3:17f) Can the land here be anything other than a figure of 'worthless' disciples who claim to know Christ but bear no fruit? . . . The reason for burning a field full of briars is not to cause pain but to destroy what is useless; and though the burnt-off land remains, those thorns and thistles are for ever gone. Is this figure intended to illustrate something directly opposite to what it pictures? (p. 171)

Similarly in the letter of James (James 1:15, 4:12, 5:1–6, 5:19), 'four times James refers to the final outcome of sin. Twice it is "death", once misery followed by "slaughter" and once "destruction." (p. 174).

Having looked in detail through the whole Bible, Fudge concludes:

> Few things are stated more often throughout the whole Bible than that the wicked will 'die,' 'perish,' 'be destroyed,' 'pass away,' 'be no more,' and 'be forgotten for ever.' The fact that we deal with the language of divine law and justice only strengthens the case for giving the words their most essential and ordinary meanings. (p. 182)

Fudge quotes William Tyndale, who came to the same conclusion: 'The true faith putteth the resurrection, which we be warned to look for every hour. The heathen philosophers, denying that, did put that souls did live for ever. And the pope joineth the spiritual doctrine of Christ and the fleshly doctrine of philosophers together, things so contrary that they cannot agree, no more than the Spirit and the flesh do in a Christian man' (p. 101).

Fudge is aware that people have often drawn other conclusions from reading the Bible: 'The conclusion is then drawn that 'destroy,' 'ruin' and 'perish' must mean eternal conscious torment, not extinction. Words which on their face would seem to suggest 'loss of life' are said to signify a 'life of loss' instead' (p. 159). The ultimate destruction of the wicked is important for what it shows us of the character of God:

> God is just and he is severe, but he does not delight in the death even of the wicked; certainly he is no sadistic torturer. This is a major difference between the Bible's picture of final punishment and that found nearly everywhere else – whether from venerated churchmen or bloodthirsty pagans. (p. 185)

Fudge also states that recovering the Biblical understanding of annihilation following the Final Judgement will renew the confidence of Christians everywhere to speak about that judgement.

'I was reared on traditionalist teaching,' writes Fudge,

> I accepted it because it was said to rest on Scripture. Closer investigation has shown this claim to be mistaken. Careful study has shown that both the Old and New Testaments teach instead a resurrection of the wicked for the purpose of divine judgment, the fearful anticipation of a 'consuming fire,'

> irrevocable expulsion from God's presence into a place where there will be 'weeping and grinding of teeth,' such conscious suffering as divine justice requires of each individual - and finally, the total and everlasting extinction of the wicked with no hope of resurrection, restoration or recovery. (p. 4)

From this summary by Fudge it is also clear that with his brilliant and detailed explanation of *Gehenna* he does not also give a detailed explanation of *Hades* as a separate reality. In various places he acknowledges the reality of an intermediate state between death and the Final Judgement, but the ultimate, rather than the intermediate, fate of the unrepentant wicked, is his focus. Some of the distress or torment which Jesus taught as being part of *Hades* Fudge understands as being part of *Gehenna,* although only briefly, as the wicked enter the fire before they are consumed.

L. E. Froom, *The Conditionalist Faith of Our Fathers* (Review and Herald, 1966)

Froom describes himself as a 'conservative, evangelical Protestant,' (p. 18) and church historian, tracing the history of 'conditionalism' - that humans attain immortality through following the specific conditions set out by God - and 'Immortal soulism' - that humans are born with an immortal soul which cannot die. His focus is both narrow and extremely broad, narrow in that he is only concerned with these two opposing doctrines, and broad in that that he includes every appropriate theologian and teacher from every century.

Froom demonstrates that conditionalism is the faith of the Old Testament, of Jesus and the New Testament writers, and of the earliest Church Fathers. He has hopes that the truth of conditionalism is at last again being widely acknowledged. Froom's work is huge: two volumes with 2735 pages (including indices). John Wenham, writing thirty years later, lamented that there had not been a serious rebuttal of Froom's arguments.

Today too Froom's work is largely ignored. His book is not in the Cambridge University Library, nor in the British Library, nor in other university libraries, except the Bodleian Library in Oxford. It could be that Froom's work is simply too extensive for people to engage with, although he gives clear chapter descriptions with charts and indices to help readers locate specific material. It could also be that Froom's work was prepared, approved and published for and by the Seventh Day Adventist Church, and prejudice against that Church prevents a serious engagement with Froom's thesis. Seventh Day Adventists, with their emphasis on the Old Testament, are unique in including annihilationism, also called conditionalism, in their official doctrine.

Froom begins with the Old Testament. He lists 'some seventy variant expressions denoting the one thought of "destruction"' (p. 108). '[I]t will be observed that in this vast array of Scripture passages there is uniform testimony as to *utter destruction* – without a single statement implying Eternal Torment for the finally impenitent wicked' (p. 111).

Froom begins his study of the teaching of Jesus with John's Gospel. Very few other writers, and especially those who support eternal torment, consider this Gospel at all, probably for the reason Froom chooses it as his starting point: 'The Gospel of John is pre-eminent in setting forth this great doctrine of *life eternal only through Christ*' (p. 196). Froom goes on to show that Jesus talked of the ultimate destruction of the wicked in *Gehenna*. Froom points out that *Hades* should be understood separately from *Gehenna*, despite translators using the same word 'hell,' as 'gravedom' 'the place of repose for the dead during their death sleep' (p. 300). Froom sees the parable of the rich man and Lazarus as fictional, not indicating that souls in *Hades* really can think, feel and communicate. He seems to be so determined to rule out the eternal existence of the soul after death that he also rules out the temporary conscious existence of the soul in *Hades* except in a death-like sleep.

Froom traces the same truths in the rest of the New Testament: God's promise of life to those who turn to Jesus, and warning of death, not torment, to those who reject Jesus: 'The *first* death cuts off from temporal life; the *second* death cuts off from eternal life. It ends all hope of further life forever' (p. 512). 'Sin is relatively incidental and passing, not integral and perpetual' (p. 519).

Froom then traces the history of 'immortal soulism' in Greek philosophy, contrasting this with the Hebrew teaching of the Old Testament and beyond. In the Dead Sea Scrolls the wicked are to be 'Found No More,' 'Cut Off,' 'Wiped Out' (p. 748).

Froom turns to and quotes from all the Church Fathers from Clement of Rome (c. 100) to Augustine of Hippo (c. 430). He demonstrates that for the first ninety years the universal teaching was that the unrepentant wicked will die, will cease to exist, after Jesus' Second Coming and Judgement.

> The concept of the Innate Immortality of the soul as a '*Christian*' doctrine did not appear in patristic literature until toward the close of the second century . . . The pathfinder on this revolutionary road was Athenagoras . . . As stated in the *Encyclopedia Britannica*, his theology is 'strongly tinged with Platonism.' However it was Tertullian of Carthage (d. c. AD 240) who gave the great impetus to this emphasis, tying in with it the dogma of the endless torment of the lost. (p. 929)

The innate immortality or not of the human soul continued to be debated, with Melito of Sardis, Irenaeus of Lyons and Athanasius of Alexandria, among others, arguing that humans are not innately immortal. Some, particularly in the East, adopted the idea of innate immortality, but argued that it meant not the eternal torment of the wicked, but their eventual restoration among all people. 'Then finally came Augustine of Hippo (d. AD 430), whose great influence brought about the general acceptance by the church at large of the belief in the deathlessness of all souls, and also its fiery corollary of the endless existence and Eternal Torment of the reprobate' (p. 930).

Froom finds few medieval theologians arguing against the innate immortality of human souls. Northern Italy had a long tradition of independence from Rome both politically and in thinking, and the belief in the ultimate destruction of the wicked seems to have been maintained there, especially among the Waldenses. Leading medieval Jewish teachers, including Moses Maimonides, taught the annihilation of the wicked. But, with printing and a far wider readership of the Bible, some teachers, beginning with John Wycliff, (c. 1324–1384) argued that '"immortalitie or undedlynesses," was for the righteous, to be received at the resurrection' (vol. 2, p. 59).

Wycliff was not widely heeded and the innate immortality of every soul continued to be assumed and taught in Protestantism as in Roman Catholicism.

The Augsburg Confession of Faith in 1530 stated: 'rejected, therefore, are the Anabaptists, who teach that the devil and condemned men will not suffer eternal pain and torment.'

By the 17th century, however, the doctrine of the immortality of the soul was strongly denied, especially in England, by a number of writers, including John Milton and John Locke. In the 18th century, Froom writes, 'there is a growing seriousness and scholarly validity that marks the overall witness of the new century . . . centred chiefly in England' (p. 243).

'The acceleration point' for Conditionalism, according to Froom, was in the 19th century. He lists and quotes from 128 'Major Witnesses to Conditionalism' mostly from England early in the century, but also many from America in the second half of the century. From the 20th century up to his time of writing in 1965 he lists and quotes from 137 'Major Witnesses'.

Froom finally turns to Spiritualism, 'the subtlest, cruellest, most devastating fraud ever perpetuated upon gullible man . . . the old original, and the most modern, the first and the last, and ever-diabolic lie' (p. 1275f). This is simply the lie of the serpent in Eden 'You shall not die.'

David Powys, *'Hell': A Hard Look at a Hard Question* (Paternoster Press, 1997)

Powys is an Australian scholar and priest. He uses Greek and Hebrew words in their original alphabets, and expresses himself in terms of developing OT Jewish and NT thought rather than 'what the Bible says.'

Powys argues that

> There is little or no New Testament warrant either for the expectation that the unrighteous will undergo ongoing post-mortem retribution, or that the unrighteous will be made righteous and restored . . . The tentative finding of this study is that the unrighteous will have no life after death, save possibly to be raised temporarily to be condemned. (p. 416)

Powys does not come to this conclusion through dismissing parts of the Gospels:

> What follows is based on the clear assumption that the four Gospels were set down by people who had access to first-hand information and whose purpose was to provide objective,

> comprehensive and accurate accounts of the life of Jesus of Nazareth. (p. 274)

For Powys our reading of Jesus' words makes more of them than Jesus intended:

> 'Gehenna', with its associations with the unrighteous, fire and destruction, had become a familiar and common expression throughout Palestine . . . Despite its imprecision as to the fate of its occupants, the term was used with no elucidation to great effect . . . Jesus, it will be argued, used the term exclusively for rhetorical purposes. (p. 276)
>
> The predominant image here is of being discarded to a fate of fiery destruction . . . His purpose was to stress the seriousness of sin by the most graphic means available: care must be taken not to confuse hyperbolic appeal with informative instruction. (p. 279)

Powys then draws out implications of his 'rhetorical' understanding of hell:

> Evangelistic proclamation which emphasises the threat of 'hell', and theology which makes 'hell' into a foundational doctrine, are both unbiblical. No positive doctrine of the fate of the unrighteous can be proclaimed with confidence: such proclamation lacks clear biblical warrant. (p. 417)
>
> The findings here ought not to be seen as in any way reducing the urgency of or need for evangelism. Biblical evangelism will be motivated by a loving enthusiasm that all might have life and have it abundantly . . .
>
> Evangelism that is grounded in biblical themes will always be primarily concerned with 'salvation to' rather than 'salvation from'. Its orientation will be a positive concern that people may enter under the saving reign of God in Jesus rather than a negative preoccupation with deliverance from hell. (p. 418)

Clark H. Pinnock and Robert C. Brow, *Unbounded Love* (IVP / Paternoster Press, 1994)

Pinnock and Brow subtitle their book *A Good News Theology for the 21st Century*. They cover the whole range of theology, stressing the primacy of the love of God, calling this theology 'creative love theism.' As part of this they see the traditional doctrine of hell as incompatible with Biblical teaching.

'Love and wrath do not exist in the life of God on an equal footing. We must say that God *is* love; we cannot say in the same way that he *is* wrath. We have to challenge this confusion in people's minds before it does them harm' (p. 9). This, they argue, is a foundation for theology.

This is not to say that wrath does not exist nor, in the end, that it is not significant, as universalists would argue. For Pinnock and Brow the Bible does not leave us that option. 'The warnings about eternal destruction are clear enough to prevent us from entertaining the hope of universal salvation. Evidently God values human freedom so much that he allows people to reject him finally' (p. 88).

Pinnock and Brow take at face value the warnings about destruction, and so teach annihilationism. The final decision, they argue, is made by each person themselves.

> God does not choose hell for people – they choose it . . . Hell is a possibility that arises from the human side out of rebellion and obduracy. God invited them to his supper, but they declined the invitation. (p. 88)
>
> If they do not say 'Your will be done' to God, they will hear God say 'Your will be done" to them. Universal salvation is implausible chiefly because God takes no for an answer. (p. 89)
>
> The criterion of judgement is not verbal profession alone . . . The criterion is words spoken and lives lived. The question is whether we have shown mercy to the poor out of an appreciation of God's love. The criterion is not so much orthodox belief as a trust in God's grace which takes the form of love in the service of others. (p. 89)

For Pinnock and Brow, hell as destruction is more Biblical, more just, more about the ultimate victory of God (as opposed to the continuing eternal rebellion of the devil).

Pinnock and Brow attribute the traditional doctrine of hell to the unwarranted adoption by Christians of the Greek concept of the immortality of the soul.

> If the soul is naturally immortal, it has to spend eternity somewhere. If there is a gehenna of fire, hell has to be a condition of torment. The conclusion flows inexorably from the Greek premise. Thus the word *destruction* gets turned into 'everlasting torment'. The idea of natural immortality seems to

> have skewed the Christian teaching about hell. It was a mistake and we should correct it. (p. 92)

Pinnock and Brow also support the view that the righteous of any religion, who live in the faith that active love for all neighbours is the right way, can be saved by this faith as the Old Testament Job was saved. 'The level of theological content is not the decisive issue' (p. 94). The other possibility is postmortem salvation:

> There are texts in the New Testament that hint at such an outcome (1 Pet. 3:18–20, 4:6) and it was commonly believed among the early church fathers. One can combine these two views and say that decisions in this life set the soul's direction in relation to God, and fuller revelation after death enables the person to pick up where things left off and decide once and for all whether to journey toward or away from God. (p. 94f.)

See also the review below of Pinnock's *A Wideness in God's Mercy* in the section on Escapism.

C. E. Chandler, *Immortalizing Evil* (self-published, 1997)

An American Evangelical argues that the fate of the unrepentant wicked is to be consumed in fire.

> For Chandler the issue is a straight conflict between tradition and Scripture. His subtitle is:
>
> The Traditional View of Hell
> (its name says it all)
> Vs
> The Biblical Teachings of:
> The Character of God
> The Very Nature of Man
> And the Fate of the Wicked

He declares that 'eternal conscious punishment' is 'false teaching.'

> There are those today within the Faith that use this false teaching as a fear tactic. They feel it is a necessity for else who would choose to be saved or live the Christian life or even bother going to church. This mentality however, reduces the Faith to merely 'fire insurance' rather than the pre-eminence of God's grace, mercy and love which is manifested in our glorious Lord and Savior, Jesus Christ. (p. 1,2)

Chandler attacks the doctrine of the immortality of the soul. 'Not only can it not be supported by the Word of God but it also gives a false hope to natural man that he is immortal, and grievously attacks the character of God, who would torture and torment individuals in a manner that far exceeds any Biblical teaching' (p. 11). He quotes many different Bible commentators all agreeing that the doctrine of the immortality of the soul is a Greek concept, not Biblical.

Chandler begins with Genesis and God's warning that the consequence of eating from the one forbidden tree is death.

> The first lie is recorded in the Bible, chapter 3 verse 4, 'and the serpent said to the woman, you surely shall not die!' It is that same lie that is the issue of this book. It is the serpent that declares that sinners will not die. It is God that declared that they will. (p. 15f., emphasis in original)

Chandler points out the importance of the story of the judgement of Sodom and Gomorrah, which both Peter and Jude state is 'an example to us of what will happen to the ungodly after judgement.' 'it would be ludicrous to believe that somewhere in this world, in that part of the Old Testament country, a fire is still burning. If this were so, we would know exactly where Sodom and Gomorrah were. This is so important to understand, for throughout much of the Bible we will read "eternal (subject)." Whenever it is written like that, it will speak of the results being eternal and not the subject itself.' He also refers to Lamentations 4:6 which describes the overthrow of Sodom happening in a moment – 'the actual burning of Sodom is notably quick – in that regard even merciful' (p. 158).

The Hebrew word nephesh (soul) is found in the O. T. 733 times. The Greek word psuche (soul) is found 105 times in the N. T. Two other Hebrew words are used one time each for soul. In these 840 passages not once do we find the expression 'immortal soul' or 'never dying soul.' (p. 66)

Chandler uses 'hell' for *Gehenna* and 'Hades' for *Hades*. 'It is important to note . . . that Hades and Hell are two separate entities and in no way compatible with one another' (p. 31).

What happens to the unrepentant wicked? 'I believe that one who seeks the truth must answer that man is mortal and he that is outside of God, will know the wrath of God, by being totally destroyed' (p. 107).

John Wenham, *Facing Hell* (Paternoster Press, 1998)
An autobiography and statement, from a leading Evangelical Bible scholar and author of a much used textbook on New Testament Greek, that neither eternal torment nor universalism are Biblical. The true teaching of Jesus and the Bible is 'conditionalism'.

Wenham describes his life, pointing out how much of a Biblical, conservative, Christian he has always been, influenced and shaped by Evangelicalism. Wenham writes to counter the charge, '"He is an Anglican who cannot stomach either the true doctrine of hell, nor an honest universalism, so he is attempting a typical compromise." But I am not a woolly liberal . . . And I am not a compromising Anglican' (p. 263).

One key influence was Basil Atkinson, a Cambridge librarian with a gift for languages 'unquestionably a fundamentalist . . . believing the very text of scripture to be inspired and infallibly true' (p. 67). Atkinson taught what Wenham calls 'conditional immortality' the doctrine that humans are not innately immortal and that the unrepentant wicked will not have immortality but 'the cessation of life for ever' (p. 69).

On hearing this teaching for the first time in 1934, Wenham recalls

> I felt deflated; it removed some of my motivation for evangelism and some of my motive for prayer. But when I came to pray over it I realized that rescue from torment was not a primary motive for evangelism, rather one wished to see God glorified through the loving response of a sinner to the one who loved him. The conviction that Basil was basically right deepened as the years went by. From this point onwards I found I had a new freedom to teach the awesome judgements of God and the perfection of his love without having to represent him as the everlasting torturer. (p. 69)

Wenham then went to teach doctrine at St John's Hall Highbury (later to become St John's College, Nottingham). 'There till 1941 I taught conditionalism with much reserve and restraint. After that I had twelve years out of direct academic work, before joining the staff of Tyndale Hall, Bristol. Here I taught with rather less reserve . . .' (p. 230f).

Wenham eventually published 'The Case for Conditional Immortality' (in N. Cameron, ed., *Universalism and the Doctrine of*

Hell, Paternoster Press, 1992, and reproduced in *Facing Hell*). Here he criticises proponents of the traditional doctrine of hell for not replying to the detailed Biblical arguments of those advocating the ultimate destruction of the wicked. He quotes Fudge at length and repeats the arguments that in many places the Bible teaches 'conditional immortality'. Wenham refers to all the places where the word *appolumi* is used. 'It is a terrible catalogue, giving most solemn warning, yet in all but one of the 264 references there is not a word about unending torment and very many of them in their natural sense clearly refer to destruction' (p. 241). Wenham recognises that one passage, and only one, can be taken to refer to eternal torment – Revelation 14:9–11. But he agrees with John Stott that the fact that this torment is in the presence of the Lamb and of the holy angels indicates that it describes the moment of judgement rather than the eternal fate. He ignores the sequence of angels which show that these verses are before the Final Judgement.

Wenham explains that understanding the ultimate destruction of the wicked enables him to speak more about sin and judgement.

> Unending torment speaks to me of sadism, not justice. It is a doctrine which I do not know how to preach without negating the loveliness and glory of God. From the days of Tertullian it has frequently been the emphasis of heretics. It is a doctrine which makes the Inquisition look reasonable. It all seems a flight from reality and common sense. (p. 254)
>
> I was drawn to conditionalism by Scripture, rather than by a horrified recoil from the other doctrine . . . I have believed the Bible to teach the ultimate destruction of the lost, but I have hesitated to declare myself in print . . . Now I feel that the time has come when I must declare my mind honestly. I believe that eternal torment is a hideous and unscriptural doctrine which has been a terrible burden on the mind of the church for many centuries and a terrible blot on her presentation of the gospel. I should indeed be happy, if, before I die, I could help in sweeping it away. (p. 256)

Wenham died less than four years after these words were published.

Guy Chapman, *All you need to know about Hell* (Ottont Books, 2005)

An English Anglican Evangelical expounds hell as a refining fire for those ready to have their sins burnt away and a consuming fire for those who hold onto their sins.

Early on Chapman asks the reader to root out the 'pernicious influence' of the doctrine of the immortality of the soul. 'There is no word anywhere in the Scriptures that teaches this doctrine. Indeed there is straightforward teaching to the contrary.' He quotes 1 Timothy 6:16 stating that God alone has immortality, and Romans 6:23 that eternal life is a free gift of God through Jesus, not something innate (p. 18).

Chapman points out the need to distinguish between *Hades* and *Gehenna*:

> These are two quite different things. If only the translators [of the King James Bible] had decided to import the Greek word Hades into the English language . . . then the English speaking world might have been saved from a lot of problems. Instead they used the English word hell for both of them, leading to great and serious misunderstanding for many generations. (p. 24)

Chapman draws out important implications of the widely recognised lack of Old Testament teaching on eternal torment. 'The New is in the Old contained. The Old is in the New explained . . . Any supposed New Testament teaching that has no background in the Old Testament is highly suspect' (p. 29f).

> The medieval doctrine of the lost being condemned to an eternity of conscious suffering in the flames of hell, is not only repulsive in concept and morally suspect, it is unbiblical and not honouring to either the love or the holiness of God. It is a terrible piece of false teaching that has caused untold distress to millions of devout Christians, and it ought to be abandoned. (p. 65)

In place of this discredited doctrine, Chapman urges his readers to pay heed to Jesus' words about body and soul being destroyed in *Gehenna* and Malachi's words about the wicked burnt up like stubble. The intense fire of God will entirely consume 'those who hold onto their sins and will not be separated from them' while 'for others it will be "the sun of righteousness with healing in its wings"' (pp. 70, 90).

William Whiston, The Eternity of Hell Torments Considered (1740)

An early and well-argued challenge to traditional doctrine, from the protégé and successor of Isaac Newton. His main work was to publicise the discoveries of Newton so that they became widely accepted. For this he has the rare distinction of having had a part of the moon named after him: Dorsa Whiston, a ridge system. He also translated the work of the 1st-century Jewish historian, Josephus. Whiston challenged the doctrine of the Trinity, believing that Jesus was not fully divine. For this, he was dismissed from his Professor's Chair at Cambridge and all his other theological writing was also dismissed.

Whiston is well aware of the two words that Jesus used and bases his understanding on the distinction between *Hades* and *Gehenna.* He also believes that *Hades* and *Gehenna* are both located in the large cavity between the internal and external rotations of the earth (p. 3)!

> In all the sacred records *Hades* is one place, and *Gehenna* another; we all go to *Hades* when we dye, but none of us go properly to Heaven or Hell (geenna) till the day of judgment. The want of distinguishing which two places in the *Old* and *New Testament,* has been the source of several pernicious mistakes, in all the later, and more ignorant, ages of the church. (p. 46)

Whiston begins by saying that Isaac Newton agreed with an earlier, shorter paper of his with the same message. Like many others, Whiston finds the doctrine of eternal torment a huge obstacle to belief:

I had many years thought that the common opinion in this matter, if it were, for certain, a real part of Christianity, would be a more insuperable objection against it, than any or all the present objections of unbelievers put together. (p. 1).

Whiston places major emphasis on the love of God shown in the Bible:

> And indeed, the astonishing Love of God to mankind so highly and frequently here celebrated, to *all* mankind; and that as to

> his own creatures, and children, and this *always* and *forever*, both *in this world* and *in the other*: And this prodigious concern for *all* their salvation and happiness; with those amazing methods of effecting their, *all* their repentance, and amendment, and future happiness, even by the death of his only begotten Son; by the ministry of his holy Angels; and by the preaching of his Prophets and Apostles; in all ages *Etc.* is so absolutely inconsistent with these common but barbarous and savage opinions, as if much the greatest part of mankind are under a state of reprobation, and must inevitably be damned: and that such their damnation is to be *coeternal* with the duration of their Creator himself; and that the torments, the exquisite torments of these most numerous and much miserable creatures, are determined without the least pity, or relenting, or bowels of compassion in their Creator, to be in everlasting fire, and in the flames of Hell; without abatement, or remission, for endless ages of ages. And all this for the sins of this short life, fallen into generally by the secret snares of the Devil, and other violent temptations; which they commonly could not wholly either prevent, or avoid; and this without any other advantage to themselves, or to others, or to God himself, than as instances (I almost tremble so much as to suppose, or repeat it,) of the absolute and supreme power and dominion of the cruel and inexorable author of their being; for all the infinite ages of eternity. (p. 18f)

Whiston says that, for Josephus, Hades was 'the place of the dead, with angels that distribute temporary judgments agreeable to everyone's behaviour and manners – intended for the correction of those lesser offenders who are curable' (p. 66f.).

Whiston argues that *Hades* is indeed a place of 'castigatory and temporary punishments'. *Hades* is terrible, but is neither eternal nor beyond the remit of God's saving love. 'God punishes the wicked and rewards the good for thousands of generations: Whence we ought to learn never to restrain the mercy, and goodness, and pardoning Grace of God; but ever to suppose him ready to forgive all truly penitent and returning sinners, *not in this world or age only, but also in the world or ages to come.*'

Whiston argues that if there is, as Jesus said, lack of forgiveness in the age to come specifically for blasphemy against the Holy

Spirit (Matthew 12:32) this implies that there is forgiveness in the age to come for other sins.

Gehenna, Whiston sees, is the place of 'destructive torments' with the emphasis on the destruction of the wicked. The burning is like the burning of 'briars' as in Hebrews 6:8, not like the burning of iron.

Whiston ends with a call to the Church so to preach that that people may be saved from punishment to come in *Hades* and extinction in *Gehenna.* He explains why he has gone to such lengths as to write about this subject:

> In order to the persuading my self and others of my brethren, whose duty it is to warn men of the solemnity of the future judgment; to preach the glorious hopes of *Paradise,* and of *Heaven*; and the dreadful fears of *Hades* and of *Hell* [*Gehenna*] to our people; And that in the most serious and affecting manner possible. (p. 143)

Silas Henn, Sunlight dispersing the shadows or the doctrine of eternal torments shown to lack reason and scripture (Elliot Stock, London, 1874)

A critique of the concept of torment as pleasing to God, and assertion of annihilation as the true meaning of the effect of the 'eternal fire'.

> We wish at the outset to state that we believe in future punishment and in the necessity and righteousness of future punishment; and we believe in it, we think, as it is taught in the Holy Scriptures. But the doctrine as it is commonly set forth . . . we cannot accept . . . because we are fully convinced that it lacks the authority of God's word. (p. 1)

Henn argues that the traditional understanding of hell is too appalling to be part of God's plan, that death normally means ceasing to exist, that human souls are not immortal, that the wicked who do not repent will be annihilated.

Henn quotes Jesus warning people to 'fear him who can destroy both body and soul in hell' (Matthew 10:28): 'a very remarkable passage, the true import of which seems to be generally overlooked.' He also points out that Jesus warned that we could lose our soul, not have it tormented (Matthew 16:26).

Universalist

Universalist writers have argued against the traditional view of hell as eternal torment and paid little attention to the arguments of Annihilationism.

Rob Bell, *Love Wins* (Harper Collins, 2011)

> A staggering number of people have been taught that a select few Christians will spend forever in a peaceful, joyous places called heaven, while the rest of humanity spends forever in torment and punishment in hell with no chance for anything better. It's been clearly communicated to many that this belief is a central truth of the Christian faith and to reject it is, in essence, to reject Jesus. This is misguided and toxic and ultimately subverts the contagious spread of Jesus' message of love, peace, forgiveness, and joy that our world desperately needs to hear. (p. viii)

Bell goes on to question particularly the assertion that belief in a traditional hell is necessary to Christian faith:

> I've written this book because the kind of faith Jesus invites us into doesn't skirt the big questions about topics like God and Jesus and salvation and judgement and heaven and hell, but takes us deep into the heart of them. (p. ix)

He does indeed then go into these questions, particularly the question of hell, without coming to answers. He poses the questions sharply and dramatically.

Bell looks in detail at many of the Biblical passages about judgement and 'hell' particularly in the gospels, recognising that Jesus used two different words, but not placing much importance on this distinction.

He also recognises the need for judgement. Great injustices happen in this world making us 'crave judgement' (p. 38).

> To summarize, then, we need a loaded volatile, adequately violent, dramatic, serious word to describe the very real consequences we experience when we reject the good and true and beautiful life that God has for us . . .
> And for that,
> The word 'hell' works quite well.
> Let's keep it. (p. 93)

Bell states, as many other have done, that the freedom to reject God, even forever, is an important human freedom: 'If at any point God co-opts or hijacks the human heart, robbing us of our freedom to choose, then God has violated the fundamental essence of what love even is' (p. 104).

Bell recognises that universalism has its flaws:

> What makes us think that after a lifetime, let alone hundreds or even thousands of years, somebody who has consistently chosen a particular path away from God suddenly wakes up one day and decides to head in the completely opposite direction?
>
> And so a universal hugfest where everybody eventually ends up around the heavenly campfire singing "Kumbaya" with Jesus playing guitar, sounds a lot like fantasy to some people. (p. 104f)

Yet, recognising the problems with universalism, especially the Biblical problems, Bell inclines towards it:

> everybody enjoying God's good world together with no disgrace or shame, justice being served, and all the wrongs being made right is a better story. . . . Whatever objections a person might have to this story, and there are many, one has to admit that it is fitting, proper, and Christian to long for it. We can be honest about the warped nature of the human heart, the freedom that love requires, and the destructive choices that people make, and still envision God's love to be bigger stronger and more compelling than all of that put together. (p. 111)

Bell, however, at the end of his book, as well as asserting that 'loves wins', comes back to the urgency of Jesus' call, with its sense of 'or else': 'Jesus reminds us in a number of ways that it is vitally important we take our choices here and now as seriously as we possibly can because they matter more than we can begin to imagine' (p. 197).

Rob Bell and David Vanderveen, The Love Wins Companion: A Study Guide for Those who Want to go Deeper (Collins, 2011/12)

Encouraged by his publisher, Bell worked with his friend Vanderveen to produce further reflections, Bible references, discussion questions and quotations from other authors.

Bell's overall message is that Jesus' loving God calls us to live in love, with Him, now. The traditional doctrine of hell is seen as interfering with this message, besmirching the character of God. Bell wants to put aside the old doctrine of hell, while also keeping Jesus' sense of urgency, of 'or else!' He encourages questioning. He stresses God's stated desire to embrace all people and gives striking stories of how Jesus has lovingly come into the lives of people outside of the 'usual church suspects.'

Bell writes that he has listed '(Almost) Everything the Bible says about Hell' (p. 40). He begins with the Old Testament and several references to *Sheol*, then lists where the names *Hades* and *Gehenna* are used. He includes no references to Old Testament teaching on the ultimate destruction of the wicked, nor to other New Testament teaching on the fate of the wicked beyond death. He invites readers to interpret the Bible verses, not in the light of their first meaning in context, but, firstly, in the light of the meanings of the respective names in Hebrew or Greek culture.

Later, Bell includes an extensive quote from Clark Pinnock expounding annihilationism (p. 177–179), but does not incorporate Pinnock's message into his teaching. Bell proclaims both the love of God and the urgent warning of Jesus with heart-felt conviction and imagination. He does not systematically connect these two truths. His questioning of the traditional doctrine of hell and emphasis on the welcoming love of God, without a coherent 'or else!', leans towards universalism.

Percy Dearmer, *The Legend of Hell* (Cassell, 1929)

Percy Dearmer was a leading Anglican clergyman, Canon of Westminster Abbey and Professor of Ecclesiastical Art at Kings College, London. Today he is best known as the author of the hymns *God is love, his the care,* and *Jesus good above all other.* Dearmer writes with great scholarship and panache. His presentation of the abhorrence of the doctrine of eternal torment has not been bettered.

> The object of our present enquiry is not so much as to refute a doctrine which in its barbarity needs little further disproof for the educated world of the present age, but rather to help clear away the taint of it which still hangs in the air, and still poisons many a conservative pulpit; and to do something towards removing the prejudice against Christianity which pervades

> large sections of people, especially in the Continent of Europe, because of that doctrine. Most of all, if it be not presumptuous, I would desire to make it clear to those who may read these pages that the charge of having fathered such a doctrine can no longer be brought against the Saviour of mankind. (p. 16)

Dearmer traces the development and history of the doctrine of hell as eternal torment with extensive quotes from the Church Fathers to the Victorians. Hell as eternal torment is taught by Tertullian and by *The Apocalypse of Peter* in the second century, although this *Apocalypse* was lost for some centuries before being discovered again. Dearmer writes that it was Augustine who fixed the idea of hell as eternal torment in the western Church, while the Eastern Orthodox Church 'accepted the punitive doctrine of hell, yet maintained its own characteristic position which was at once more spiritual and less defined, and never lost sight of its own Greek Fathers with their less legalistic ideas and their strain of universalism' (p. 55).

Differing views continued, however,

> 'What might seem almost incredible is the uncertainty and inconsistency of the Holy Fathers on this subject from the very times of the Apostles down to the pontificate of Gregory XI [1370] and the Council of Florence [1439], that is for the whole of fourteen centuries. For not only do they differ the one from the other, as commonly happens in such questions not yet defined by the Church, but are not even consistent with themselves.' H. B. Workman, *Christian Thought in the Reformation*, Duckworth, 1921, p. 150ff. (p. 102)

From the late Middle Ages, hell as eternal torment was fully part of all official Roman Catholic teaching. Dearmer quotes the *Catechismus Romanus* issued in 1564 as ordered by the Council of Trent:

> The most loathsome and dark prison, in which the souls of the damned together with the unclean spirits are tortured in everlasting and inextinguishable fire. This place is also called Gehenna, the bottomless pit, and in its literal signification, hell. (Part 1, art. 5). (p. 24f)

Dearmer stresses how infants were particularly included among the tormented: He quotes St Fulgentus:

> Also little children who have begun to lie in their mother's womb and have there died, or who, having been just born, have passed away from the world without the sacrament of holy baptism, administered in the name of the Father, Son and Holy Ghost, must be punished by the eternal torture of undying fire. De Fide, 70. (p. 53)
>
> This doctrine of the damnation of infants, which had been first formally decreed by the Council of Lyons in 1274, the year of Aquinas' death, was further ratified in the same words by the Council of Florence, also of oecumenical authority in the Roman Catholic Church. (p. 54)

A Victorian Roman Catholic priest wrote this in a book for children in the middle of the 19th century:

> 'You are going to see again the child about which you read in the *Terrible Judgment*, that it was condemned to Hell. See! It is a pitiful sight. The little child is in this red-hot oven. Hear how it screams to come out. See how it turns and twists itself about in the fire. It beats its head against the roof of the oven. It stamps its little feet on the floor of the oven. You can see on the face of this little child what you see on the faces of all in Hell – despair, desperate and horrible!'
> Rev J Furniss *Books for Children,* Book 10: *The Sight of Hell* C.SS.R. (Dublin, Duffy, c.1850). (p. 44f)

Dearmer also writes about the doctrine of purgatory, 'doubtfully suggested by Augustine . . . and horribly developed . . (c. 582) by Pope Gregory the Great' (p. 62)

> It is a common mistake to suppose that the doctrine of **purgatory** mitigates that of hell. The truth is that it vastly increases the horror of future punishment; for it does not hold out any help to those who are to be damned (whether for their sins or because they are heathen, excommunicants, or unbaptised), but only adds torment to the future state of the just. The torment is the same for those in purgatory as for those in hell, according to the authoritative Thomas Aquinas . . . exceeding anything we have experience of, and only differs from that of hell in not lasting for ever. (p. 61).

Such miserable uncertainty about the departed brought enormous wealth to the Church: 'The fire of purgatory,' ran an old proverb, 'boils the monk's saucepan' (p. 63).

The Church of England, newly independent of Rome, proclaimed in 1543 that infants and young children shall be saved ('The Kings Book'), and in 1563 decided to remove an earlier teaching that it was unacceptable to hold the opinion that all men shall at length be saved.

After this detailed and knowledgeable account of the history of hell as eternal torment, Dearmer turns to examine the New Testament. He writes that the verses in the Gospels which indicate the torment of the wicked are shown by modern scholarship to have been inserted, into Matthew's gospel particularly, by an early Church believing ideas which they found in Jewish apocalyptic writing and had not heard from Jesus himself.

Jesus himself, according to Dearmer was never harsh:

> His most solemn warnings are not of eternal punishment, but are like the friendly and liberating advice of a physician, who says to a patient, 'If you go on living as you are now doing, you will contract a terrible illness which will bring pain and misery upon you.' (p. 261)

Dearmer sees this pain and misery not as lasting eternally but as always able to be healed: 'ready and instant forgiveness is always shown. Why should that activity cease towards a man merely because he has passed into another life? What is there so frightful in committing the crime of dying that God's forgiveness should thenceforeward be refused?' (p. 263). '[C]hoice, rescue and reform are possible as before, and surely no less in that clearer light than now' (p. 270).

Dearmer believes that because Jesus must the same yesterday, today and forever, in this life and beyond this life, in the end He will save all people. He does not know how this will come about. He ignores the distinction between *Hades* and *Gehenna,* and the many other places in the Bible where the final end of the wicked is described not as salvation but as extinction.

Gregory MacDonald, *The Evangelical Universalist* (Wipf and Stock 2006, SPCK 2008)

Gregory MacDonald is the pseudonym of Robin Parry. Parry was Commissioning Editor for Paternoster Press, an Evangelical Publisher. Worried about the reputation of Paternoster in the eyes of their authors and readers, he considered it best not to make the public connection between Paternoster and universalism. He was concerned also that some people would dismiss his other writings because of his universalism. Three years after his book was published, Parry decided 'It's going to come out some time – better to reveal my identity myself than be "exposed".'[4]

'I hope that this book may persuade some at least to tolerate evangelical universalism as legitimate Christian position – a view that is true to the message of the gospel – even if they themselves feel unable to accept it' (p. 176). This is MacDonald's tentative hope for his book, reflecting his whole argument, which is one of tentative hope. Yet he also here casually writes of others who 'feel unable to accept' what he is saying, almost accusing them of basing their position on feelings rather than good logical Biblical arguments. MacDonald tries not to be fiercely critical of those who hold to a traditional view of hell, but sometimes his criticism comes through. He recognises the annihilationist view but does not pay it much attention. His summing-up pits universalism against traditionalism with no mention of annihilationism (p. 176).

MacDonald begins with 'philosophical problems with traditional Christian teachings on hell' (p. 7). His universalism solves these problems. He goes on to 'provide a fairly detailed biblical metanarrative that fits very nicely with the teachings of Christian universalism' (p. 7). This involves plotting the story of redemption with its increasingly wide scope across humanity, and highlighting those passages which refer to the salvation of 'all'. MacDonald is aware that he is drawing out particular threads in the Bible rather than asserting that universalism is the overall message of the Bible. He ignores the repeated Old Testament teaching on the ultimate destruction of the wicked.

MacDonald goes on to 'argue that it is legitimate to understand the biblical teaching about hell as compatible with an awful *but temporary* fate from which all can, and ultimately will, be saved' (p. 7). He is remarkably frank about the weakness of his argument. He knows that 'orthodox churches worldwide (Orthodox, Catholic, and Protestant) have more or less universally rejected universalism' (p. 173). He recognises that many Biblical passages,

[4] http://theologicalscribbles.blogspot.com/2009/08/i-am-evangelical-universalist.html

especially words of Jesus, seem to indicate an 'or else' which is incompatible with universalism. 'I think that it is quite clear that Jesus' contemporaries would not have thought that he was a universalist of any variety' (p. 145). 'The purpose of most of the hell texts is to serve as a warning to avoid it at all costs. This is what God wished to accomplish by means of Jesus' words, and, *in such a communicative context*, to add a "p.s., it'll work out OK in the end" was not only unnecessary but also counter-productive' (p. 149).

MacDonald goes on to argue that in a later context, with the rational arguments against eternal torment, and the wide scope of some threads in the Bible, it is now legitimate to add "p.s., it'll work out OK in the end." Not necessary, but only legitimate; only an option which should be respected. But this option is tantamount to saying that Jesus wasn't able to communicate the full picture, wasn't able to portray hell truly as a place of horrendous and painful purifying, best avoided. MacDonald thinks that this could well be what Jesus would say today, even though He couldn't at the time. But how does this tie in with a Jesus who is the same yesterday, today, and forever, and with a Bible which is seen by all Evangelicals as the unchanging word of God for all times?

MacDonald tries very hard to portray universalism as an Evangelical option but, in order to make this portrait, he has to use the Bible in a way that is not properly Evangelical. MacDonald does not want to jettison the Bible, he wants to respect it highly. But to achieve his aim of producing an account of universalism that respects the Bible he cannot treat the Bible as fully authoritative. MacDonald writes that the language of the Bible is influenced too much by the culture of its day and not enough by the Christian theology which he espouses (p. 155). By contrast, Evangelicals generally see the language of the Bible as divinely inspired 'when the time was right'[5] and the source of Christian theology rather than to be moulded by any theology. In the end MacDonald demonstrates how far apart universalism is from the Bible, especially if the Bible is treated as the authoritative word of God.

[5] Romans 5:6, I Timothy 2:6 (NRSV).

Keith Wright, *The Hell Jesus Never Intended* (Northstone, 2004)
Wright promotes a liberal view of Hell as incompatible with God's love. He argues against substitutionary atonement. He never mentions the concept of hell as annihilation.

Traditionalist

Traditionalist writers hold to the traditional definition of hell as eternal torment, generally including all the elements of hell as detailed in the Introduction.

Francis Chan and Preston Sprinkle, *Erasing Hell* (David C. Cook, 2011)
Chan and Sprinkle explain their holding to the traditional doctrine of hell, particularly in response to Rob Bell's *Love Wins.*

Chan and Sprinkle begin by stating that they do not want to believe in eternal torment, but consider they have to from what the Bible says. Later they explain that when human standards of logic and morality do not fit with what is taught about God's standards, we have to abandon the human rather than question the understanding of the divine 'because we are the clay and He is the Potter.' But instead of then looking directly at Scripture, they look at universalism and point out several problems with it. They also go into detail about scholarly understanding of the views of 1st-century Jews about the ultimate fate of the wicked, seeing this as an important background to Jesus' words. This shapes their understanding more than the 'ears to hear' meaning of Jesus' words and more than the teaching of the Old Testament.

When they come to the words of Jesus they state that 'hell is described in imagery of fire and darkness, where people lament' (p. 74). This indicates that they have not grasped the distinction between *Hades* and *Gehenna,* despite also writing 'hades, like sheol, is where the wicked await their judgment. Hades is not hell' (p. 157). Later they write 'These metaphors of fire and darkness are clearly mixed – where there's fire, there cannot be complete darkness.' But instead of taking this logically and questioning whether the combination of fire and darkness is a true conclusion from the teaching of Jesus, they write, 'The mixing of metaphors suggests that these images are just that: *metaphors*' (p. 155).

Neither realities nor metaphors work well when they are, at first sight, in contradiction to each other.

They do acknowledge that the parable of the Rich Man and Lazarus 'doesn't refer to the final state of the wicked – only to a temporary state where the wicked await judgment' (p. 81). Even with combining references to *Hades* and *Gehenna*, they state, 'In almost every passage where Jesus mentions hell, He doesn't explicitly state that it will last forever' (p. 81). Chan and Sprinkle finally say that they are not certain about the duration of torment but they 'lean heavily on the side that says it is everlasting' (p. 86). This is because of their understanding of 'eternal punishment' and of some people suffering the same fate as the devil. 'If they go to the same place, they probably suffer the same fate – never-ending punishment in the lake of fire' (p. 106). They make no distinction between the nature of humans and the nature of the devil and his angels, despite later writing that the devil and his angels are 'spirit beings' unlike humans (p. 155).

As well as affirming the traditional view of hell as eternal torment, Chan and Sprinkle state that it is belief which is the key factor in determining a person's fate. 'Are you sure that you're on the right side? What evidence do you have that you *know* Jesus?' (p. 119). Immediately after this they quote Jesus: 'I never *knew* you; depart from me' (Matthew 7:23). They fail to see that these words were said to people who would have said that they knew Jesus, for they called him 'Lord, Lord.' It is one thing to claim to know Jesus, it is another for Jesus to know us. For Jesus to know us, and to avoid judgment, we have to do the will of His Father in heaven (Matthew 7:21). Here, as in many places, the Bible teaches us that we will be judged on our deeds, not on our beliefs.

At the same time Chan and Sprinkle take seriously Jesus' warning in the parable about the sheep and goats, calling people to live responding to the needs of others. 'Racism, greed, misplaced assurance, false teaching, misuse of wealth, and degrading words to a fellow human being – these are the things that damn people to hell? According to Scripture, the answer is yes' (p. 124). 'In the light of this truth and for the sake of people's eternal destiny, our lives and our churches should be – no, they must be! – free from the bondage of sin, full of selfless love that overflows for neighbours, the downcast, and the outsiders among us' (p. 146). Whatever our understanding of the outcome of the Final Judgement, we can all say Amen to that.

Christopher Morgan and Robert A. Peterson (eds), ***Hell Under Fire*** **(Zondervan, 2004)**
Morgan and Peterson gather essays from various writers to defend the traditional doctrine of hell. This book was republished in 2011 under the title *Is Hell for Real or Does Everyone Go to Heaven?* This second title shows that the writers do not engage with annihilationism. *Is Hell for Real . . .* omits the chapter on the Old Testament, perhaps because it shows how hell as eternal torment has no support from the Old Testament.
Albert Mohler, Jnr, laments and criticises 'The Disappearance of Hell' in modern theology.

> The revision or rejection of the historic doctrine of hell comes at great cost. The entire system of theology is modified by its effect, even if some revisionists refuse to take their revisions to their logical conclusions. Essentially, our concepts of God and the gospel are at stake. What could be more important? (p. 40)

Mohler mentions Fudge's work but passes over him, concentrating on others (p. 33f.). He mentions too the exhaustive work of the UK Evangelical Alliance in producing *The Nature of Hell,* but goes into no detail, simply commenting: 'Sadly, the picture was not much clearer' (p. 33). He makes nothing of the distinction between *Hades* and *Gehenna.*
Daniel I. Block examines 'The Old Testament on Hell'. 'What does the Old Testament teach about hell? The simple answer to this question is, "Very little"' (p. 44). He glimpses that the Old Testament views *Sheol* and the ultimate judgement of God separately and differently: 'although Sheol is never linked with eschatological judgment elsewhere [other than Isaiah 66] . . . the motif of fire as an instrument of divine judgment is a common motif in the Old Testament' (p. 61). But he concentrates on *Sheol* and, not seeing any mention of destroying fire in *Sheol,* ignores the many mentions elsewhere. 'Although rhetorically persons could refer to death as the end of existence, any tendency toward contemporary theories of annihilationism, either for the wicked or the righteous, would have been rejected' (p. 65).

Having not found eternal torment in *Sheol,* Block also finds 'very little' in the rest of the Old Testament. All he can see is in Isaiah 66, the vision of the worm that never dies and the fire that is not quenched, and in Daniel 12, the 'eternal disgrace' of the wicked.

> Prior to Daniel 12:2 we find no clear evidence of belief in hell, if by hell we mean a place of eternal torment and judgment for the wicked. It would be left to later revelation in the New Testament to develop this image. (p. 65)

Robert W. Yarbrough examines 'Jesus on Hell'. He makes no distinction between *Hades* and *Gehenna*. It seems that he has not read Block's assessment of the Old Testament: 'Christ's teaching on hell . . . draws persuasive force from its basis in the Old Testament witness and not only from the scattered references to the actual word "hell" discussed above' (p. 77).

Yarbrough focuses on the Rich Man in *Hades* in Luke 16, and on the eternal fire prepared for the devil and his angels in Matthew 25. In combining these descriptions of *Hades* and *Gehenna,* Yarbrough sees 'his clear teaching on eternal conscious punishment' (p. 75). Yarbrough explains away the even clearer teaching in Matthew 10 about body and soul being destroyed in *Gehenna.* Of Matthew 10:28 he writes, 'in Jesus' usage "destroy" can also mean to inflict enduring torment . . . *apollymi* can also be parallel with *basanizo.*' Yarbrough's case is built on an occasional and unusual use of language as opposed to the obvious meaning, in Greek as any other language, of 'destroy'. He then quotes, in support of his case, what the unclean spirits in the Gadarene man say (Matthew 8:29 and parallels). Torment after judgement for unclean spirits does not indicate that there will be torment after judgement for humans. And no good theology can be even partly built on what comes from the minions of the father of lies.

Yarbrough concludes: 'Jesus did not find the concept of eternal conscious punishment intolerable. On the contrary, it was much on his mind and on his lips.' Most other scholars, including those who argue for eternal torment, would say that eternal torment was not a frequent part of Jesus' teaching.

Douglas J. Moo examines 'Paul on Hell'. He also seems not to have read what Block wrote on the Old Testament, for he writes of it: 'many passages emphasize the reality of God's judgment for sin. At least two (Isa. 66:24 and Dan. 12:2) present the judgment in terms of eternal punishment' (p. 95). Block was very clear that these two passages can be taken to refer to eternal torment, but, as we have seen, this may not have been in the mind of the writers. Nowhere else in the Old Testament is eternal torment even hinted at.

Moo details the language that Paul uses to talk about judgement and sees it as referring to eternal torment, not in its plain or surface meaning but in a more convoluted way: 'We would suggest that the "destruction" of which Paul here speaks may just as likely refer to "ruin"' (p. 106). It is far more likely that 'destruction' means destruction. Moo criticises Fudge for connecting Paul's description of those under a curse as *anathema* with the Old Testament concept of something devoted to destruction: 'Fudge errs in thinking that the original connotations of the imagery must be present in Paul' (p. 93, footnote). How Moo thinks that the rabbinic-trained Jewish Paul could have connotations in mind which are specifically not from the original Old Testament is a mystery.

Moo comes to the conclusion that 'the evidence that we do have from Paul suggests that he agrees with the larger New Testament witness in portraying hell as an unending state of punishment and exclusion from the presence of the Lord' (p. 109). He does not explain what this supposed larger New Testament witness is, probably relying on the assumption that as eternal torment has been taught so much by the Church, it must be in the New Testament.

Gregory K. Beale examines 'The Revelation on Hell'. He looks particularly at Revelation 14:9–12 and 20:7–15. He sees the Revelation 14 passage as a description of final judgement and its consequences, ignoring the fact that it is a description of what happens when the third angel blows his trumpet, before the cloud appears carrying 'one like the Son of Man'. Beale writes, 'it is just possible, if not probable, that this passage concerns the final judgment of all unbelievers throughout history' (p. 115). Note also his description of those facing judgement as unbelievers rather than the wicked.

Beale then argues that humans thrown into the lake of fire in Revelation 20 suffer in the same way as the devil, the beast and the false prophet, despite Revelation 17:8 describing the beast ascending from the pit, certainly not a place from which humans originate. Beale asserts

> It is hard not to resist the conclusion that only someone with a prior theological agenda to defend a particular view of divine love and justice could deny that the judgment of all unbelieving humans in Revelation will be different from that of the devil and his angels. (p. 134)

It is not a theological agenda, but Jesus and Scripture both show that humans are not in the same category as the devil and his angels. In Matthew 25, Jesus describes the eternal fire as prepared for the devil and his angels, not for humans. It is a tragedy that some humans end in the fire but Jesus does not treat the devil and humans in the same way, as Beale does.

Christopher W. Morgan, lastly, examines 'Biblical Theology: Three Pictures of Hell'. The pictures are Punishment, Destruction and Banishment. Morgan chooses two pictures which can support eternal torment and one which is made to support eternal torment by being placed only with these other two. A more common Biblical picture, from Genesis to Revelation, is Death. 'Blotting out' 'being consumed' are other Biblical pictures which Morgan does not choose.

Morgan, unlike Yarbrough, does refer to John's Gospel, but without the much repeated reference to death and perishing. Instead he writes: 'John describes future punishment as "condemnation" and the continuation/culmination of God's wrath on those without faith in Christ (3:36)' (p. 141).

Morgan recognises that his interpretation, ignoring any distinction between *Hades* and *Gehenna*, does stretch believability in what it tries to combine: 'At times, the pictures of hell even seem irreconcilable. How can burning fire coexist with the blackest darkness, for example? How can someone experience intense torment and yet perish?' (p. 142) Morgan does not investigate this further. He, like the other contributors to *Hell Under Fire,* holds unquestioningly to his received understanding of hell as one place of eternal torment.

Bruce Milne, The Message of Heaven and Hell (IVP, 2002)

Milne conveys the traditional understanding of both heaven and hell. With such a large remit he cannot cover the whole Bible in detail so he selects passages which he considers significant.

Milne writes as a typical Evangelical treating the whole Bible without distinction as the Word of God. 'Without apology we need to start where the Bible starts – with its opening section, the Old Testament and with its opening words' (p. 25). He also equates rejecting accepted Evangelical doctrine with rejecting God:

> The fact of hell is highly unpalatable to our human sensitivities and its proclaimed eternal duration a heavy cross to our intellect, but its dismissal is far more problematic. It means the rejection of God's word, and hence the dismissal of his revealed character. It is nothing less than a repetition of the primal sin – a rejection of God himself. (p. 64)

Starting with the Old Testament, however, Milne finds little evidence of eternal torment. 'The overall impression of *Sheol* as something of an "un-place" certainly finds support in the Old Testament. There is not much here, it would seem, to enrich our understanding of heaven and its joys, or of hell and its miseries' (p. 28). Milne ignores the many places in the Old Testament, beginning in Genesis 3, which teach that the ultimate fate of the wicked is to die, to be destroyed. He describes the serious implications of the Fall: 'breakdown in relationship with God, banishment from his presence, the threat of his just wrath' (p. 68). Milne, however, fails to mention the one implication clearly taught in Genesis 3: death.

Milne states that humans will suffer the same fate as the devil.

> Satan (and his minions) – will be brought to final and everlasting punitive judgment. That this same fate awaits human moral agents who have arrived at the same degree of settled impenitence is the clear witness of every one of these passages just cited. (cf. Matt. 25:41; 2Pet. 2:1–3, 10–22; Jude 7–16, Rev. 20:7–9, 15). (p. 60)

As we have seen, humans thrown into the same lake of fire as the devil and his angels are, unlike the devil, destroyed – as Jesus said in Matthew 10:28.

Milne goes on to examine the New Testament. Again he ignores images of destruction in favour of continuing existence: 'the darnel was used in Palestine as fuel' (p. 118). The only possible use for weeds as fuel is in lighting a fire. Weeds burn to nothing so quickly that they cannot be used for cooking, warmth or even lighting. Milne writes that he is aware of the arguments of John Stott and other 'conditionalists' but does not go along with them: 'the case for a revision of the traditional understanding concerning the meaning of the texts in question appears to fall short of compelling demonstration' (p. 153).

Milne recognises 'the apparently contradictory image of "darkness" used of hell' but writes that it is 'a reminder that we are dealing here with metaphors.' A contradictory metaphor is a very bad metaphor, unlikely to have come from the world's greatest story-teller. Later Milne writes 'it is clear that Gehenna, with its "eternal burnings", had come [in Jesus' time] to be distinguished from *Hades*' (p. 154). He makes no use of this distinction, preferring to obliterate it.

'Jesus' primary image of "fire", or "hell, where the fire never goes out" . . . It is impossible to eliminate the element of conscious suffering from this image' writes Milne (p. 149). A greater imperative is to give to this image the primary meaning that Jesus gave to it, as the place where body and soul are destroyed. Instead, Milne writes, '"fire" regularly occurs in phrases which appear to stress the endless duration of the experience of those so consigned' (p. 152). He gives no references to back up his word 'regularly'. Later he writes, 'A condition of agonizing personal self-consciousness is at the core of this picture' [of the lake of fire.] (p. 302) but offers no evidence to support this view.

As part of Milne's examination of Romans, he asks 'What has the wrath of God to do with hell? The answer is "just about everything", for hell is simply the locational expression of God's wrath in post-mortem experience. Hell is the eternal form of God's wrath' (p. 216). But 'His anger is but for a moment' (Psalm 30:5) and 'He will not keep his anger for ever' (Psalm 103:9). The doctrine that there is an eternal form of God's wrath is not Biblical.

David Pawson, *The Road to Hell* (Hodder and Stoughton, 1992)
A robust defence of hell as eternal torment. Pawson shows detailed Biblical knowledge and a great ability to grasp and convey both major themes and telling detail in the Bible. But his

presentation of hell as eternal torment is confused and, at times, illogical.

Pawson writes in the context of the debate sparked by John Stott's publication of his view that the unrepentant wicked are to be annihilated. Pawson acknowledges that others before him have written asserting hell as eternal torment, but his focus is slightly different:

> the warnings of Jesus about hell were rarely aimed at sinners; they were occasionally directed at religious hypocrites (like the Pharisees) but usually at his own disciples, particularly the twelve. This contextual fact seems to have been totally overlooked, even by those who still believe in, preach on and write about hell. Drawing attention to it is probably the unique contribution of this book to the present debate. (p. 6)

But despite knowing that Jesus rarely talked to sinners about hell, Pawson immediately goes on to write, 'The gospel has always been bad news (about God's wrath) before it is good news (about his love) – Paul's letter to the Romans is a good example' (p. 7). This may be true of the gospel message as Pawson has heard it himself, but even he acknowledges that it is not true of the gospel message of Jesus. The letter to the Romans is not a 'gospel message' but a reply to Christians who are questioning Paul's emphasis on the grace and forgiveness of God. Paul begins by agreeing with them that sin is terrible and widespread, leading to death, before repeating his 'good news' about the free gift of God's forgiveness leading to life.

Pawson begins by celebrating the historical standing of the doctrine of eternal torment. 'The medieval concept of hell has survived almost intact, in spite of the Protestant Reformation' (p. 11). Early on, he dismisses the view of annihilationists like Stott and others: 'if hell is not conscious and continuous torment but simply nothingness, there is really no point in preaching it any more' (p. 17). 'Support is usually found in the vocabulary of scripture, rather than any specific statements' (p. 24). Pawson passes over Matthew 10:28: 'Fear him who can destroy body and soul in *Gehenna*.' Later he quotes that verse with his own peculiar interpretation: 'fear him who can destroy (ruin) both body and soul in hell' (p. 82).

Pawson says that objections to hell as eternal torment are firstly personal and subjective, and secondly theological and objective. He deals with them in that order. Unusually for an Evangelical, he does not begin with Scripture. He considers arguments that hell is incompatible with God's love, justice and power. 'In fact all these arguments contain the same fatal flaw. They exalt one divine attribute at the expense of others, they emphasise one part to the detriment of the whole.' (p. 20f) Yet it is the Bible which describes God as being love, exalting that attribute as part of the divine being, while also saying that God's wrath lasts only for a short while and is in no way part of His being.

Pawson then turns to the Bible, particularly the teaching of Jesus. He shows how the New Testament transforms the Old Testament concept of *Sheol* ('described as a station waiting-room at midnight with no trains due until the morning! There is little or no expectancy of any consciousness or communication there'; p. 32) to now show that, after death, human personality survives.

Turning to the ultimate end of the unrepentant wicked, Pawson asks

> To put it bluntly, even crudely, is being 'thrown into hell' more akin to being incarcerated in a concentration camp or being incinerated in a crematorium? When biblical language and imagery are first read, the immediate impression is that life is extinguished in hell. (p. 36)

Later, he writes 'At first sight, this phrase [lake of fire] might be thought to imply the extinction of persons' (p. 164). A good rule in understanding language, including and especially listening to Jesus' words, is that the immediate simple meaning is the correct one, unless there is excellent reason for thinking otherwise. Pawson breaks this rule.

Pawson points instead to the stories of the burning bush which Moses saw and the fire in which Shadrach, Meshach and Abednego walked, to indicate that

> it would be perfectly possible for God to limit the 'physical' effect of fire to intense heat and discomfort (which seems to be the exact situation of the poor rich man in Luke 16 . . .) . . . So the concept of 'fire' in hell is ambiguous. (p. 37)

Pawson also concludes that the meaning of *appolumi* is 'ambiguous'. He creates this ambiguity by giving the same weight to a few occasional instances as to many repeated instances.

After also acknowledging the debate about the meaning of 'eternal', Pawson leaves Scriptural arguments to challenge annihilationists with four questions:

'Why should the wicked be "raised" (i.e. given new bodies) for the Day of Judgement, only to have them destroyed again immediately afterwards?' (p. 39). He can see no purpose in such an arrangement, despite it being clearly described in Revelation 20. The horrendous experience of *Hades* has not brought the wicked to repentance and to seek Jesus. Maybe the experience of judgement will? Here is the final opportunity, before the judge.

'Why "prepare" a place called "hell" after all?' (p. 39) Jesus and Revelation give the clear answer. The place is prepared for the devil and his angels, to burn them. Pawson later acknowledges this, but assumes that the fire which continuously burns the devil also continuously burns humans, despite humans being, as Pawson writes, different in only being 'capable of receiving immortality' rather than 'inherently immortal' (p. 40). Later he simply writes 'Presumably the same fate awaits those who join him [the devil] in the fire' (p. 114). Having seen the great difference in nature between the devil and humans, it would be more logical to write 'presumably the same fate does not await'.

'What is to be made of the clear statements that the fire, smoke, and even worms of hell are permanent?' (p. 40) The agents of destruction will complete their work, there is no possible reprieve. The agents of destruction were created to deal with the devil, not humans.

'Why should the thought of oblivion inspire fear? . . . sinners who have had their fling would probably be glad of it' (p. 40). This seems to assume that the most important effect the church is to have on people is to instil fear. Anyone who has ministered to the dying or taken a funeral knows that one of the deepest human desires is to see our loved ones again after death. The removal of that hope for ever is a terrifying prospect to most people. To this is added the fearful prospect of *Hades* before the Final Judgement.

Pawson comes to Revelation 14:9–11, which he sees as conclusive. He gives the impression that the picture of torment here is both final, as opposed to being intermediate (inaugurated by the third angel out of seven, not by Jesus, and happening in the presence of Jesus) and widespread, as opposed to being unique (other pictures in Revelation 20 are of the Final Judgement by Jesus, leading to a future away from His presence). Later Pawson studies Revelation 20 in depth, while also including Revelation 14, assuming the two passages describe the same thing (p. 164). 'The fact that much of the clear evidence comes from the book of Revelation is no reason for dismissing it' (p. 43). But if the only 'clear evidence' he sees is from Revelation, does this not rather indicate that the whole traditional picture needs be to be reassessed?

Pawson then elaborates many of his points at greater length. 'There are only two future destinies open to the whole human race – heaven or hell . . . They could not be more different, they are exact opposites . . . Heaven is the reverse of hell' (p. 65). Pawson here is implying that as people live in heaven for ever, so they live in hell for ever. This argument is based on the assumption, which he nowhere demonstrates as Biblical, that all that can be said of one, can also be said of the other, but in an opposite way. This is contradictory, for he is arguing that heaven and hell are completely different, but also the same. If they were truly completely different they would not mirror each other. This dualist thinking owes more to Manichaeism than to Jesus or the Bible.

Pawson states that in the Old Testament there is 'a paucity' of information about future punishment (p. 123). It is certainly true that there is no information about eternal torment awaiting the wicked, but there is considerable information about the wicked being destroyed, as the outcome of their judgement. Despite acknowledging his 'paucity', Pawson also writes, 'Since the first preachers were addressing Jews, it could be assumed that they already understood and believed in the concept of hell.' If the Old Testament does not teach hell, where does this assumption come from?

Similarly Pawson writes, 'Another point is that Jesus neither describes nor defines hell on this occasion. [Matthew 10:28] This can only mean that his hearers were already quite familiar with the concept and needed no further explanation; he could take it for granted' (p. 97). If, as Pawson knows, the Old Testament does not teach hell as he understands it, Jesus' hearers cannot have been familiar with it. Jesus was never in the habit of going into detailed descriptions and definitions. Jesus gave us cornerstone words from which we, with the guidance of the Holy Spirit, develop descriptions and definitions. Jesus' cornerstone here is that *Gehenna* is a place where body and soul are destroyed. This cannot be developed logically into a place of everlasting torment.

Pawson mostly ignores the distinction between *Hades* and *Gehenna,* specifically early in his book, drawing lessons about hell from the parable of the Rich Man and Lazarus. But he also acknowledges that *Hades* is an intermediate place distinct from the final:

> scripture treats the intermediate as an interlude – and so should we. To become excessively curious about the present whereabouts of the dead might lead us into that desire to have contact with them which God, in his wisdom, has declared distracting and dangerous for us. (p. 34)

Later, he acknowledges that in the parable Jesus uses *Hades* but argues 'Hades is not here a specific title for the intermediate state, but a general term for posthumous existence' (p. 128). Pawson redefines *Hades* to suit his purposes.

Pawson is also aware of the tradition of Jesus descending to the dead but seems confused about it: 'with the keys of hades in his hand (Rev. 1:18), Jesus could move freely in and out of the abode of the departed. The gates of hades could not be bolted and barred against him – or his church (Matt. 16:18)' (p. 33).

> *He descended into hell.* This is not something that happened after his death (as older versions of the Apostles' Creed seem to imply; modern versions rightly change 'hell' to 'hades' or simply 'the dead', that is, the world of disembodied spirits). No, he experienced hell while still in his body, for the last three of the six hours he hung on the cross. (p. 57)

These two passages contradict each other. In the second Pawson states that Jesus experienced hell while still alive, which is a modern understanding of hell in this life, neither the traditional understanding of hell, nor the better understanding of *Hades* which he commends earlier.

J. Casey, After Lives: A Guide to Heaven, Hell and Purgatory (OUP, 2009)

A modern Catholic presentation of traditional teaching with much exploration of other religions and traditions.

Casey explains the value of holding to hell:

> Although the doctrines of eternal punishment and eternal bliss did have a use in persuading the faithful to lead virtuous lives, fearing punishment or looking for justice in the next world, that was not all they did. In the case of hell the immense effort that went into imagining what it must be like was also an effort in persuading people to see their sins in all their loathsomeness – as they are seen by the eyes of God. (p. 9)

Although Casey appeals mostly to the teaching of the Church, he does also refer to the teaching of Jesus and to 'three crucial passages in which Jesus is represented as teaching an eternity of punishment for the wicked'. He quotes Mark 9:43–48, the parable of the Rich Man and Lazarus (Luke 16:19–31) and the parable of the sheep and the goats (Matthew 25:34–36). Casey does not make any distinction between *Hades* and *Gehenna.*

Casey recognises that the traditional doctrine of hell cannot be derived from Paul's letters:

> Paul, although he promises an eternity of rewards to the good, never threatens the wicked with an eternity of punishment. His thought about the fate of the reprobate hovers between a hope that even they will somehow eventually be reconciled with God, and the sterner expectation of their ceasing to exist.

Casey is aware, however, that *Hades* may be distinct from *Gehenna*, for he refers to William Whiston making this distinction:

> Dives is brought by this punishment to true repentance, and this shows that forgiveness is sometimes denied in this world and granted in Hades. With this saving of Dives – the parable about whom has always been taken as the strongest evidence that Jesus did believe in an eternity of suffering for the lost – the English tradition of free religious enquiry reaches the point of no return. (p. 222)

Casey understands this point of no return to be a dead end, indicating the futility of going down the road of 'free religious enquiry' as opposed to accepting the doctrine of the Church. But it can also be read as the point of no return to the doctrine of hell as eternal torment. Once we have seen, as Whiston did, the distinction Jesus made between *Hades* and *Gehenna*, and its importance, we cannot return to the discredited view of the one place of eternal torment for the wicked after death.

Piers Paul Read, *Hell and Other Destinations* (DLT, 2006)

A defence of the traditional Roman Catholic doctrine of hell against liberal modernising.

Read recognises that hell as eternal torment is not found in the Old Testament, nor in much of the New Testament. 'When we come to the Gospel of John . . . Damnation means extinction: the soul dies with the body. The same less terrible definition of Hell can be found in the epistles of St Paul' (p. 20) Even in examining Matthew, Read's case is weakened by misquoting Matthew 10:28, described as an exhortation to 'fear God who, as Jesus taught "can punish soul and body together in hell"' (p. 40).

For Read the important issue is not what the Bible says, but that the Church has taught hell as eternal torment. He quotes the Council of Constantinople of 543: 'If anyone says or holds that the punishment of devils and wicked men is temporary and will eventually cease, that is to say that devils or the ungodly will be completely restored to their original state, let him be anathema.' This teaching has been preserved by the Roman Catholic Church up to the Catechism of 1994. But nowadays, to Read's dismay, the doctrine of hell is held more lightly. John Paul II said, in a General Audience in 1999: 'Eternal damnation remains a possibility, but we are not granted, without special divine revelation, the knowledge of whether or which human beings are effectively involved in it' (p. 40).

W. G. T. Shedd, *The Doctrine of Eternal Punishment* (1885; republished Banner of Truth, 1986)

A fierce critique of universalism and the doctrine that divine punishment is merely remedial and temporary.

Shedd shows that he is aware of Jesus' use of the two words *Hades* and *Gehenna*, quoting the Schaff-Herzog encyclopedia (article: 'Hades'):

> Hades was identified with Gehenna, and hence both terms were translated alike in the Protestant versions. The English (as also Luther's German) version of the New Testament

> translates Hades and Gehenna by the same word 'hell' and this obliterates the important distinction between the realm of the dead (or nether-world, spirit-world) and the place of torment or eternal punishment; but in the Revision of 1881 the distinction is restored, and the term Hades introduced.

Shedd himself makes little use of the awareness of Jesus' terminology, preferring to use the common language of the translators: 'Fear him who after he hath killed hath power to cast into hell; yea, I say unto you, Fear him' (p. 13).

Shedd is also aware of other scholars who argue against the traditional doctrine of hell: He refers to Rothe as an annihilationist[6] and quotes Julius Müller, 'We may venture to hope that in the interval between death and the judgment many serious misconceptions, which have hindered men from appropriating truth in this life, will be removed.'[7] Shedd, however, does not take these views seriously. Instead he asserts the validity of the traditional doctrine.

Shedd states that the eternal torment of the wicked was the accepted Jewish understanding at the time of Jesus: Edersheim (*Life of Jesus*, vol. II, p. 789) asserts that the schools of Shammai and Hillel both taught the doctrine of eternal punishment' (p. 14). More recent scholarship has shown that the nature of God's ultimate punishment was a matter of debate between the two rabbinic schools, one teaching torment, the other annihilation.

Shedd sees hell taught clearly in the Old Testament without giving references and argues that the Old Testament *Sheol* must also be hell. 'But it is utterly improbable that the final judgment would be announced so clearly as it is under the Old Dispensation, and yet the place of retributive suffering be undesignated.' Most scholars today recognise that hell is not taught in the Old Testament and that *Sheol* is not a place of tormenting punishment.

Shedd states with confidence, but with no biblical references, that the traditional doctrine of hell is 'nowhere formally demonstrated because it is everywhere assumed' (p. 50f.). Several later writers have pointed out that we cannot build doctrine on what the Bible is supposed to 'assume' but instead on what the Bible asserts, which is the death and destruction of the impenitent

[6] Rothe, *Dogmatics*, Th, II, Abth., ii, para 46-49, 124–131.

[7] *Sin*, II, 191, 418, 425.

wicked. The assumption was not in Scripture but in Shedd's mind and culture.

Jonathan L Kvanvig, *The Problem of Hell* (OUP, 1993)
Kvanvig gives a philosophical analysis commending a 'Self Determination Thesis': 'Those in hell are there because of their determination to avoid the company of the redeemed and the God who redeems' (p. 158).

His conclusion is that 'although it is possible for persons to have hell as a place of residence or state of existence, it is also possible that those consigned to hell undergo a complete and total eradication of being' (p. 159).

Alyssa Lyra Pitstick, *Light in Darkness* (Eerdmans, 2007)
An affirmation of traditional Roman Catholic teaching about Christ's Descent to Hell, as against the revisionist teaching of Hans Urs Balthasar. Pitstick asserts the true doctrine of the Church to be

> First, Christ descended in His soul united to His divine Person only to the limbo of the Fathers. Second, His power and authority were made known throughout all of hell, taken generally. Third, He thereby accomplished the two purposes of the Descent which were 'to liberate the just' by conferring on them the glory of heaven and 'to proclaim his power.' Finally, His descent was glorious, and Christ did not suffer the pain proper to any of the abodes of hell.

According to this view a very limited number of people, in the very outer part of hell, were rescued by Jesus, but the vast majority of humankind outside the Church in the other parts of hell came to know Jesus' power and authority and not in any way his desire or ability to save. The souls of the damned cower in terrified respect at the awareness of Jesus, knowing that for them there is no salvation.

Jonathan Edwards, *Sinners in the Hands of an Angry God* (Whitaker House, 1997)
The classic American presentation of hell as eternal torment, 'America's most famous sermon', preached on 8 July 1741. It has been continuously in print. Why this sermon has struck such a strong a chord with Americans is a puzzle. It might have been expected that people in the New World would have looked afresh

at the Bible, free from old dogmas and the authority that imposed them. Yet this sermon is a virulent restating of the old oppressive dogma, leading people to be afraid, very afraid, of the torturing God. Perhaps Americans had brought with them into the New World the fear, mostly justified, of what had driven them from the Old World and, as pioneers in a strange land, also lived in precarious fear. Did the fear within them make Edwards' call to be afraid of God seem appropriate?

Despite quoting Psalm 73 ('Thou castedst them down into destruction') and saying that 'they will fall into destruction' (p. 17), Edwards gives greater weight to his own understanding of justice: 'Rather, justice calls aloud for an infinite punishment of their sins' (p. 19). His picture of God is of Him angry for ever.

> The God who holds you over the pit of hell, as one might hold a spider or some loathsome insect over the fire, abhors you and is dreadfully provoked . . . you are ten thousand times more abominable in His eyes than the most hateful, venomous serpent is in ours. (p. 39f)

Hell is the place where 'the Devil stands ready to fall upon them, and seize them as his own' (p. 22), rather than the eternal fire prepared for the devil and his angels. This hell is also God's doing.

> He will have no regard for your welfare, nor will He be at all concerned about your increasing suffering . . . God will have no other use to put you to, except to suffer misery; you will be allowed to exist for no other end. (p. 48f)

> You will be tormented in the presence of the holy angels, and in the presence of the Lamb, and when you are in this state of suffering, the glorious inhabitants of heaven will go forth and look on the awful spectacle, that they may see what the wrath and fierceness of the Almighty is. Then, when they have seen it, they will fall down and adore that great power and majesty. (p. 54f)

> There will be no end to this exquisitely horrible misery. (p. 56).

Dante, *Inferno* (c. 1314)

The incredibly detailed journey through twenty-four Circles of increasing torment, each one ingeniously designed to fit the crime, ending with Satan himself endlessly flaying and munching the very worst sinners, including Judas Iscariot. A famous mixture of

Graeco-Roman Pagan mythology, (Virgil is the Guide), Biblical references, Roman Catholic elaboration, and a vivid imagination.

Geoffrey Rowell, *Hell and the Victorians* (Clarendon, 1974)
This is an interesting book which does not argue for any particular doctrine of hell.

Rowell describes and summarises the intense debate in 19th-century England about hell. 'There were few issues which figured more prominently in the nineteenth-century theological debate than those of the everlasting punishment of the wicked and the immortality of the soul' (p. 1).

Early in the century, belief in a hell of eternal torment was common, widely accepted and taught in the Evangelical revival stemming from the earlier ministry of John Wesley, which had spread through every town and village and among all classes.

Criticism of the traditional doctrine of hell grew stronger through the century. The philosopher John Stuart Mill has been widely quoted: 'I will call no being good, who is not what I mean when I apply that epithet to my fellow creatures; and if such a being can sentence me to Hell for not so calling him, to Hell I will go' (*Examination of Sir William Hamilton's Philosophy*, 1865, p. 103)(pp. 113–14).

Debate raged mostly between those who held to the traditional doctrine, as part of a traditional, biblical, faith, and those who believed that, in the end, God would welcome all people to heaven. This debate came to a climax with the publication by J. W. Parker, in 1860, of *Essays and Reviews*, including an essay by the Revd H. B. Wilson, in which he wrote:

> we must rather entertain a hope that . . . all, both small and great, shall find a refuge in the bosom of the Universal Parent, to repose, or to be quickened into higher life, in the ages to come, according to His Will.[8]

In 1862 Wilson was brought before the Church of England's Court of Arches and found guilty of promoting teaching which was incompatible with the Athanasian Creed, a Latin Creed of the late 5th or early 6th century. Wilson was suspended from his post, and from his income, for one year. Wilson appealed. In 1864 the Judicial Committee of Queen's Privy Council, including the

[8] *Essays and Reviews*, p. 205-6.

Archbishops of Canterbury and York, declared that there was 'nothing in Church formularies so certain as to make expression of universal hope incompatible.' The Privy Council referred back to the decision in 1563 when a statement critical of the hope that all would be saved was removed from Church teaching. Wilson was vindicated, reinstated and, a prominent newspaper proclaimed 'Hell was dismissed with costs.'

This apparent capitulation to universalism so concerned Anglican clergy that 11,000 signed a Declaration affirming that the Church of England believed and taught 'in the words of our Blessed Lord, that the "punishment" of the "cursed" equally with the "life" of the "righteous" is "everlasting"'(p. 121).

The debate between traditionalism and universalism was the most prominent one and it takes up the majority of Rowell's book. Rowell does also mention annihilationism / conditionalism, which, unlike the two more prominent positions, denied the immortality of the soul. Rowell sees this as emerging first in the 1840s through Congregational and Baptist Ministers, especially the Congregationalist Edward White, who published *Life in Christ* in 1846. White made a distinction between physical death, which the soul survives, and spiritual death, in which the soul is destroyed. He taught that there is an intermediate state, between death and Final Judgement, where repentance is possible. Conditionalism became more widespread in the 1870s. The Prime Minister, William Gladstone, studied the debate carefully and declared himself also a conditionalist.

Rowell himself concludes:

> We cannot do without a doctrine of hell, for it stands as a vitally important reminder of the reality and seriousness of the experience of alienation, isolation, and estrangement, and the consequences of evil in human life, though to speak of hell can so easily make God thoroughly obnoxious and repellent. (p. 221)

Escapist

The writers referred to so far, with others, focus on the ultimate fate of the wicked. A few have written also about the intermediate state of the wicked and their ability still to repent and be rescued by Jesus. These writers would probably welcome the title 'escapist' as an appropriate focus on the real and wonderful opportunity for escape from *Hades.* Their opponents probably call them 'escapist' with at least something of the connotation that these writers are fleeing from reality. 'The Wider Hope' is another term which has been used to describe the same position as 'escapism'.

C. S. Lewis is the most well known 'escapist', affirming his belief with increasing force through various books. Lewis does not base his view on the distinction between *Hades* and *Gehenna,* but on the eternal loving, saving, ministry of Jesus and His Church.

C. S. Lewis, *The Great Divorce* (Collins 1946, 1977)

A tour de force of supernatural and psychological imagination depicting hell as a bleak, dreary town full of rancour and bitterness, out of which a bus takes any who want to board, to the outskirts of heaven. Some shake off the habits which have taken them to hell. Many don't and choose to board the bus for the return journey to hell. The 'habits' are 'personified' as clinging animals, mostly reptilian, daemons as in Greek mythology, or demons. Their role is to keep people from the repentance which would enable them to move on to heaven. Once these daemons are renounced and killed, they are resurrected as angelic helpers, also animal-like.

Lewis supports the idea of hell as somewhere horrendous in which people are trapped - but by their own doing - while also affirming that it is possible to escape from hell. This is his latest treatment of hell, closest to his final word.

C. S. Lewis, *The Problem of Pain* (Collins 1940, 1977)

Lewis devotes a chapter to hell, asserting human free will and its eternal consequences:

> the Divine labour to redeem the world cannot be certain of succeeding as regards every human soul. Some will not be redeemed. There is no doctrine which I would more willingly remove from Christianity than this, if it lay in my power. But it has the full support of Scripture and, specially, of Our Lord's own words. (p. 106)
>
> And here is the real problem: so much mercy, yet still there is Hell.

> I am not going to try to prove the doctrine tolerable. Let us make no mistake; it is *not* tolerable. But I think the doctrine can be shown to be moral. (p. 108)

Lewis suggests the example of the most depraved, unrepentant man, forever choosing not to accept any guilt, and therefore blocking any possibility of forgiveness. 'Finality must come some time' (p. 112).

In detailing Jesus' words about hell, Lewis ignores the distinction between *Hades* and *Gehenna.* This leads him to the common misconception that Jesus 'combines the idea of torment and destruction' (p. 113). He holds to the immortality of the soul and tries to make sense of the immortal suffering destruction. 'If soul can be destroyed, must there not be a state of *having been* a human soul?' (p. 113). This 'state' could possibly be a conjecture, but the concepts of a state of something and something not being any more are most naturally in contradiction to each other. 'What is cast (or casts itself) into hell is not a man: it is "remains"' (p. 113). Lewis here plays down the Biblical language of utter destruction which leaves no such remains. He compares it with burning a log, when Scripture compares it with burning stubble, or weeds in a furnace.

> I notice that Our Lord, while stressing the terror of hell with unsparing severity usually emphasises the idea not of duration but of *finality.* Consignment to the destroying fire is usually treated as the end of the story – not as the beginning of a new story.

But despite this recognition of the import of Jesus' words, Lewis illogically continues to hold to the innate immortality of the soul. 'That the lost soul is eternally fixed in its diabolical attitude we cannot doubt: but whether this eternal fixity implies endless duration – or duration at all – we cannot say' (p. 115). Lewis is clearly struggling here, contradicting himself, writing of something eternally fixed which may have no duration at all. If he had accepted that human souls are not innately immortal, he would have been able to argue more logically his main point, that we are free to turn away from God, and our true home in heaven, turning to a place made not for humans but for the devil and his angels, and that ultimately God will allow us to choose to turn away from life into death and destruction.

Lewis also writes of the objection to hell that death ought not to be final, that there ought to be a second chance. 'I believe that if a million chances were likely to do good, they would be given' (p. 112).

C. S. Lewis, *The Pilgrim's Regress* (Collins 1933, 1977)

An allegory of a soul wandering through all the false philosophies of the world before coming to 'Mother Kirk' and the true faith. Here Lewis tries to explain Hell as putting a limit on evil (albeit a seemingly never-ending 'limit'). He also writes, briefly, of the possibility of repentance beyond what is normally thought.

The wanderer is called John. He begins living in Puritania, where he is taken to see the Steward, the representative of the Landlord. The Steward

> was an old man with a red, round face, who was very kind and full of jokes, so that John quite got over his fears and they had a good talk about fishing tackle and bicycles. But just when the talk was at its best, the Steward got up and cleared his throat. He then took down a mask from his wall with a long white beard attached to it and suddenly clapped it on his face, so that his appearance was awful. 'And,' he said, 'Now I am going to talk to you about the Landlord. The landlord owns all the country, and it is *very, very* kind of him to allow us to live on it at all – very, very kind.' He went on repeating 'very kind' in a queer song-sing voice so long that John would have laughed, but that now he was beginning to be frightened again.

The Steward then shows John an 'enormous' list of 'all the things the Landlord says you must not do' with the warning, from behind the mask, that if John breaks even one of these rules 'He'd take you and shut you up for ever and ever in a black hole full of snakes and scorpions as large as lobsters – for ever and ever.' With the mask off the Steward finally whispers 'I shouldn't bother about it all too much if I were you' (p. 30f).

At the end of the journey John is shown by his angel Guide that there truly is a black hole which is chosen by people themselves. 'The Landlord does not condemn men to lack of hope; they have done that themselves' (p. 226). The Guide then sings:

> God in His mercy made
> The fixed pains of Hell,
> That misery might be stayed. (p. 227)

The Guide explains that

> The Landlord has taken the risk of working the country with free tenants instead of slaves in chain gangs; and as they are free there is no way of making impossible for them to go into forbidden places and eat forbidden fruits . . . You must not try to fix a point after which a return is impossible, but you can see that there will be such a point somewhere. (p. 228)
>
> The Landlord does not make the blackness. . A black hole is blackness closed, limited . . . evil is fissiparous and could never in a thousand eternities find any way to arrest its own reproduction . . . The walls of the black hole are the tourniquet on the wound through which the lost soul else would bleed to a death she never reached. It is the Landlord's last service to those who will let him do nothing better for them. (p. 228f)

John Sanders, *No Other Name* (Eerdmans, 1992 / SPCK and the C. S. Lewis Centre, 1994)

'What John Sanders offers us in this book is a careful and impressive exposition and defence of what he calls "inclusivism", that is, the possibility of the accessibility of salvation to the unevangelised' (p. xv). So writes Michael Green in his Foreword. The possible salvation is a salvation beyond death. Sanders asserts 'all unevangelized will be given an opportunity after death to receive Christ' (p. 5). He describes this as 'an idea developed in the early church and currently being revived in popularity' (p. 4).

Sanders argues that the traditional view of hell, which he labels 'restrictivism', 'seriously puts in jeopardy . . . the great love of God for all humanity.' 'Restrictivism gives far too much ammunition to the critics of Christianity' (p. 6). Sanders seeks 'to challenge those involved in missions to develop sound motivations' and to 'give those who now meekly believe in the wider hope the theological muscle they need' (p. 7). He also provides 'a comprehensive typology and survey of the literature in this important topic' given that he is 'not aware of any comparable English-language works written this [20th] century' (p. 7).

Sanders affirms 'two essential truths' which are foundational to Christian thinking, and which also give rise to 'the problem of the unevangelised.' 'The first is God's universal salvific will . . . The second is the particularity and finality of salvation only in Jesus' (p. 25). He goes on to assure readers that he is in every way a conservative Evangelical, holding that 'the Bible is the final authority for faith and practice' (p. 32).

After presenting and countering the arguments of both restrictivism (traditionalism) and universalism as 'in their own way incompatible with the key premises of God's universal salvific will and the finality of Jesus' (p. 131), Sanders turns to 'wider hope' (escapist) views.

> The idea that people will receive an opportunity after death to hear about Christ and to accept or reject him is not a new one on the theological scene. It became well known through the Alexandrian theologians Clement of Alexandria and Origen but fell out of favour after the time of Augustine. It was revitalized in the nineteenth century and is now finding increasing popularity among Lutheran theologians and even some noteworthy evangelicals. (p. 177)

Sanders lists twenty theologians of the 20th century and their works supporting escapist views. Sanders notes that in the Apostles' Creed millions of Christians every Sunday affirm the descent of Christ into hell. 'Few doctrines are as familiar but as little discussed as this one' (p. 206).

'The idea of an intermediate state and the possible release from hell of sinners were common among both Jews and Gentiles in the New Testament era' (p. 182). 'Liturgies involving prayers for the dead were widespread throughout the entire geographic range of the early church' (p. 183). 'That the doctrine was taken for granted by A.D. 150 is evident from the fact that the heretics Marcion and the Valentinians, who were criticised on most of their beliefs by the early Church Fathers, were not challenged at all on this point' (p. 183). '[T]he doctrine of Christ's descent into hell and the release of souls therefrom was well established by the end of the first century. The only question through this time involved *who* was released' (p. 184).

> Early Christians, such as Ignatius of Antioch, Irenaeus and Tertullian, limited 'the dead' who benefited from Christ's redemptive work to the Old Testament patriarchs and prophets . . . The second school of thought held that Christ released any who desired salvation from the realm of hell . . . This view was put forward as early as the second century by Melito, and later by Hippolytus, Clement of Alexandria, Origen,

Athanasius, Gregory of Nazianzus, Ephraem and Ambrose. (p. 184)

Sanders also lists five other Fathers who 'perhaps' put forward the same view.

'By far the most important and controversial texts used in support of postmortem evangelism are 1 Peter 3:18–20 and 4:6' (p. 185). Sanders, and others, make little of Jesus holding the keys of *Hades.* Sanders presents the thinking of three 'Leading Defenders' of escapism: Joseph Leckie in the early 20th century, Gabriel Fackre, an American Theological School professor writing in the 1980s, and George Lindbeck, a Professor at Yale University, writing in the 1970s and 1980s. All of these, like Sanders, see the strongest arguments for escapism as from Biblical truths rather than from particular Bible texts.

Despite setting out to give 'theological muscle' to those who believe in the 'wider hope', Sanders ends his book meekly. 'I am merely suggesting that these positions have more biblical warrant and theological plausibility than either restrictivism or universalism and that the wider hope also has a venerable history in the church' (p. 281).

Clark Pinnock, *A Wideness in God's Mercy* (Wipf and Stock, 1992)
Pinnock argues that 'a grace-filled postmortem encounter with Christ' will be available to 'those who sought God during their earthly lives and loved him, though they had not heard of Jesus' (p. 171). These people will be faithful Jews and followers of other religions or none. Pinnock argues in the context of the encounter between Christianity and other faiths and the need to affirm both God's universal will to save all people, and Jesus Christ as the one mediator between God and humanity. He explores various approaches to how Christians should understand and relate to people of other faiths, commending his assurance that the saving will of God will continue to be worked out by Jesus beyond death.

Pinnock does not draw a clear distinction between *Hades* and *Gehenna*. He sees the possibility of the saving encounter with Jesus happening when people meet Jesus at the Final Judgement. This means that Pinnock is unable to build on Jesus saying that He has the keys of *Hades*, a verse which Pinnock does not mention.

Without being able to draw on much of what the Bible teaches about *Hades* / *Sheol*, Pinnock concludes 'The exegetical evidence may not be plentiful, but the theological argument is strong' (p. 172). Pinnock argues that it is generally accepted that the Old Testament Job will be saved, although he was not a believer in the God of Israel. Other 'holy pagans' are similarly commended by the Bible. Faithful Jews from Abraham onwards are also counted among the 'saved'. Jesus spoke of those being saved who had responded with compassion to His poor brothers and sisters. Cornelius is described in Acts as 'righteous' before he had heard about Jesus from Peter. Babies who die in infancy are generally now regarded as 'in heaven'. Apart from the later Cornelius, none of these expressed specific faith in Jesus in this life, but are regarded as among the faithful in the next life. If, as Pinnock asserts, only Jesus can bring people to heaven, Jesus must have, for all these people, another way of salvation than through people declaring their allegiance to Him in this life. We know therefore that such a way exists, through Jesus, and we can be sure that the loving, generous, God will use this way to bring many to know and enjoy Himself for ever.

> God allows us a generous hope, however we may explain it, however the mechanics work. God boosts our morale by sharing with us the information that salvation will be large and generous in the end. This hope coheres well with the picture of God's love for the whole world and the universal covenant he made with all flesh. (p. 154)

Some people, such as Hitler, Pinnock argues, will refuse all Jesus' offers of salvation and will be destroyed. But Jesus' invitation to salvation will be extended to all people either in this life or in the next.

Pinnock quotes a statement of the Roman Catholic Second Vatican Council:

> They also can attain to everlasting salvation who through no fault of their own do not know the gospel of Christ or his church, yet sincerely seek God, and, moved by grace, strive by their deeds to do His will as is known to them through the dictates of conscience (*The Church,* chap.16). (p. 159)

J. A. MacCulloch, *The Harrowing of Hell* (T&T Clark, 1930)

MacCulloch argues that the concept of Jesus rescuing people from *Hades* is consistent with Scripture:

> From at least the second century there was no more well-known and popular belief, including the Descent to Hades, the overcoming of Death and Hades, the Preaching to the Dead, and the Release of Souls, and its popularity steadily increased. After a detailed investigation, we shall see that, as expressed then and later, the belief owes little or nothing to Pagan myths, though the form in which it is expressed is mythical, *i.e.* in accordance with current conceptions of the Other World. (p. 45)

MacCulloch points out that the descent of Jesus into death, the place of the dead, *Hades,* is clear in the Epistles: Ephesians 4:9, Romans 10:7, Hebrews 13:20. He sees this as 'a natural development of Palestinian Jewish thought – Jesus in Hades, and he cannot keep quiet any more than he did in this life . . .'

MacCulloch concludes boldly: 'The Cross, the Crucified Saviour, is active in the Other World as on this earth.'

Revd George Bartle, DD, DCL, *The Scriptural Doctrine of Hades* (4th edn, London, 1874)

A presentation of *Hades* as distinct from *Gehenna*. The book was published at a time of intense controversy about the nature of hell and, running to at least four editions, must have been widely read at the time. The copy I read in Cambridge University Library, however, had many pages uncut, the book having not been read at all in the previous 136 years. This is one small indication of the lack of attention to the distinction between *Hades* and *Gehenna* throughout the 20th century.

Bartle, like Whiston a century before, teaches that *Hades* is the place before the Final Judgement, *Gehenna*, for which he, also like Whiston, uses the word 'hell', the place after the Final Judgement:

> The souls of men at death enter upon a state of happiness or misery, according to the manner in which they lived and the condition in which they died, and this happiness, or misery, is neither so complete nor intensified as it will be after the Great Judgment, into heaven or hell.

Bartle states that this is historic Anglican teaching as shown by the prayer for the departed in the *Book of Common Prayer*. He criticises those who teach that people enter either heaven or hell at death as either ignoring or making too little of the intermediate states. He criticises the Authorised Version (the King James Bible) for confusing matters, not only by translating *Hades* and *Gehenna* with the one word 'hell' but also by translating the one word *Sheol* variously as hell (Job 26:6), grave (Genesis 42:38) or pit (Psalm 88:4).

Joel Buenting (ed.), The Problem of Hell: A Philosophical Anthology (Ashgate, 2010)
Thirteen essays by various authors arguing both for and against the traditional doctrine, with two essays suggesting rescue from *Hades*, although they too fail to see the significance of the distinction between *Gehenna* and *Hades.*

Buenting states that, 'The problem of hell . . . poses a problem for anyone who believes (a) there is life after death and (b) some people suffer for eternity' (p. 1).

In his final essay he argues 'there is no non-problematic version of the doctrine of hell' (p. 6).

Claire Brown and Jerry L Walls, in 'Annihilationism: A Philosophical Dead End?' dismiss annihilationism as based mostly on philosophy and a patently 'new' interpretation of Scripture. They claim to have won the philosophical argument, showing serious flaws in annihilationism, and state that the onus is still on the annihilationists to prove their interpretation of Scripture. They do not respond seriously to the work of Fudge and others which does indeed provide the detailed exposition of Scripture in favour of the ultimate annihilation of the wicked.

Brown and Walls argue that the annihilationist view equates God to a child unable to reach certain levels in a video game (*sic*) and then simply unplugging the machine, behaviour which they see as childish, and therefore not divine. But, using the same analogy, the traditional view of hell is that the characters in the game have become truly and irredeemably stuck in a horrible low level, and God does not even have the option to unplug. The game has to 'go wrong' for all eternity. Where then is divine omnipotence?

Andrei A. Buckareff and Allen Plug Value, in 'Finality, and Frustration: Problems for Escapism?', argue that there is the possibility of escape from hell, an argument they call 'escapism'.

In a previous publication they

> defined escapism as the conjunction of the following two claims:

> 1. Hell exists and might be populated for eternity.
>
> 2. If there are any denizens of hell, then at any time they have the ability to accept God's grace and leave hell and enter heaven. (p. 78)

Buckareff and Plug acknowledge the argument that there is little specific Scriptural backing for such a view, but argue that it is consistent with the character of God as shown throughout Scripture: 'we should expect that God would make provision for persons to convert in the eschaton [age to come] and that the opportunities for persons to convert should not be exhausted by a single post-mortem opportunity' (p. 78).

Buckareff and Plug argue that escape from hell is a possibility which people may or may not use. It may be that all people take this escape route out of hell (universalism) or it may be that some, even many, do not, and stay tormented in hell.

Stephen T. Davis, in 'Hell, Wrath, and the Grace of God', offers 'a proposal (or, better, conjecture) - postmortem evangelism' (p. 97).

> Beginning with Clement of Alexandria, (AD ca. 150 - ca. 213), several of the Church Fathers (e.g. Gregory of Nazianzus in his *Orations,* 45.23, and Cyril of Alexandria in his *Paschal Homily,* 7) argued that the descent into Hades had the effect of rescuing righteous pagans as well . . . In Hades, Christ (or, Clement suggested, perhaps the apostles) preached the gospel to them; some accepted and so were rescued. (p. 98)

Davis quotes Clement:

> I think it is demonstrated that the God being good, and the Lord powerful, they save with a righteousness and equality which extend to all that turn to Him, whether here or elsewhere. For it is not here alone that the active power of God is beforehand, but it is always and everywhere at work. (p. 99)

Davis suggests rather than argues with conviction:

> Perhaps they live in the post-mortem (but pre-last judgment) state that Paul seems to speak of in 2 Corinthians 5:8 and Philippians 1:23,24. And in John 5:28–9 Jesus is even reported to have said that the dead will hear the message of the Son of God. (p. 99)

Davis, like Whiston, points to the implication of forgiveness in the age to come in Matthew 12:32. He points out that Jesus' ability 'for all time' to save those who approach God through him, as in Hebrews 7:25, applies to every conceivable time, or all ages. For Davis also the picture of the heavenly Jerusalem with gates always open in Revelation 21 points to the continuing openness of God to those who call to Him, in this life and in the life to come.

Davis, however, remains tentative:

> perhaps some who die in ignorance of Christ will hear the good news, repent, and be rescued. Perhaps even some denizens of hell will do so too. Again the key word here is *perhaps.* There are no grounds to dogmatize here. (p. 102)

Experience

Christian doctrine has been described as derived from Scripture, Tradition, Reason and Experience. These four elements form the Wesleyan Quadrilateral, identified by Albert C. Outler in 1964 as a summary of the sources of doctrine used by John Wesley. Scripture is seen as the most important source and the other three sources are useful in interpreting and applying Scripture. In the terms used in this book, we begin by listening to Jesus, listen also to the rest of the Bible, and to the Holy Spirit communicating through the Church (including in previous years), through Reason, and through Experience. So far we have examined Scripture, Tradition, and Reason. It is important also to examine Experience. As in the book of Acts, this Experience includes visions, coincidences, and lives changed to become more holy.

At first sight, it would seem unlikely that there is any human experience in this life of life beyond death. However a surprising number of people have reported what they understood as an experience of life beyond death, commonly called a 'near-death experience'. Although, as with any subjective experience, these accounts cannot be verified, it is good to include them as part of the whole picture.

Howard Storm, *My Descent into Death* (Clairview, 2000)

A detailed account of a lengthy near-death experience, beginning with darkness and torment and ending in the light of Jesus and His angels.

Visiting Paris in June 1985, Storm felt that he had been suddenly and inexplicably shot in the stomach. A hole had suddenly formed in the wall of his stomach. Acid leaked out attacking everything around. Later Storm was told that if he had had the necessary surgery within five hours, he would have survived. For various reasons he had to wait at least ten hours before surgery. Despite all his efforts, he died.

He found himself being drawn by hidden voices down a long dark corridor. After a while he became suspicious that their promises of going to a better place were empty. The voices mocked him, tormented him and finally set upon him in a gruesome way. 'Now I was a worm cast into the outer darkness and had neither strength nor power, nor my inner rage to protect me' (p. 25). 'Little strength was left to resist becoming a creature gnashing his teeth in the outer darkness' (p. 28).

Eventually Storm remembered a song from Sunday School. For many years as an adult he had dismissed all Christianity and had nothing to do with it. But, as the words 'Jesus loves me, this I know' came back to him from somewhere, he thought that maybe there could be hope for him.

> A ray of hope began to dawn in me, a belief that there really was something greater out there. For the first time in my adult life I wanted it to be true that Jesus loved me. I didn't know how to express what I wanted and needed, but with every bit of my last ounce of strength, I yelled out into the darkness 'Jesus, save me.'
>
> Far off in the darkness I saw a pinpoint of light like the faintest star in the sky. I wondered why I hadn't seen it before. The star was rapidly getting brighter and brighter. At first I thought it might be some *thing* not someone. It was moving towards me at an alarming rate. As it came closer, I realized that I was right in its path and I might be consumed by its brilliance. I couldn't take my eyes off it; the light was more intense and more beautiful than anything I had ever seen. It was brighter than the sun, brighter than a flash of lightning. Soon the light was upon me. I knew that while it was indescribably brilliant, it wasn't just light. This was a living being, a luminous being approximately eight feet tall and surrounded by an oval of radiance. The brilliant intensity of light penetrated my body.

> Ecstasy swept away the agony. Tangible hands and arms gently embraced me and lifted me up. I slowly rose up into the presence of the light and the torn pieces of my body miraculously healed before my eyes. All my wounds vanished and I become whole and well in the light. More importantly the despair and pain were replaced by love. (p. 29f)

Storm knew that this being was Jesus, who had heard him and did love him.

> I cried and cried from joy and the tears kept coming. Joy upon joy billowed through me. He held me and caressed me like a mother with her baby, like a father with his long lost prodigal son. I cried all the tears of a lifetime of hopelessness and shame due to my unbelief. I cried all the tears of joy and salvation. I cried like a baby and couldn't stop crying. He held me close and stroked my back. We rose upward, gradually at first, and then, like a rocket, we shot out of that dark and detestable hell. (p. 31)

All around was an intense loving light. While Storm was in that healing, soothing embrace, he was shown his life and especially the effect he had made on other people. He was ashamed and humbled, but assured throughout by Jesus that he was forgiven. Storm had many questions to which Jesus and the angels gave specific answers. Then, with great reluctance, he returned to this life, and to the hospital recovery room, where no one expected him to live.

Storm talks of his experience as having been in hell and in heaven. He seems not to know the distinction between *Hades* and *Gehenna.* But he writes of the ultimate end of those in 'hell' not to be there for ever but to be annihilated:

> For some people this may culminate in the ultimate annihilation of their being after they have existed in this eternity without seeking their way back to God. For some there can be a possibility of salvation. In the Christian tradition, Jesus Christ journeyed into the depths of Hell and saved lost souls. This could happen again. The terrible truth is that the deeper people are into degradation the less willing they are to want salvation. Too many desire annihilation as relief from the torment. (p. 129)

The torment Storm describes is very similar to the torment of Hades described by Jesus in the parable of the Rich Man and Lazarus. Storm's experience shows that people in this place of darkness and torment can be quickly delivered by calling out for Jesus to rescue them. '[T]he reason why God gave me a second chance was because God loves me. God gives all of us second, third, fourth, fifth, sixth, seventh, and more chances' (p. 91).

Storm, now a Christian minister, is keen that people should understand the eternal consequences of what they do in this life. 'As we live in God's love or opposed to God's love, we are making our choice' (p. 151). '[W]hether people claim they are a Christian or not is not what is ultimately important. What is important is whether one loves as He loved' (p. 154).

Bill Wiese, *23 Minutes in Hell* (Charisma House, 2006)

The account of an extraordinary night time 'visit' on which the writer was taken during the night of 23 November 1998. It seems that he didn't actually die, but was taken away in spirit.

Wiese found himself firstly in an intensely hot prison cell with powerful aggressive demon warders. He was shielded somewhat from the full effects of the pain the warders tried to inflict on him. He crawled out of the cell, into overwhelming darkness, making his way down to a pit of fire in which people were in torment, with huge demons all around. He then saw an opening in the roof.

> It was the entrance to an upward tunnel, approximately thirty-five feet in diameter. The fiendish creatures lined the tunnel walls as well. They were distinctly wicked. Their eyes were cauldrons of evil and death. Everything was filthy, stinking rotten and foul. There was one other distinguishing aspect about these creatures – they all seemed to possess a hatred for mankind. They were the epitome of evil. The creatures seemed to be chained, or attached in some fashion, to the cavern walls. I was relieved to know that they could not reach me. (p. 30)

Wiese was then lifted out through the opening and the tunnel, into the healing embrace of Jesus, into an intense and marvellous light. From this perspective the huge intimidating demons looked like tiny ants. 'Looking back, I now realise that the light that was present when I was dropped into the cell was, in fact, the Lord's presence. When He left, it resumed its normal state of darkness' (p. 32).

Wiese understood that his mission is now to tell people about what he saw and to warn them of the reality of hell. At first he was reluctant to describe such an unlikely experience, but eventually he told a few people. These people told others and Wiese was invited to a few small groups and churches to tell his story. One church recorded his account and copies were passed far and wide. Without seeking any publicity, Wiese has spoken in many churches and on radio, and his book became a New York Times best-seller.

Wiese himself has questioned why he should have been selected for such an extraordinary experience and mission. He describes himself as a suit-and-tie wearing estate agent ('realtor' in the US), old-fashionedly conventional. Maybe Jesus thought that the best person to show people round a place where they might be living was an estate agent? And all the better if this estate agent is not known for any flights of imagination of his own.

Wiese calls the place he went to 'hell'. He writes with a traditional understanding of the meaning of hell. He seems not to know the distinction between *Hades* and *Gehenna.* Twice in his book he stresses, however, that the place he visited was 'Sheol / Hades'. The darkness and torment are consistent with Jesus' words about *Hades.* The prison-like nature of the place is consistent with this being a remand prison for those awaiting final judgement. The hidden presence of Jesus in that place protected him from the full effects of the attacks of the demons. The opening through which he was lifted out of that place was a permanent opening in the roof, around which the demons had been chained so as not to be able to stop people leaving. Wiese's experience shows a place of terrible affliction for people. His experience also indicates that Jesus can make His presence felt in that place and that there is a way out which leads directly to Jesus and His light.

Richard Kent and Val Fotherby, *The Final Frontier* (Marshall Pickering, 1997)

Kent and Fotherby present the near death experiences of twenty-five people, in order to help people to see the reality of heaven and hell and turn to Jesus. Some, not all, of these people had an experience or vision of 'hell'.

Ian McCormack received a fatal sting from jellyfish while scuba-diving.

> I had acknowledged God as my Lord and Shepherd just before I died and He led me through the valley of death, but at the moment of deepest blackness a brilliant light shone on me and drew me straight out . . . Looking back I was able to see the darkness fading either side and could feel the power and presence of the light drawing me up into a circular opening far above me, like a speck of dust caught in a brilliant beam of sunlight. (p. 6)

Dr Dick Eby fell through a rotten railing onto a concrete pavement. 'By the time the paramedics arrived I was a bloodless corpse hanging by its feet in the bush with my scalp torn loose' (p. 41). After a wonderful experience of heaven, he came back to life. Five years later he was in Israel visiting 'the tomb of Lazarus'. He felt again the heavenly presence of Jesus who took him briefly to visit hell.

> 'My son,' said Jesus, 'I want you to know that the present hell is a holding tank for the unsaved souls, pending the eventual judgement. God is not there. People who elect to go to hell do not want him to interfere with their plans, they just tell him one way or another to stay out of their lives. My Heavenly Father said He will give the desires of their hearts to all of His creatures. He grants their desires by placing them in a holding tank apart from him until that day when they will be called and judged before Him.'

Eby describes:

> The terror was unbelievable . . . I was surrounded by demons and they seemed to be so excited they were doing a fancy rock and roll dance in honour of getting me there. Thousands of them shouted to me that I would never get out . . . I wanted to get out of there and screamed and yelled . . . Suddenly however, I was snatched out of there and I found myself standing before the great white throne which St John describes in the book of Revelation. (p. 48f)

Christine Eastell was fatally injured in a car crash.

> While I was in this limbo state with the machines in effect keeping my body alive, my spirit left my body . . . I began to go down into a very deep pit . . . I was desperate to get out and when I saw what I thought was a small opening I began to claw desperately. But the more I tried to get to this opening the

> more distant it became. It was an impossible situation. All around there were ordinary people and they were in such deep pain and despair. They seemed to be tormented by an enormous sense of guilt which was reflected in their faces . . . In the darkness I became aware of an even more evil presence than I had already felt and there, high up above anything, was this creature I just know was Satan . . . What could I do? There I was in hell, with Satan and in total despair. I had thought I was a Christian, but I had not committed my life to Jesus. At that point I thought, 'Lord, please just rescue me.' I prayed for forgiveness . . . Jesus heard my prayer and He lifted me up from hell into His presence. I looked up and there stood Jesus in all His glory. (p. 79f)

Oden Fong overdosed on LSD.

> I remember my heart beating fast and then ceasing. I peacefully nodded off into death. Then everything started to get dark because I couldn't see any longer. I looked for the light and wanted to head for that light. That was what the mediums and psychics had told me to expect. When I could see no light, in desperation I cried out 'Jesus, if you're real, save me.' Then something extraordinary happened. In that darkness, there was light, flashing light that became brighter and brighter. Pretty soon I woke up and could make out the figure of a man in front of me. The brightness was such that I couldn't bear to look at Him. (p. 118)

George Ritchie, *Return from Tomorrow* (Kingsway / Chosen Books, 1978)

In December 1943 Ritchie developed double pneumonia while at army training camp. He was pronounced dead but returned to life. Ritchie went on to become a doctor and psychiatrist.

Ritchie found himself outside his body not realising that he had died. He was consumed with his desire to be home for Christmas and dashed off in what he thought was the direction of home. Eventually he realized that he was indeed 'only' a spirit whom other people could not see, although, like all near-death experiencers he felt very much alive. He returned to the army hospital.

As Ritchie stood by his own body, the room filled with light and he knew that he had to stand in the loving presence of *'the* Son of

God.' '[A]long with His radiant presence – simultaneously, though in telling about it I have to describe them one by one – had also entered every single episode of my entire life' (p. 49). Ritchie responded with 'self-pity and self-excuse . . . wanting to justify myself' (p. 55).

Ritchie was taken, with Jesus, to a large city on earth where he could see the spirits of the dead desperately and unsuccessfully trying to communicate with living people. 'Lay not up for yourselves treasures on earth! For where your treasure is, there will your heart be also,' came unexpectedly to mind. He questioned whether his own heart had been fixed on earthly treasure. Then he saw other spirits of the dead also desperately unable to communicate. When he looked at Jesus, he understood that these were suicides 'chained to every consequence of their act' (p. 59). Then he saw the spirits of dead alcoholics in a bar desperately wanting to drink alcohol but unable. One or two were able to step into a living man when the living one passed out in a stupor. In all these places Ritchie could see Jesus there, but the others could not. 'Maybe whenever our center of attention was on anything else, we could block out even Him' (p. 63).

Next Ritchie and Jesus went to a wide, flat plain with no living people.

> The plain was crowded, even jammed with hordes of ghostly discarnate beings . . . And they were the most frustrated, the angriest, the most completely miserable beings I had ever laid eyes on . . . everywhere people were locked in what looked like fights to the death, writhing, punching, gouging. (p. 63)

'If I suspected before that I was seeing hell, now I was sure of it . . . These creatures seemed locked into habits of mind and emotion, into hatred, lust, destructive thought-patterns.' Their thoughts could be heard by all, mostly 'yelps of envy and wounded self-importance' (p. 64f).

> Perhaps it was not Jesus who had abandoned them, but they who had fled from the Light that showed up their darkness. Or . . . were they as alone as at first appeared? Gradually I became aware that there was something else on that plain of grappling forms . . . That entire unhappy plain was hovered over by beings seemingly made of light . . . I could see that these immense presences were bending over the little creatures on

> the plain. Perhaps even conversing with them. Were these bright beings angels? . . . In a realm where space and time no longer followed any rules I knew, could He be standing with each of them as He was with me?
>
> I didn't know. All I clearly saw was that not one of these bickering beings on the plain had been abandoned. They were being attended, watched over, ministered to. And the equally observable fact was that not one of them knew it . . .
>
> . . . now that I had become aware of these bright presences, I realised with bewilderment that I'd been seeing them all along, without ever consciously registering the fact, as though Jesus could show me at any moment only so much as I was ready to see. Angels had crowded the living cities and towns we had visited . . . where nobody had been any more conscious of their existence than I myself had. And suddenly I realized that there was a common denominator to all these scenes so far. It was the failure to see Jesus. Whether it was a physical appetite, an earthly concern, or absorption with self – whatever got in the way of His Light created the separation into which we stepped at death. (p. 66f.)

The last place Ritchie was taken to see was like a huge university, with people 'caught up in some all-engrossing activity: not many words were exchanged among them. And yet I sensed no unfriendliness between these beings, rather an aloofness of total concentration.' Ritchie writes 'I'd prided myself a little on the beginnings of a scientific education' (p. 69). As he looks, he isn't sure if he is seeing heaven or hell.

> Were these selfless, seeking creatures also failing in some degree to see Jesus? . . . obviously it was the truth that they were so single-mindedly pursuing. But what if a thirst for truth could distract from the Truth Himself, standing here in their midst while they searched for Him in books and test tubes . . . ? (p. 71)

This place of academic absorption was very close to the places of torment. Nine years later Ritchie recognised one of these places in an illustration in *Life* magazine of the factory for the US's second atomic submarine engine.

Ritchie was then lifted far above the earth from where he saw, at a great distance, a city which he knew to be heaven. With great reluctance he returned to his body.

Raymond A Moody, *The Light Beyond* (Rider / Random House, 1988, 2005)

In 1965, at university studying philosophy, Moody heard George Ritchie tell his story. He went on to hear and study many other such experiences, coin the phrase 'near-death experience' or NDE, and write authoritative books.

Moody quotes a 1982 Gallup poll which showed that eight million adult Americans, about one in twenty of the population, had experienced NDEs. This correlates with Moody's own research.

One of the common features of NDEs is an encounter with 'the Being of Light'. For some this is identified as Jesus, for others another figure or just a being. With such a range of people having these experiences, there are a large range of understandings of what has happened and what conclusions to draw. But 'upon their return, almost all of them say that love is the most important thing in life' (p. 38). The NDE is, overall, an experience of being loved, and people return to this life with a renewed impetus to love as they have been loved.

In the presence of the Being of Light, NDEers take part in a Life Review. 'When they see the review of their life, NDEers realise that the being of light loves and cares for them. They realise that he is not judgmental, but rather he wants them to develop into better people. This helps them to eliminate fear and focus instead on becoming loving people.

> You have to understand that the being of light isn't telling them that they have to change. My summation, after hearing hundreds of these cases, is that the people change willingly because they are in the presence of the standard of goodness, which makes them want to change their behavior radically. (p. 36f)

Moody states that only about 0.3 per cent of NDEs include an experience of darkness, torment, 'hell' of some sort – or, according to Gallup, 24,000 adult Americans (p. 25). Each of these people returned from 'hell' or were taken out of 'hell', usually into the presence of the Being of Light, before returning to this world.

CHAPTER SEVEN

HISTORY: HOW DID THE TRADITIONAL DOCTRINE OF HELL DEVELOP?

See to it that no one takes you captive through philosophy and empty deceit, according to human tradition, according to the elemental spirits of the universe, and not according to Christ.

Colossians 2:8

The assertion that the traditional doctrine of the Church on hell is incompatible with the Bible to such an extent that it should be described as a lie, is striking. How could what has been believed and taught for centuries be so misguided? How did this happen? The short answer is that the Church did not heed Paul's warning in Colossians and paid too much attention to philosophy and human tradition. In this we can maybe discern, behind the scenes, the hand of the 'elemental spirits of the universe'.

Greek Philosophy

The detrimental influence of Greek philosophy, Greek ways of thinking, in the early Church has been much acknowledged in recent years. Many of the first Christians came from backgrounds within Greek culture, naturally bringing with them Greek concepts and prejudices. These concepts were often unquestioned. After the early years, few Christians came from Jewish backgrounds so that the influence of Jewish, Old Testament, concepts and prejudices was very weak. D. W. Gundry puts it this way:

> although St. Paul mentions Judaism in *Galatians* as a schoolmaster to bring us to Christ, within the apostolic period itself Hellenistic philosophy soon appears as another schoolmaster. Nor, indeed did it prove any exception to the failing of schoolmasters at large – that of becoming an intellectual tyrant whose domination of the pupil lingers long after the pupil has left school.[1]

[1] *Scottish Journal of Theology*, 18, no 2 (1965): quoted in ACUTE, *The Nature of Hell*, p. 164.

The struggle between Greek and Jewish culture did not begin with the New Testament. The efforts of Alexander the Great and his successors to incorporate the peoples they had conquered, not only politically but also culturally, were fiercely resisted by some Jews. The Greek rulers tried to make even the Temple in Jerusalem at least partly Greek, with a Greek image alongside the traditional Jewish ones. This was 'the abomination of desolation' warned about in the book of Daniel. This Greek image led to the revolt led by Judas Maccabeus and his family. Eventually and miraculously the Temple was preserved and cleansed, a victory celebrated by Jews to this day in the festival of Hannukah. This Jewish tradition of being wary of and fighting against Greek influence, commended by Paul, was, however, not preserved in the increasingly gentile, Greek, Church.

The Greek-speaking writers of the New Testament were careful not to translate *Gehenna* with an equivalent Greek word but instead wrote the Hebrew, or Aramaic, word in Greek letters. This was probably because no equivalent Greek word existed. The original writers, with their Jewish backgrounds, indicated that here was a concept which was not found in Greek culture. Fudge comments:

> The word would mean nothing to Gentiles – it appears only once in the New Testament outside the Gospels, and that is in the very 'Jewish' epistle of James. It is not found in the pagan literature, or even the Septuagint or Josephus.[2]

Subsequent generations read the word *Gehenna* and assumed, from quite early on, that it referred to the same place as *Hades. Hades* was a word they understood, a common Greek word used to describe the abode of the dead, especially the wicked. These Greek Christians had a concept of *Hades* fairly clearly in their minds from before they were Christians, and it was 'natural' for them to understand the *Gehenna* which they did not know in terms of the *Hades* which they did know. Part of this concept was that there was only one abode of the dead, in the same way that there is only one abode of the living. 'Knowing' that there is only one place for the dead, especially the wicked, it was hard for them to take in the concept of two places: *Hades* before Final

[2] *The Fire That Consumes*, p. 96.

Judgement, and *Gehenna* after Final Judgement. Philosophy and human tradition were beginning to prevail. Those who copied the New Testament and those who translated it into Latin were faithful to the language of the writers and preserved the word *Gehenna* – now in Latin letters as well as Greek letters. But there the distinction ended. *Gehenna* was understood as another name for *Hades.*

Other writers have pointed in particular to the influence of Plato within the Church. The philosophy of Plato was, in some ways, a precursor to the insights of Jesus and the New Testament, and early Christians could take some of the arguments and concepts of Plato and use them to affirm Christian truths. But, in this welcome of the teaching of Plato, not enough care was taken to filter out concepts which were not compatible with Jesus and the rest of the Bible, especially the concept of the immortality of the soul. H. Constable, in 1886, put it this way:

> When the latter [the New Testament] says the soul shall die, Plato says it shall not die; when the latter says it shall be destroyed, Plato says it shall not be destroyed; when the latter says it shall perish and suffer corruption, Plato says it shall not perish and is incorruptible. The phrases are the very same, only that what Plato denies of all souls alike, the New Testament asserts of some of the souls of men.[3]

S. D. F. Salmond wrote in 1895 that the immortality of the soul was not a concept peculiar to Plato but part of the wider Greek way of thinking. As we noted in relation to Genesis chapter 3, the idea that the human soul survives death is common to nearly all human cultures.

> The idea of annihilation, says Plutarch, was intolerable to the Greek mind. If they had no choice left to them between entire extinction and an eternity of torment in Hades, they would have chosen the latter; almost all, men and women both would have surrendered themselves to the teeth of Cerberus, or the buckets of the Danidae, rather than to nonentity.[4]

Froom, however, points out that, according to Tertullian, the schools of the Greek philosopher Epicurus and the Roman Seneca

[3] H. Constable, *The Duration and Nature of Future Punishment London* (Hobbs, 1886), p. 42.
[4] S. D. F. Salmond, *The Christian Doctrine of Immortality* (1895), p. 608f.

taught that there is nothing after death,[5] although this was probably a minority view.

More recently, the UK Evangelical Alliance, in their book *The Nature of Hell,* also point to the influence of Plato in fixing the traditional doctrine of hell: 'Plato . . . commended the immortality of the soul on the basis that a soul which ceases at death cannot pay the punishment due for its wickedness'. A footnote reads: 'An early attack by a Christian on this and other related Platonic ideas comes from Aeneas of Gaza, in his dialogue *Theophrastus*.'[6] The same book quotes Pinnock and Brow: 'Why would anybody have turned the notion of destruction into everlasting life in hell, creating this monstrous problem? We attribute it to the influence on theology of the Greek idea of the immortality of the soul.'[7]

For many years, as Froom and others have demonstrated, Jesus' Jewish teaching about the ultimate destruction of the wicked also prevailed in the Greek Church. Not until Athenagoras, writing about 130 years after Jesus, is there teaching on the immortality of the soul, and therefore the continuing existence of the wicked, as a Christian doctrine. Athenagoras was a Greek philosopher who converted to Christianity. His idea was later embraced in the Greek Church and, more strongly, in the Roman Church.

One Greek concept was of *Hades* as a place of punishment, after which cleansed, immortal, souls can take their place among the righteous. Origen, an influential Greek teacher and writer of the 3rd century, wrote:

> There is a resurrection of the dead and there is punishment, but not everlasting. For when the body is punished the soul is gradually purified, and so is restored to its ancient rank . . . For all wicked men, and for daemons too, punishment has an end, and both wicked men and daemons shall be restored to their former rank.[8]

Origen was declared to be a heretic, but his more universalist teaching was preserved and built on in the Eastern Greek / Orthodox Churches. In Eastern Christianity, to this day, hell is seen

[5] Froom, *Conditionalist Faith*, vol. 1, p. 950.
[6] ACUTE, *The Nature of Hell*, p, 12.
[7] Pinnock and Brow, *Unbounded Love*, p. 92.
[8] Origen, *First Principles* 146, quoted in Dearmer, *The Nature of Hell*, p. 141.

as the one place of eternal torment but the fate of those in hell is not fixed eternally and absolutely.

Roman Imperialism

As well as the general influence of Greek culture and the specific influence of Plato, scholars have pointed to the influence of the experience of persecution on early Christians, especially the second century Roman writer Tertullian. In *De Spectaculis* Tertullian describes the Roman games, or spectacles, in which Christians were pitted against gladiators or lions in a fight to the death. He sees these games of persecution as inspired by demons. One day, Tertullian assures, God will turn the tables on the tormentors. The persecutors will, in God's judgement, be themselves persecuted. The delight that the Romans have taken in watching the torments of Christians will be replaced by the delight of Christians watching the torments of those who promoted the games.

Tertullian's words were clearly meant for his time, and are at odds with the teaching of Jesus about love for enemies. Percy Dearmer writes of *De Spectaculis* 'But it is quite unique at this early period (c. AD 200); there is nothing like it, so far as I have discovered, in the Fathers.'[9] Froom also shows that Tertullian's teaching on eternal torment, building on Athenagoras, was a departure from all pervious Christian teaching. Later, however, Tertullian's words were accorded more weight and taken to show that eternal torment was part of the Church's teaching from the beginning.

The Roman Empire superseded the Greek Empire, welcoming and absorbing Greek culture, which was very similar to Roman culture. The Romans had very similar gods to the Greeks, although with different names. The Romans had very similar concepts to the Greeks. The understanding continued that there was one place for the wicked after death, a place where they could not die, now called '*Infernum*' instead of *Hades*. *Infernum* originally meant 'the lower place or places' but, by combining this with the image of fire from Jesus' teaching about *Gehenna, infernum* came to mean a place of tormenting fire. Some Christians challenged this adoption

[9] Dearmer, *The Legend of Hell*, p. 33.

of Roman thinking into the church and the immortality of the soul was a matter of debate. But when, in the 4th century, the Church moved from being the persecuted minority within the Roman Empire to being the honoured majority, there was less willingness to challenge Roman ways and concepts.

Another Roman trait, which influenced the Church centred in Rome, was anti-semitism. The Roman Empire had a particular antipathy to the Jews, against the Jews' insistence on preserving a separate cultural identity. The Romans expended more energy and military manpower in crushing the Jewish revolt in AD 70 than would have been expected on objective imperial or military grounds. The Jewish revolt was very unlikely to have influenced other conquered peoples; the Jews wanted to be as separate from every other nation as from the Romans. The usual Roman way of dealing with other peoples was to demand submission, with some compromise, achieved through harsh military threats, often half hidden. With the Jews, the Romans went much further, destroying Jerusalem and exiling most Jews, as Jesus had foreseen when He wept over Jerusalem.

This antipathy to the Jews was also shown in other, less obvious ways, and is hinted at in the Gospels' description of the excessive scourging inflicted on Jesus as 'the King of the Jews.' As the Church became allied to the Empire, something of this anti-semitic attitude influenced the Church, perhaps more at first in what the Church did not do than in what it did. The Church did not look to Jewish thinking, to the Old Testament, for help in resisting the philosophies and human traditions of its age. The Church was so distant from the Jews and influenced by such antagonism to them that this was unthinkable. As Froom points out, even before the alliance with the Empire, the doctrine of eternal torment was developed specifically by Latin-speaking, Roman theologians, starting with Tertullian.

Froom himself explains the connection between Roman thinking and eternal torment as due not so much to anti-semitism, but to the prominence of legal ways of thinking in general and of punitive punishment in particular. Roman Christians related to God primarily as the Judge. They built more upon the Scriptural passages which explain salvation as the Judge reversing the verdict, particularly in Paul's letters, than on the passages which explain salvation in terms of God as Father buying back His children from the slavery in which they were trapped. Pinnock and Brow also see Roman thinking as responsible for the dominance of the legal metaphor over the family metaphor. Roman Law was a severe law, enforced by and justifying severe treatment of offenders. Those who saw the Roman Law and Roman penal practice as good and civilising were more inclined to see the same attributes in God, even in the Christian God, once that God was adopted by the Romans.

The Church, once allied to the Empire, was also increasingly comfortable in using threats and even violence for its own ends. The formal justification and limitation of the violence of war came through Augustine (354–430), and it has been commonly noted that the threat of hell was also very useful to a dominating Church. The later development of the doctrine of Purgatory, and the teaching that the prayers of the Church could relieve souls of the torments of Purgatory, ensured the Church considerable wealth from people keen to ensure that prayers were said for them after their death. Even before this development, the threat of hell was a useful tool to use against anyone threatening the authority of the Church. It is sad to relate also that the Church acquiesced and colluded in the Roman practice of torture – torture akin to what had been inflicted on Jesus by the Romans. Christians justified their use of torture by claiming that a good result would relieve the victim of many, many years of torture in hell. It was the opponents of the Church, particularly in the 18th century, who began the abhorrence and outlawing of torture which is more common today.

Manichaeism

Augustine of Hippo (now part of Algeria) was described by his contemporary Jerome as 'the one who has established anew the ancient faith.'[10] Augustine's teaching has been much revered, more in Western than Eastern Christianity, both by Roman Catholics and Protestants. Augustine's teachings on Original Sin and on Just War have been particularly influential. Another element which Augustine understood to have been part of the

[10] Jerome, *Epistola* 195.

ancient faith and which he established anew was the nature of hell as the one place of eternal torment.

Before Augustine's dramatic conversion to Christianity in 387 he had been much influenced by both the philosophy of Plato, as expounded by a later disciple Plotinus, and by the Persian religion Manichaeism. The latter was the earlier influence, more fundamental to his ways of thinking. Although Augustine understood his conversion as a radical break with his past, he consciously built on the work of Plotinus, and also retained elements of the thinking of Manichaeism, whether or not he was aware of this latter influence.

Manichaeism was developed from the work of the Persian Mani, who in the 3rd century combined some elements of Christianity and Judaism with other Eastern religions and philosophy. In Manichaeism the world is influenced and controlled by two opposing forces, Light against Darkness, Good against Evil. These two forces are almost equal and mirror each other. The realm of Good has exact counterparts in the realm of Evil. God, the 'Father of Greatness' and origin of Light and Good, is not omnipotent, but is forever locked in a battle with the powers of Darkness.

Augustine rejected the Platonic idea, taught by Origen, that all punishment must lead to the cleansing of the soul. Instead he taught that God's punishment is simply punitive, the response of an infinitely powerful being to a creature who has entered into an alliance with the eternal enemy, Satan. Augustine also taught that hell must be an eternal counterpart or mirror of heaven. As souls in heaven live forever in bliss, so souls in hell live forever in torment: 'To say, in the same context "Eternal life will be without end, eternal punishment will have an end", is utterly ridiculous.'[11] In this trenchant teaching Augustine was influenced more by the assumptions of Manichaeism than by the Bible, with its insistence on the end of evil and the ultimate complete victory of God and His Son. Even before Jesus' final victory, the devil, in the book of Job, does not have his own rival court, but is a part of the court of heaven. In Revelation 12 the devil is pictured as a great red dragon who 'swept down a third of the stars of heaven.'[12] These

[11] *City of God*, XXI.23.
[12] Revelation 12:4 (NRSV).

stars are understood to be the angels who 'fell' with the devil. Although the devil has angels working with him, there are twice as many angels working for and with God.

Following Augustine, in Western Christianity, the teaching of hell as the one place of eternal torment, presided over by the eternal enemy of God, became normal. However Percy Dearmer and others have noted that the doctrine of hell as eternal torment was not fully fixed until about the 12th century.[13] One strong influence, which questioned hell as eternal torment, was the tradition of the the Harrowing of Hell. Early Christian pictures and icons of 'hell' often showed Jesus rescuing people from this hell (or *Hades*.) This is clearly a different picture from the theological picture of eternal torment from which there is no escape. Early Christian pictures of the devil do not show him as a great power rivalling God in his opposing kingdom of hell, but as a small tempter, more like what came to be the standard picture of a demon, without any 'domain' of his own.[14] In pictures of the Harrowing of Hell, the devil is not significant. It is only later in the Middle Ages, and in the West, that hell was painted as the eternal, tormenting, domain of an eternally powerful devil.[15] Eastern European Christianity, with its emphasis on icons, including the Harrowing of Hell, retained a sense of ambiguity about hell, with the possibility of rescue from hell.

In Western Europe drama developed, instead of icons, as a primary means of teaching Christian stories and truth to an illiterate population. From early on, this Christian drama, especially the very widespread 'mystery plays', depicting the story of the whole Bible, contained scenes of the Harrowing of Hell. The earliest text we have is the *Book of Cerne* from the 8th century. Subsequent mystery plays also included a depiction of Jesus going down into hell and rescuing people from hell. The Church officially taught that these rescued people were only the righteous from the times of the Old Testament, but the popular tradition indicated a greater hope of rescue from hell.

[13] See above, pp. 118–21.

[14] See, for instance, the fresco in St Mark's Basilica, Venice, of the temptation of Jesus.

[15] See, for instance, the hell section of the Last Judgement fresco in the Cathedral or Duomo in Florence.

The Lichfield Mysteries is a modern revival of a medieval Passion Play using surviving medieval texts. After His crucifixion, Jesus descends to hell. He commands:

> Open up hell gates yet I say,
> Ye princes of pain that be present,
> Let in the King of Bliss this way
> That He may fulfil His intent.

The stage directions continue:

> The gates of hell burst open. Jesus, the Archangel Michael and angels enter.

Jesus addresses Adam:

> Peace to thee, Adam, my darling,
> And so to all thy offspring
> That righteous were on earth living.
> From me ye shall not be severed.
> To bliss now will I you bring,
> There you shall stay without ending.
> Michael, lead them, singing,
> To bliss that lasteth ever.

The devil is left with one woman, a tavern-keeper and brewer, who persistently mixed ashes and grass along with the hops and malt, and never sold a full, measured, pint of beer. The devil leads her away.[16]

Hymns, as well as plays, celebrated and taught the Harrowing of Hell, for instance 'Ye Choirs of New Jerusalem' quoted in the Introduction, written by St Fulbert of Chartres, in France, who died in 1028:

> For Judah's lion burst his chains, and crushed the serpent's head
> and brought with him from death's domain, the long-imprisoned dead.
> From hell's devouring jaws the prey alone our leader bore;
> his ransomed hosts pursue their way where he hath gone before.

The Harrowing of Hell contributed to the continuing ambiguity about hell, in both Western and Eastern Europe. The Bible

[16] *The Lichfield Mysteries*, selected and edited by Robert Leach Clydesdale (1994).

probably also contributed to this ambiguity, and, in particular, the Latin Gospels which preserved *Gehenna* as 'Gehenna', distinct from *infernum,* and described Jesus as having the keys of *Hades.* By the 13th century, however, even this continuing ambiguity disappeared, under the influence of another tradition from outside Christianity.

Islam

In the Koran, hell as eternal torment is taught clearly and repeatedly. Hell as 'an awful doom', a place of fire in which unbelievers (more than the morally wicked) dwell, from which there is no escape, is a constant part of the message of Mohammed. Surah 2, which is described by Moslems as the Koran in miniature, contains such references to this abiding hell in 20 out of 286 verses. The absolute certainty of the Koran about hell as the place of eternal torment for unbelievers carried over into Christian thinking and removed the last traces of uncertainty or ambiguity in the Church's teaching on hell.

In Southern Spain and Portugal, from 711 to 1249, Christians and Muslims lived together under Moslem rule. Political rulers were keen play down any historic antagonism between the two faiths. Encouraged by these leaders, theologians from the two communities engaged in dialogue. Christians and Moslems talked together and studied together. Moslem scholars, especially two men known by their Latin names, Avicenna (11th century) and Averroes (12th century) were respected. Moslem teaching, developing the work of Aristotle, was particularly influential. (The work of Aristotle, a pupil of Plato, had been lost in the West but preserved in Islam.) Thomas Aquinas, a Roman Catholic theologian of the 13th century, drew on this teaching in his influential and authoritative *Summa Theologica*. The thought of Aristotle was embraced by the Church through Islam. Other Moslem concepts were also welcomed if they were seen to fit in with Christian concepts, such as hell as the place of eternal torment.

R. W. Southern, an eminent Cambridge historian, wrote that Islam was influencing Christianity long before the 11th century:

> It is a remarkable fact that every single important novelty we shall touch upon can be traced back in its origin to Spain . . .

> The large constructions, the great systems and elaborations of ideas, were produced elsewhere, but the seminal ideas, whether apocalyptic or scientific or synoptic, came out of Spain.[17]

Southern quotes Paul Alvarus writing c. 860 in a biography of Eulogious, Bishop of Toledo, who was martyred in 859:

> The Christians love to read the poems and romances of the Arabs; they study the Arab theologians and philosophers, not to refute them but to form a correct and elegant Arabic . . . Alas! All talented young Christians read and study with enthusiasm the Arab books; they gather immense libraries at great expense; they despise the Christian literature as unworthy of attention.[18]

Southern continues: 'On a central theological issue Western theologians of all shades of opinion did not scruple to re-examine traditional views in the light of Islamic philosophy, or at least to restate traditional views in the language of these philosophers.' Hell was also restated with the vehemence and certainty found in the Koran.

Southern continues:

> It is tempting to linger over this fascinating prospect of Christian theology being influenced in its views and language by Islamic philosophy. And this scholastic influence was only one aspect of a wider penetration. It seems now, for example, quite certain that a work translated into French and Latin from Arabic at about this time, giving an account of Mahomet's journey through the heavens, had an influence – perhaps a profound influence – on the plan of Dante's *Divine Comedy*.[19]

The work referred to by Southern was *The Night Journey of Mohammed to Heaven* by Ibn Arabi. The certainty of Southern and others as to the specific influence of *The Night Journey* on Dante has been challenged and continues to be a matter of debate.[20] But the general influence of Islamic thinking on the development and final fixing of the Church's doctrine of hell is clear. The doctrine of eternal torment was already, before Islam, a central part of the

[17] R. W. Southern, *Western Views of Islam in the Middle Ages* (Harvard University Press, 1962).
[18] *Ibid.*, p. 21.
[19] *Ibid.*, p. 55.
[20] http://en.wikipedia.org/wiki/Divine_comedy, section on Islamic philosophy.

teaching of the Western Church. The certainty of this hell in Islam, and the forceful confidence with which it was taught, served to reinforce and strengthen the teaching of the Church.

The largest surviving medieval painting of hell in England is the Doom fresco in St Thomas' Church, Salisbury. On the right side of Jesus we see angels blowing trumpets to wake the dead from their graves and to lead some to Jesus seated in judgement and heaven above. On the left of Jesus we see demons leading the souls of the dead into the gaping, many-fanged, fiery mouth of hell. Many elements of this painting are common in medieval times. Painters did not portray what they wanted but adhered faithfully to the teaching of the Church. In the Doom painting, the souls of the damned are chained together, led to their terrible fate. Nowhere in the Bible do we find this picture of the souls of the damned chained together. Rather, Christian teaching is that each individual will be judged and dealt with on their own. In the Koran, Surah 14:49, we read of the day of judgement by Allah: 'Thou wilt see the guilty on that day linked together in chains.'[21]

The 'turning of the tables' on the perpetrators of the Roman games envisaged by Tertullian, and proclaimed by Augustine, was confirmed and strengthened by the Koran. So in the 12th century, Peter Lombard could write: 'Therefore the elect shall go forth . . . to see the torments of the impious, and seeing this they will not be affected with grief, but will be satiated with joy at the sight of the unutterable calamity of the impious.'[22] Those condemned are specifically the 'impious', similar to the 'unbelievers' in the Koran, rather than the 'wicked' referred to in the Bible.

For Thomas Aquinas in the 13th century, hell as punitive eternal torment was a given. His role was to explain and justify it:

> The magnitude of the punishment matches the magnitude of the sin . . . Now that a sin against God is infinite; the higher the person against whom the sin is committed, the greater the sin – it is more criminal to strike a head of state than a private citizen – and God is of infinite greatness. Therefore an infinite punishment is deserved for a sin committed against him.[23]

[21] M. M. Pickthall, *The Meaning of the Glorious Qur'an* (UK Islamic Mission Dawah Centre, 1997) p. 225.

[22] *Sententia*, Book 4, dist 50, para 7.

[23] *Summa*, 1a2ae; p. 27.

The revered and influential Italian writer Dante, took most of his theology from Aquinas, according to Dorothy Sayers introducing her translation of *The Divine Comedy*. Dante's *Inferno* replaced the mystery plays' Harrowing of Hell as the strongest popular picture of hell. The gates of hell burst open by Jesus were replaced with an eternal one-way gate over which were the words 'Abandon hope all you who enter here'.

The picture and understanding of hell, the one place of eternal torment for unbelievers, presided over by the devil, was now fixed.

Simplicity

The last contributory factor to the development of traditional hell was its simplicity. It was, and still is, easier to talk of one place for unbelievers after death than to talk of two. Jesus' use of two names can be seen as an unnecessary complication. The warning of *Hades* and *Gehenna*, combined with the hope that Jesus has the keys of *Hades,* can be deemed too ambiguous. Literate theologians can understand such a distinction, but, patronisingly, they can deem it too complex for 'the masses'. When clarity is needed in combating heresy, defending the faith, warning waverers, it is not natural to speak of a severe warning and yet, at the same time, of a hope of release. Preaching and teaching hell as eternal torment is the easier option.

Christian ethics, however, teach us that usually the path that seems more difficult at first proves to be less fraught in the end. So it is with the doctrine of hell. The simple warning of eternal torment has led to huge problems for the Church through the ages and particularly in our present age. The inconsistency of a God who Jesus teaches is 'kind to the ungrateful and the wicked'[24] and yet who tortures the ungrateful and wicked for eternity, is harder to explain than a God who initially allows the wicked to go to a remand prison to which His Son has the keys, before having the same Son judge them and, if they continue not to repent, send them to their destruction.

[24] Luke 6:35 (NRSV).

Spiritual Influence

The teaching of Jesus and Revelation is that *Gehenna* is an eternal fire prepared for the devil and his angels, a lake of fire into which the devil, as the victim, will the thrown, and in which he will suffer torment. The teaching of the Church has been that hell is where the devil is in charge and where he torments others while not in any way himself tormented. This turning round of truth, from one teaching to its opposite, is an astonishing feat. In people's eyes, the devil rises from the place of the victim to the place of the eternal ruler. The development took many years, many people, many influences. Is it possible that one influence was the figure who most benefited from the lie of hell, the devil himself?

Although the devil is clearly mentioned by Jesus and other New Testament writers, modern teachers tend not to mention him. Some do not believe that there is such an independently existing personified force of evil. Some are happy to pray often 'But deliver us from evil', knowing that this means 'from the evil one,' but do not bring the concept of the devil into rational discussion and debate. Listening carefully to what Jesus said, however, leads us to continue, however unfashionably, to talk of the devil as Jesus did.

The hidden nature of the devil is clear from the Gospels. The devil who tempts Jesus in person in the wilderness is clearly working behind the scenes at Jesus' crucifixion. He prompts people to say what he has said before, in almost exactly the same words. Yet in the accounts of the crucifixion, the devil is not mentioned, except as the influencer of Judas' thinking. The devil remains hidden so that it is difficult to talk of him. Earlier, when Peter tells Jesus that He surely cannot suffer as He expects, Jesus responds not directly to Peter but to the 'satan' whom he discerns hiding behind Peter's words. It took Jesus' gift of discernment to detect the devil hidden in and behind normal human behaviour. Today too, those of us who believe in the devil as a potent, although defeated, force in the world can rarely identify anything as being clearly his work. Human action, human participation, is always involved and is always the obvious factor. We can only tentatively, with the help of the Holy Spirit, glimpse the devil behind the human.

Paul's warning from Colossians encourages us, however, to point to the work of the devil behind the scenes. Paul warns that, as well as philosophy and human tradition seeking to trap us into 'dead end' ways of thinking, we need to beware 'the elemental spirits of the universe' acting not according to Christ. Spirits acting not according to Christ are working against him, working to enslave rather than to free. The chief and ruler of these spirits is the devil:

He was a murderer from the beginning and does not stand in the truth, because there is no truth in him. When he lies, he speaks according to his own nature, for he is a liar and the father of lies.

John 8:44 (NRSV)

The first lie recorded in the Bible is the serpent telling Eve that if she eats the one forbidden fruit, she will not die.[25] The serpent, in whom Christians see the devil, contradicts what God has said. The words of the serpent are proved to be a lie: Adam and Eve go on to die. The rest of the Bible affirms the truth that humans, especially the wicked, die – the death of body and, eventually, soul. As many scholars have said and written, the doctrine of the immortality of the soul, that human souls cannot and will not die, is a foundation for the doctrine of hell. We see here the hand of the devil, continuing to spread the serpent's lie that humans cannot die through 'philosophy and human tradition'. In Genesis God makes sure that Adam and Eve can no longer live for ever by removing them from the Tree of Life. God does not want his human creatures living forever at odds with Him. He does not want them to die either and goes to unimaginably great lengths to rescue them from the death to which they are now heading. But if, in the end, they refuse His rescue, they will not suffer for ever, but will have a merciful release from the horrendous life they have chosen. In propagating the lie that people will not die, the devil continues the work he had already started with Eve, making people believe that God is not good, but cruel.

If such a devil, described by Jesus and Genesis, exists, it is not surprising that he would do his best to spread the lie that he is not defeated, not the ultimate victim of Jesus, but that he has power over human life which will continue for ever. This devil would understandably want people to be more afraid of himself than

[25] Genesis 3:4.

they need to be. He would want people trapped in believing that there is no eternal hope for themselves, and particularly for their unbelieving friends, relatives or ancestors. This devil would be happy for people to see God as the eternal torturer giving the devil his eternal role, and for many to be put off coming close to such a God. This devil would equally be happy with making Christians so uneasy about talking about eternal torment as the consequence of the judgement of Jesus, that they fail to talk about judgement at all. Christians have reason to see the lie of hell originating in the father of lies.

Some Christians will find it hard to accept that God could allow such a lie, such deception, to take so firm a hold within the Church. One common insight from teaching about hell, *Hades,* and *Gehenna*, is the high value God places on human freedom.[26] All people are free to deny and reject God. If this possibility does not exist, humans are not truly free. God wants people to come to Him, to listen to Him, to live according to His word. But God will not force people to listen. He warns of the dangers that lie ahead for those who refuse to listen, especially death. But he refrains from forcing people into His ways. The father of the Prodigal Son wants and longs for his son to return, but he does not force him home. We can apply the same insight about God to the development of the doctrine of hell. The Church has failed to listen properly to Jesus and to the Bible and has become 'captive through philosophy and empty deceit, according to human tradition, according to the elemental spirits of the universe, and not according to Christ', as Paul warned the Christians in Colossae. God has graciously allowed this to happen, respecting human freedom, even to the extent of a lie penetrating the heart of the Church.

[26] For example: 'Hell is necessary not to ensure the triumph of justice and retribution to the wicked, but to save man from being forced to be good and compulsorily installed in heaven', Nicolas Berdyaev, *The Destiny of Man* (1937) pp. 266–7.

CHAPTER EIGHT

HADES EXPLORED

Then Death and Hades were thrown into the lake of fire.

Revelation 20:14 (NRSV)

The words of Jesus about *Hades* have been the most ignored part of His teaching. Several scholars ('annihilationists') have shown clearly the nature of *Gehenna*, the consuming fire where body and soul are destroyed. *Hades* as a separate place has not been expounded. At the risk of repeating some points from earlier in this book, it is good to fill this gap.

Expounding truths taught by Jesus and the rest of Scripture means both listening carefully to their actual words and also working out what follows from these words. We believe that the Holy Spirit is with us, guiding us into more truth. The words of Jesus and Scripture point us in certain directions. The Holy Spirit then shows us how to go further in these directions. The Holy Spirit guides us through logic. If we see, and others recognise, that something follows logically from Jesus' words, either necessarily or coherently, we can be confident that the Holy Spirit is guiding our thinking. The Holy Spirit also guides us through prophecy, dreams, visions. This guidance is more open to debate and cannot be relied on entirely by itself. Prophetic and visionary guidance is to be welcomed as part of the whole process, contributing to the final understanding.

Distinct

Hades is distinct from *Gehenna.* Jesus used two different words to indicate two separate places. *Hades* will eventually be destroyed in *Gehenna.* It is wrong to combine the characteristics of both places as though they were the same place.

Hades is not eternal. It is not a geographical place in this life, this Universe, this era. *Hades* is a place in the life beyond death, in the era beyond, even in 'eras to come.' But we know clearly from Revelation that *Hades* will be destroyed one day.

Hades will be destroyed at, or shortly before, the Final Judgement. It is a place where people go before the Final Judgement, pending that Judgement. *Hades* is a remand prison for people awaiting the ultimate trial.

Hades is the same place which the Old Testament writers named *Sheol.* Their understanding was that it is a place where all the dead, wicked and righteous, go. The fate of the wicked in *Hades* is, however, more fixed. Jesus talked more about *Hades* as the place for the wicked. It is possible to combine the understanding of Jesus with that of the Old Testament, by seeing different parts of *Hades*, for different categories of people. Jesus spoke of 'the outer darkness.' It is logical to think that there is also an 'inner darkness' and even a 'middle darkness' also.

The distinct nature of *Hades* has, mostly, been half recognised. Jeremias, the German Biblical scholar, in the article on *Hades* in *The Theological Dictionary of the New Testament,* sees a sharp distinction between *Hades* and *Gehenna*. *The Nature of Hell,* the report by the UK Evangelical Alliance, states, 'Given their belief that death and resurrection to final judgement are distinct events separated by a clear period of time, evangelicals have generally accepted that there must be *some* sort of intermediate state between the two.'[1] Evangelicals generally, and other writers, have not paid much attention to this intermediate state and its nature.

Affliction

The most striking element in Jesus' references to *Hades* is the deep distress of people in *Hades.* In the story of the Rich Man and Lazarus, Jesus states that the Rich Man is 'being tormented' in *Hades.* The Greek word translated 'torment' is *basanos.* Elsewhere in the Gospels the same word is translated as 'afflicted' with diseases and pains (Matthew 4:24), 'in distress' from paralysis (Matthew 8:6), 'battered' by waves, 'straining at oars against an adverse wind' (Matthew 14:24; Mark 6:48.) Of the range of seriousness that this Greek word can convey, 'torment' is at one extreme. A less extreme translation, which still conveys the sense of experiencing a powerful distressing effect (of fire, sickness, waves), is 'affliction'. The same Greek word is used in Revelation

[1] *The Nature of Hell* p19

14:11 for the fate of people in *Hades.* This can be translated 'the smoke of their affliction goes up to ages of ages'. In English 'torment' always reminds people of the discredited hell. For the truth of *Hades*, 'affliction', without connotations of hell, is better.

The affliction of the Rich Man in *Hades* is severe thirst caused by intense heat, and the sight of Abraham far away, alongside the beggar whom he had spent his life ignoring. The Rich Man had spent his life in great physical comfort; his callousness has ensured that in *Hades* he experiences great physical discomfort. To this affliction is added the knowledge that he is far away from the place and the fellowship which he had probably, like all his fellow Jews, hoped or expected to join after death. The Rich Man's first concern is for himself, showing that he has not learnt any lesson from his experience. His second concern is for his immediate brothers. It seems that the affliction of *Hades* has only confirmed his selfish mindset.

In Luke 13:28 Jesus warns all His hearers 'There will be weeping and gnashing of teeth when you see Abraham and Isaac and Jacob and all the prophets in the kingdom of God, and you yourselves thrown out' (NRSV). Elsewhere Jesus speaks of the same 'weeping and wailing and gnashing of teeth' by people in 'the outer darkness'. This darkness is therefore in *Hades* or part of *Hades.* Weeping is a response to pain of body and heart. We can weep in sympathy for others and we can also weep in deep self-pity. Wailing is also an expression of pain, and of grief, disappointment or despair. Wailing can also be an expression of intense self-pity. Gnashing of teeth is more an expression of anger and resentment.

People in *Hades*, like the Rich Man, experience and express pain, grief, despair, self pity, anger, resentment. Their affliction comes both from what is being done to them from outside themselves, and also from what they conclude inside themselves from seeing others not in such affliction. The darkness limits their sight and, probably, their understanding. They rage against whoever has put them in the miserable darkness. The little that they can see of another life affects them deeply, causing more weeping, wailing and gnashing of teeth.

Jesus took the Old Testament understanding of *Sheol,* the place of the dead about which little is known, and added to that understanding, showing that it is a place of dark affliction. Whereas in the Old Testament, *Sheol* is mostly a place of 'soul sleep', for Jesus *Hades* is a place of affliction. As we have noted, this could be that Jesus was talking particularly about the deepest darkest parts of *Hades.* It is clear that, especially for all who listen to Jesus, *Hades* is a place to be avoided at all costs.

Edward Fudge notes that at least one Jewish writing from outside the Bible but from roughly the time of Jesus shows a similar understanding to that of Jesus.

> In 4 Ezra 7:80–87 the damned weep seven ways during their intermediate detention before the judgment: in shame and remorse for the past and in fear and dread of the future, but most of all as they glimpse the glory of God, before whom they will soon be judged.[2]

The 1st-century Jewish historian Josephus also had a similar understanding. His understanding helped inform the view of *Hades* of William Whiston, Josephus' translator.

Fudge continues:

> In scriptural usage the expression 'weeping and grinding of teeth' seems to indicate two separate activities. The weeping reflects the terror of the doomed as they begin to realize that God has rejected them and as they anticipate the execution of his sentence. 'Grinding of teeth' seems to express their bitter rage and enmity towards God, who has sentenced them, and towards the redeemed, who will for ever be blessed.[3]

Jesus has Been in *Hades*

Hades and death go together. In Revelation they are described hand in hand. Death, according to Paul, is 'the last enemy'.[4] Death came into the world through sin. Death was not part of the original creation by the Author of Life. The power of sin and death is in opposition to the power of God and His Son. *Hades* is the place where this power is most at work. Death puts people in *Hades. Hades* is the place of death. When we look at *Hades* we see death and the outworking of death, the outworking of sin. When

[2] *The Fire that Consumes*, p. 104.
[3] *The Fire that Consumes*, p. 105.
[4] 1 Cor. 15:26 (NRSV).

we look at death and its outworking we see *Hades.* The outworking of sin, the power of death, was seen most clearly in the crucifixion of Jesus. It is likely that when we look at the death that Jesus suffered we also see something of the nature of *Hades.*

Hades is also the place of darkness. In *Hades* the power of darkness afflicts people. Jesus spoke to the chief priests who had had Him arrested. 'When I was with you day after day in the temple, you did not lay hands on me. But this is your hour, and the power of darkness!'[5] 'This', this arrest, this trial, and all that follows from it, is the power of darkness. When we look at the crucifixion we see the power of darkness more clearly than anywhere else. We can therefore also say that when we look at the crucifixion we see *Hades*, the place of darkness, more clearly.

In being crucified Jesus was 'handed over' to other powers. Jesus the independent man of action, the man whom no one, not even His own family, could understand, let alone contain, is now, by His own volition, bound, arrested, accused falsely, afflicted with whips, insults, and all the pain of crucifixion. W. H. Vanstone, in his book *The Stature of Waiting*, demonstrated that 'being handed over' was a key element in Jesus' crucifixion.[6] Jesus is handed over to be afflicted by the powers of death and darkness.

In the Bible people are usually described as being 'handed over' to suffer the consequences of their own wrongdoing. The wicked are handed over into the very pit that they have dug for others.[7] In Jeremiah 38 the prophet warns that the nation will be handed over into the power of the Babylonians as a consequence of their wickedness and unfaithfulness. On the cross Jesus is in the place of 'having been handed over'. Although He has done nothing to deserve this fate, He has placed Himself in the position of being afflicted for sin. The cross shows what happens to people when they are handed over to suffer the consequences of their own wrongdoing. *Hades* is also a place where people, like the Rich Man, are handed over to suffer the consequences of their own wrongdoing.

On the cross, Jesus is handed over to the power of darkness, the power of sin and death. Behind and in these powers, we glimpse

[5] Luke 22:53 (NRSV).
[6] W. H. Vanstone, *The Stature of Waiting* (DLT, 1982).
[7] Psalm 7:15, 57:6, Proverbs 26:27 (NRSV).

also the hidden work of the devil. The devil, who openly tempted Jesus in the wilderness with the words 'If you are the Son of God, throw yourself down from this Temple,' is behind the people challenging Jesus to save himself and come down from the cross if He is the Messiah. The crucifixion is orchestrated by the devil. The power of darkness is the power of the evil one. The power of sin and death is wielded by the devil. When we look at the cross we see more clearly than anywhere else the devil at work. If the devil is in and behind Jesus' crucifixion and this crucifixion shows us the nature of *Hades* we can say also that the devil is in and behind the darkness of *Hades.* In Hades, as on the cross, people are handed over to suffer the consequences of their own wrongdoing, handed over into the power of the 'accuser of our comrades'.[8] The devil delights in trapping people into the consequences of sin so that he can then freely accuse them. The devil, in and through the powers of sin, death and darkness is the agent behind the crucifixion. As we know that *Hades* is a place of sin, death and darkness, the same agent is at work in and through *Hades.*

The devil also has his minions, the beings whom Jesus called 'unclean spirits', and who were generally known as 'demons' or, occasionally 'evil spirits'. Like their master, these spirits live and work hidden in and behind human behaviour. The devil is the orchestrator or conductor, the unclean spirits are the individual 'players' working in and on individual people. In His ministry, Jesus had complete power and authority over these unclean spirits. In His ministry, spirits, which had been hidden, manifested themselves, were shown for what they were and were decisively dispatched. At His crucifixion, Jesus is handed over to the power of these spirits, to their petty resentment, accusation and derision. These same spirits will also be at work in *Hades.*

People who in this life have become infected with spirits of selfishness, greed, fear, hatred, and many others, go down to *Hades* with these accompanying spirits, making their life and the life of those around them an intense misery as they wait for the Final Judgement. The unclean spirits are not restrained and hidden as in this life. Within the darkness of *Hades* they are freer to attack, accuse, deride and afflict.

[8] Revelation 12:10 (NRSV).

When we look at Jesus on the cross we see Jesus in *Hades*, Jesus already handed over to the power of sin, death, darkness, evil. The first truth we can affirm from this is simply that Jesus has been in *Hades.* This is confirmed by Peter's speech in Acts 2 and Paul and Peter writing of Jesus' descent to the dead.

Jesus has been in *Hades* as a man suffering alongside others. Jesus has been in *Hades* as the crucified one. Jesus has not been in *Hades* as the Judge or the confirmer of people's fate. Jesus has been in *Hades* as silently as He hung on the cross between two thieves. Jesus has been in *Hades* as thirsty as He was on the cross, thirsty like the Rich Man in *Hades.* Jesus has been in *Hades* as one afflicted with pain, derision, callousness, vindictive anger and all the worst that is in and behind human nature.

Jesus has been in *Hades* as a man suffering alongside others, and promising to one person an almost immediate place in Paradise. One thief on the cross responds to Jesus suffering alongside him with sympathy and respect. 'Truly I tell you,' said Jesus to him, 'today you will be with me in Paradise'.[9] Jesus has chosen not to save Himself but He promises salvation to one man suffering alongside him. The other thief alongside Jesus has a very different attitude. This thief joins in the general, derisive, devilish, affliction of Jesus. To him Jesus says nothing. This man remains in the grip of sin, death, darkness and evil.

Jesus was Raised From *Hades* and Now Has the Keys of *Hades*

This man, handed over to you according to the definite plan and foreknowledge of God, you crucified and killed by the hands of those outside the law. But God raised him up, having freed him from death, because it was impossible for him to be held in its power.

Acts 2:23,24 (NRSV)

So Peter proclaims in Acts 2. Peter goes on to explain that this raising, specifically from *Hades,* was foretold in Psalm 16. If God raised Jesus up from *Hades,* this confirms that Jesus has been in *Hades.* This accords with the understanding of Jesus having descended 'into the lowest parts of the earth' as Paul writes in

[9] Luke 23:43 NRSV

Ephesians 4:9. The lowest parts of the earth are the parts associated with the grave or to which the visible grave is the entrance: *Hades / Sheol.*

Jesus Himself adds to the truth about His having been raised from *Hades* in a remarkable way:

Do not be afraid; I am the first and the last, and the living one. I was dead, and see, I am alive for ever and ever; and I have the keys of Death and of Hades.

Revelation (1:17,18 NRSV)

So proclaims Jesus to John at the beginning of Revelation, with the instruction to write down all that John sees and hears for everyone to know.

Jesus was in *Hades* but He was raised up from *Hades.* Jesus descended to the depths, to the lowest place, the place of the dead, but He then ascended on high. For Jesus there was a way out of *Hades.*

'I have the keys of Death and of Hades' is a simple powerful statement, which forms part of the foundation and cornerstone of our thinking about what happens to the unrepentant wicked after death. But this statement has been, mostly, put to one side as insignificant. As we have seen, even Clark Pinnock, the theologian most convinced that people are given an opportunity to be saved after death, does not mention this statement of Jesus. This statement needs to be given its true significance. We need to keep it uppermost in our minds and to work out, with the guidance of the Holy Spirit, what leads up to it and what follows from it.

Jesus says that He has THE KEYS of Death and *Hades.* He does not say that He has some keys, those related to certain people or groups of people. Jesus has THE keys, all the keys. There are no keys which are not now in Jesus' hands. There is no single person locked in *Hades* to whom Jesus does not have the key.

The simple surface meaning of someone having the keys to a place is that they control access to and from that place. Jesus, alive for ever, controls access to and from *Hades.* Jesus' control of access to *Hades* is confirmed later in Revelation. In Revelation 6:8 the power of death is limited, by the Lamb breaking a seal on the scroll, to one quarter of the earth's population. Jesus is shown to be ultimately in charge of who goes into *Hades.* At the end of Revelation 20, when Jesus comes again to sit on His throne as

Judge, everyone is taken out of *Hades.* They leave *Hades* when Jesus is ready, at Jesus' command. Jesus is also shown to be ultimately in charge of who goes out of *Hades.*

Moreover, Jesus' assertion that He has the keys of death and *Hades* is not in any way specifically limited to certain times and places. He does not say that He has access to the keys of Death and *Hades*, but simply that He has them. He holds them in His hands permanently. He can use these keys at any time and in any way He chooses. Jesus has been in *Hades.* Now He can return there at any time. This is part of our doctrinal foundation and cornerstone.

Jesus' assertion is not that He 'has had' the keys of *Hades.* A universalist interpretation would be that Jesus has opened *Hades* so completely that everyone is now free to leave without any further intervention on the part of Jesus. In such a scenario Jesus would have no further use for His keys. He would not continue to hold them. Jesus saying that He has the keys implies, rather, that He has not finished using them. Jesus has complete access to anyone in *Hades* but this does not mean that *Hades* is already empty or redundant. *Hades* continues in existence and people continue to be imprisoned in *Hades* until Jesus' Father decides that the time for Judgement has come. All people in *Hades* have the potential to be released, saved, by Jesus, but for this they need the specific intervention of the key holder.

Jesus Chooses to Use His Keys

The question then arises: Does Jesus choose to return to *Hades?* He did not say specifically what He does with the keys. Jesus did not say 'I now go in and out of *Hades* whenever I want, bringing with me whoever I want.' He leaves that for us, with the Holy Spirit, to work out. Maybe Jesus chooses not to re-enter *Hades,* saving only those whom He has chosen to save in this life. This would appear to be the traditional understanding of conservative theologians, both Protestant and Catholic. Does anywhere else in the Bible indicate that Jesus exercises His authority to go in and out of *Hades*?

Revelation 14 gives us the clearest answer:

Then another angel, a third, followed them, crying with a loud voice, 'Those who worship the beast and its image, and receive a mark on their foreheads or on their hands, they will also drink the wine of God's wrath, poured unmixed into the cup of his anger, and they will be tormented with fire and sulphur in the presence of the holy angels and in the presence of the Lamb.

Revelation 14:9,10 (NRSV)

Despite what many who believe in tormenting hell have stated, these verses, as we have seen, show clearly torment or affliction before the Final Judgement, the torment of *Hades.* The affliction is that they have been handed over by God to face and feel the consequences of their own wrongdoing. Yet this affliction is 'in the presence of the holy angels and in the presence of the Lamb.' Jesus chooses to use His keys to go to those who are afflicted in *Hades,* being there with them. Revelation 14:10 does not say that the afflicted are in *Hades,* while a message of judgement or forgiveness, is preached to them, either by Jesus or by anyone else. Revelation 14:10 only says that Jesus is with the most afflicted people in *Hades.* Jesus may be speaking to them or He may not. As Jesus was with the thieves at the crucifixion, so He is with others in *Hades.* He does indeed choose to use His keys before the Final Judgement.

Jesus the Lamb is described the first time He appears in Revelation:

Then I saw between the throne and the four living creatures and among the elders a Lamb standing as if it had been slaughtered, having seven horns and seven eyes, which are the seven spirits of God sent out into all the earth.

Revelation 5:6 (NRSV)

The Lamb, who is with those in *Hades,* looks as if He has been slaughtered. Presumably He is bloodstained and drained. He looks afflicted by death. He is with those afflicted in *Hades* as one who looks afflicted Himself. He does not come to those in *Hades* with power and authority. He comes in weakness and humility, to be with the afflicted, beyond death.

The Lamb in the New Testament is pre-eminently 'the Lamb of God who takes away the sin of the world.'[10] He is the Passover lamb, killed for the sins of His people and all people. He is the one perfect sacrifice for sin, making all other sacrifices obsolete. Jesus,

[10] John 1:29 (NRSV).

with people in *Hades*, is there as the one who offers to take away their sin and the consequences of their sin, as He did with the sympathetic, repentant, thief on the cross.

Jesus in *Hades* is still 'Jesus', 'Yeshua', 'God saving'. Jesus in *Hades* cannot stop being Jesus, being the Saviour, for that is His nature. Jesus' presence in *Hades* must be a saving presence, not a condemning presence. Jesus Christ is the same yesterday and today and for ever.[11] For the Son of Man came to seek out and to save the lost.[12] He uses His keys of *Hades* to continue to seek and save the lost. He continues to seek in humility. He comes to His own people, and to all people, as one who can be, and is, rejected. But to those who receive Him, who believe in His name, He gives power to become saved children of God.[13] Jesus came to people during His time on earth and continues, through His Spirit and through His Church, to come to people in this life. Jesus, the key holder of *Hades,* also comes to people in the life beyond death and before the Final Judgement.

If Jesus chooses not to use His keys, why did Jesus proclaim and have recorded in Scripture that He has the keys of *Hades*? It could be that Jesus has the keys but they hang on His wall in heaven unused. But this is completely inconsistent with the name and nature of Jesus. If Jesus does not use the keys of *Hades*, the only reason He would tell the world is to impress people with His power and His hard-heartedness. Again, this is so uncharacteristic of Jesus as to be impossible. If, on the other hand, Jesus does use His keys, this is a wonderful, heartening, continuation and extension of the Good News. Christians, surely, who know the loving, saving, Jesus are compelled to conclude that Jesus announces that He has the keys because He has every intention of using them whenever He can.

One striking indication of the power, ability and willingness of Jesus to rescue people from *Hades* is the raising of Lazarus in John 11.

[11] Hebrews 13:8 (NRSV).
[12] Luke 19:10 (NRSV).
[13] John 1:11,12 (NRSV).

Jesus stood outside Lazarus' grave, prayed, and cried with a loud voice, 'Lazarus, come out!' The dead man came out, his hands and feet bound with strips of cloth, and his face wrapped in a cloth.

John 11:43,44 (NRSV)

The Jews present understood Lazarus was in *Sheol / Hades* awaiting the general resurrection. Martha has told Jesus that she knows that her brother will rise again in this resurrection. He is clearly not already in 'heaven' but waiting his call from God. The place of waiting was called *Sheol* in the Old Testament. The same place is *Hades* in the New Testament. Presumably Lazarus was not in 'the outer darkness' but in a less remote, less afflicted, waiting area, but it was all known as *Sheol / Hades.* When Jesus spoke to Lazarus, He was speaking into *Hades.* Jesus' command was heard and obeyed in *Hades.* Nothing could stop Jesus raising, saving, Lazarus from *Hades.* Jesus had explained to Martha that this power and authority came from His being 'the resurrection and the life.' These words echo closely Jesus in Revelation 1 saying that He is 'the first and the last, and the living one. I was dead, and see, I am alive for ever and ever'; Jesus' action in raising Lazarus was a foretaste of His action in raising all people. Jesus can and will call all people out of *Hades* for the Final Judgement. Jesus can and does call people out of *Hades* before then, as He did with Lazarus. Jesus does choose to use His keys to bring those who respond to Him out of *Hades.*

Matthew describes a similar event in his account of the crucifixion and resurrection:

At that moment the curtain of the temple was torn in two, from top to bottom. The earth shook, and the rocks were split. The tombs also were opened, and many bodies of the saints who had fallen asleep were raised. After his resurrection they came out of the tombs and entered the holy city and appeared to many.

Matthew 27:51-53 (NRSV)

The many people raised from the dead along with Jesus are described as 'the saints'. This is often understood to indicate people who had begun to follow Jesus, had been part of the company around Jesus, but had died, like Lazarus. Like Lazarus too, they were made alive again, body and soul. They too had come out of the waiting place before the expected time, before the general resurrection. Their deliverance from *Hades* was through the death and resurrection of Jesus. These saints, also presumably not in 'the outer darkness', were the first to be 'unlocked' by Jesus using His keys. They were probably the ones most ready and willing to leave *Hades*. Matthew's description also indicates that Jesus can and does choose to use His keys during the lengthy interval in which *Hades* exists, until, at the Final Judgement, it has no more use.

There is one further indication from the teaching of Jesus that people in *Hades* can be forgiven:

Whoever speaks a word against the Son of Man will be forgiven, but whoever speaks against the Holy Spirit will not be forgiven, either in this age or in the age to come.

Matthew 12:32 (NRSV)

Jesus implies that, as long as people have not spoken against the Holy Spirit, they can be forgiven in *Hades*, which is in the age following the current age of the living, although before the ultimate age beyond the Final Judgement. Beyond the Final Judgement there can be no forgiveness because a binding, irrevocable, verdict has been issued. But there is 'an age' before this Judgement, an age that is stretched out, Peter tells us, by the patience of God:

The Lord is not slow about his promise, as some think of slowness, but is patient with you, not wanting any to perish, but all to come to repentance.

2 Peter 3:9 (NRSV)

Because of this patience in delaying the Final Judgement, and because of Jesus' desire that all should come, or at least be given the opportunity to come to repentance, forgiveness is available to people even to people in *Hades.*

The Church Joins the Mission of Jesus in *Hades*

The truth of *Hades* is greater than that which has been generally explained and proclaimed by the Church. God is always the one who is able to accomplish abundantly far more than all we can ask or imagine.[14] In the Passover liturgy, Jews recount the blessings of

[14] Ephesians 3:20 NRSV

God, more than they could possibly have expected, using the word *Dayenu* which means 'it would have been enough'.

> If God had only brought his people out of Egypt and not fed them with manna in the wilderness: *dayenu*, it would have been enough. If God had only fed his people with manna and not given them the Law: *dayenu*, it would have been enough.

These reminders continue, forming a great list. Christians can say 'If God had only sent his Son to die for our sins, and not raised Him to life: *dayenu*, it would have been enough. If God had not raised Him to life, and not given him the keys of *Hades*: *dayenu*, it would have been enough.' But it continues.

And I tell you, you are Peter, and on this rock I will build my church, and the gates of Hades will not prevail against it. I will give you the keys of the kingdom of heaven, and whatever you bind on earth will be bound in heaven, and whatever you loose on earth will be loosed in heaven.

Matthew 16:18,19 (NRSV)

Not only do Jesus and His angels, as Revelation shows, have free access to *Hades*, His Church also has free access. The gates of *Hades* try to keep the Church out. They will not prevail. As we have noted before, this saying has often been misunderstood as the supposed 'powers of hell' not being able to defeat the Church in this life. This is not the plain meaning. Gates serve to restrict access to a place. The gates of *Hades* restrict access to *Hades*, but for the Church, they will not prevail. The Church will have access to *Hades*. The Church of Jesus, the ones who know that He is the Messiah, the Son of the Living God, will be able, like Him and with Him, to go in and out of *Hades* despite the strength of the gates.

The mission of the Church is to continue and to participate in the mission of Jesus and of His father, the mission to seek and to save the lost, to redeem humankind. The Church's ability to reach people, according to Jesus, is not confined to this life, but includes people in *Hades*. How exactly this mission is carried out we probably cannot know until after this life. But we know for certain, as part of the foundation and cornerstone of all our thinking, that the gates of *Hades* will not prevail against the Church.

The only possible reason for the Church to have the power to open the gates of *Hades* is to use this power to save people, not to assure people that there is no hope for them, not to rejoice over their suffering. Jesus is the Judge and the Church is not to judge anyone.[15] Peter said that the Church is commanded to preach that Jesus is the Judge but this is so that the Church can help people realise their need to believe in Jesus and receive forgiveness through His name.[16] The main thrust of the Church's message is to urge people to seek forgiveness from Jesus. The idea that the Church is to preach to people either in this life or in *Hades* their sure and irrevocable condemnation is contrary to the nature of the Gospel as 'Good News' and contrary to all of the New Testament. The idea that the Church has the power to triumph over the gates of *Hades* but chooses not to use this power is similarly heretical. The Church, as the body of Christ, acts like Jesus, seeking and saving the lost wherever they are.

People in this life can be trapped in bad, selfish ways and habits, as trapped as behind the gates of *Hades.* The Church can use Jesus' keys, His individual keys for each person, to enable people to be open to Jesus and His forgiveness. This ministry in this life is a beginning of the ministry of the Church in the next life, when people will have placed themselves beyond the gates of *Hades*.

The only possible reason for Jesus to tell Peter about the Church's power to go through the gates of *Hades* is that He wanted to encourage Peter and the Church to use that power when appropriate. Why would Jesus let the world know that no power in or of *Hades* can stop the Church entering, if this too were not a confirmation and extension of the Good News? The power of Jesus and His Church to seek and to save the lost is far greater than has been commonly realised.

Biblical Confirmation that Jesus Uses His Keys

Jesus has the keys of *Hades*. Jesus has already raised some saints from *Hades.* Jesus has talked about the forgiveness of sins in the age to come and the gates of *Hades* not being able to prevail

[15] Matthew 7:1
[16] Acts 10:42.43

against His Church. This is the foundation onto which we can add the 'useful' insights of the rest of Scripture.

Writing about licentious, lawless, idolatrous Gentiles, Peter continues:

But they will have to give an account to him who stands ready to judge the living and the dead. For this is the reason the gospel was proclaimed even to the dead, so that, though they had been judged in the flesh as everyone is judged, they might live in the spirit as God does.

1 Peter 4:5,6 (NRSV)

The Gospel which Peter is recorded preaching in Acts 10 is that Jesus will judge all people, but that by believing now in His name, that He is 'God Saving', all people can receive forgiveness now. Peter now states that this Gospel has been proclaimed to the dead, that is, to those in *Hades.* The proclamation must have been an invitation to receive salvation, or else it would not have been the Gospel, the good news. This proclamation had been made by the time Peter wrote. The full Gospel, as in Acts 10, was unknown before Jesus' death and resurrection. Therefore the Gospel must have been preached to the dead between the ascension of Jesus and the time that Peter was writing. Peter does not specify who exactly made the proclamation. Peter confirms that Jesus, who has the keys of *Hades,* has used them to go into *Hades* with a message of salvation, or has sent His Church into *Hades* with the same message of salvation.

A little earlier in his letter, Peter has specifically written of Jesus making a similar proclamation:

For Christ also suffered for sins once for all, the righteous for the unrighteous, in order to bring you to God. He was put to death in the flesh, but made alive in the spirit, in which also he went and made a proclamation to the spirits in prison, who in former times did not obey, when God waited patiently in the days of Noah, during the building of the ark, in which a few, that is, eight people, were saved through water.

1 Peter 3:18-20 (NRSV)

This may well be the same proclamation that Peter refers to later. This proclamation was to 'spirits in prison'. Some commentators have understood these to be angels, but in Genesis it was not the disobedience of angels which promoted the flood, but the disobedience of people. It is more likely that Peter is referring to human spirits or souls in the prison of *Hades*, awaiting the Final Judgement. Peter seems to be saying that Jesus made a proclamation specifically to people from immediately before the flood. Maybe Jesus sought out these people particularly, with a particular Gospel message. It could also be that Peter is referring to Noah's contemporaries because they were often seen as the archetypal thoroughly wicked generation. Peter is explaining how Jesus' death was for the unrighteous. He explains how far-reaching this death was. Jesus' death, His going to the place of the dead, *Hades,* made it possible for Him to preach even to Noah's contemporaries. If even these unrighteous people were not beyond the reach of Jesus' saving mission, then no one is or will be beyond salvation until the Final Judgement. Jesus has used His keys to access some people in *Hades.* Jesus can, does, and will use His keys generally to access people in *Hades.* This is a logical consequence of what Peter wrote.

To these strong indications from Peter that Jesus does indeed use His keys to access people in *Hades* we can also add a slightly weaker indication from Paul:

> what will those people do who receive baptism on behalf of the dead? If the dead are not raised at all, why are people baptized on their behalf?
>
> *1 Corinthians 15:29 (NRSV)*

Paul's readers practised baptism on behalf of those who had died. From early Church writings it is likely that those who had died were Christians, who had begun preparation for baptism but died before the actual event.[17] This indicates that the people in Corinth, at least, understood that the saving work of Jesus, mediated through baptism, was effective beyond death. Paul did not correct this understanding, but explained that it was based on the general understanding of the resurrection. This echoes Jesus explaining that He has the keys of *Hades* as the living one who was dead and is now alive.

[17] Described by John Chrysostum, and Ephiphanius is reporting the practices of others. These others were deemed heretics, but this particular practice was not condemned as heretical. See Jonathan, *Grace Beyond The Grave* p. 81, 82.

As well as the specific New Testament indications that Jesus does use His keys to seek and to save the lost, there are general indications that this is characteristic of Him. We have already explored some of these indications in describing the unchanging nature of Jesus, His name and His mission.

Steve Jonathan, Senior Pastor of Tamworth Elim Church in England, has written a doctoral thesis exploring the arguments that Jesus and His Church seek out those who have died with the message of salvation. Jonathan calls this ministry after death Post-Mortem Evangelism. Jonathan is writing a book with the same name as his thesis, *Grace Beyond the Grave.* Jonathan argues that Post-Mortem Evangelism is highly consistent with the character of Jesus as portrayed in the Gospels and the teaching of Jesus in the parables of the lost sheep, the lost coin, and the prodigal son in Luke 15. 'Whilst none of the above passages explicitly teach of post-mortem opportunity, they do portray Christ as a Saviour who will not be deflected from his mission to the lost, but will continue seeking until he finds.'[18] Jonathan points out that Jesus states God to be Father, kind to the wicked. As God cannot change, this kindness must continue to those in *Hades.* He quotes G. Fackre pointing out Paul's assertion in Romans 8 that even death cannot separate us from the love of God.[19] Jonathan also argues that, as Jesus taught His disciples to practice unlimited forgiveness, He must Himself practice what He preached.[20] Clark Pinnock also argued strongly that the possibility of people being forgiven and saved beyond death is shown by the whole character of Jesus and the nature of the Gospel.

An argument can also be made from the extent of humanity saved by Jesus, as proclaimed by the four living creatures and the twenty-four elders in Revelation:

> You are worthy to take the scroll and to open its seals, for you were slaughtered and by your blood you ransomed for God saints from every tribe and language and people and nation.
>
> *Revelation 5:9 (NRSV)*

[18] *Grace Beyond The Grave* p117

[19] Fackre, G., "The Scandals of Particularity and Universality," *Midstream* 22 (Jan.1983), 32-52, [51], *Grace Beyond The Grave* p118

[20] *Grace Beyond The Grave* p152

If these words are to be taken literally, there will be people saved by Jesus from every human tribe, language, people and nation who have ever existed. This includes tribes and peoples who lived in Old Testament times but who died out or were assimilated into other cultures before the time of Jesus. This includes languages and nations who have lived since the time of Jesus, but who died out or were assimilated into other cultures before the Church reached them with the Gospel. Any other understanding is not truly 'from every tribe and language and people and nation.' The wording here is specific: it does not include all people who have ever lived, only some people from 'every tribe and language and people and nation.' This specific language states 'every'. How can it be that some Girgashites from Old Testament times, and some people from Amazonian tribes long ago defeated and absorbed by other tribes are ransomed by Jesus? The only way is through Jesus saving them, as Peter wrote that He saved Noah's generation, through using His keys to be with them in *Hades* with His message of forgiveness.

The New Testament, from the foundation of Jesus, His words, life, death and resurrection, to the letters and Revelation, indicates strongly that Jesus and His Church have free access to *Hades* and choose to use that access to continue to save people.

The Old Testament, also, as we have seen, glimpses this wonderful scope of God's redemptive action, referring to *Hades* in the equivalent Hebrew term *Sheol.*

God delivered Jonah from *Sheol*:

Then Jonah prayed to the Lord his God from the belly of the fish, saying, 'I called to the Lord out of my distress, and he answered me; out of the belly of Sheol I cried, and you heard my voice.

Jonah 2:1,2 (NRSV)

Sheol and Abaddon lie open before the Lord

Proverbs 15:11 (NRSV)

Sheol lying open could mean that God sees everything that happens in *Sheol* or it could mean that He has free access to *Sheol* as to anywhere else. Psalm 139 states that God makes use of this access:

If I ascend to heaven, you are there; if I make my bed in Sheol, you are there.

Psalms 139:8 (NRSV)

God is present in *Sheol* as God's Son is present in *Hades.* God also will raise people from *Sheol* so that they sing for joy:

Your dead shall live, their corpses shall rise. O dwellers in the dust, awake and sing for joy! For your dew is a radiant dew, and the earth will give birth to those long dead.

Isaiah 26:19 (NRSV)

The joy indicates that this resurrection is not the resurrection to face Final Judgement and condemnation, but resurrection to salvation and new life. Such raising is within God's power and is promised by God. Such rescue of people from *Sheol / Hades* is part of his nature and character:

The Lord kills and brings to life; he brings down to Sheol and raises up.

1 Samuel 2:6 (NRSV)

A Great Chasm has Been Fixed

Jesus, the rest of Scripture, and logical thinking of what follows from Jesus and Scripture, all point to Jesus not only having the keys of *Hades*, but using them. In the Parable of the Rich Man and Lazarus, however, we read of Abraham saying to the Rich Man in *Hades*:

Child, remember that during your lifetime you received your good things, and Lazarus in like manner evil things; but now he is comforted here, and you are in agony. Besides all this, between you and us a great chasm has been fixed, so that those who might want to pass from here to you cannot do so, and no one can cross from there to us.

Luke 16:25,26 (NRSV)

If what Abraham says is true for all time, Jesus is not able to go into *Hades* as we have been arguing: Jesus may want to cross the chasm into *Hades* but no one, not even He, can.

We should not, however, build such a case based solely on what Abraham says. Abraham speaks as a character in a story by Jesus, so we must take these words seriously as part of our listening to Jesus. But we should not make the mistake of attributing to an author the opinions of one of his or her characters. Jesus was careful to put the words describing the great chasm in the mouth of Abraham. Jesus sets it out as Abraham's understanding, not necessarily His own. As we have seen, Jesus spoke at others times affirming the same truths about *Hades* as in the parable. We have no record that He repeated on another occasion, speaking as Himself, the impossibility of anyone crossing the great chasm.

Jesus' choice of Abraham as the person to speak in this parable is also significant. Abraham is a father figure, one who calls the Rich Man 'child'. He is not a great teacher, lawgiver, or prophet. Abraham is looked to as an example of a man of faith, not as an authoritative source of truth about God and people. (Despite being a man of faith, Abraham was also known to lie - particularly saying that his wife Sarah was his sister.) If Jesus had wanted to convey that the great chasm was indeed uncrossable even for Him, He could have put these words in the mouth of Moses or Elijah.

The truth as spoken by Abraham is the truth of the Old Testament. In general, the truth of the Old Testament is the truth which Jesus commanded us to retain, but to which He also added in a way that changes the truth. Jesus added to Old Testament teaching about marriage by stating that divorce was only a concession and not God's preferred way for people. Jesus added to Old Testament teaching which limited response to injury to 'an eye for an eye and a tooth for a tooth' by stating that His followers, His brothers and sisters, are to go further and love their enemies.[21] The words of Abraham in this parable are not necessarily true for all time, but can be added to by Jesus.

Jesus added to Abraham's words by saying 'I have the keys of Death and Hades.' This preserves the sense of a great chasm, but adds that, because He has been into *Hades* and come out again, He now has the ability to cross that chasm. Jesus' proclamation that He has the keys came after His death, resurrection and ascension. At the time when He told the parable, Jesus did not explain His access to *Hades*, either because at that time He had not forged that access, or because this was a truth more than His disciples, and others, could bear. This truth was communicated by the Holy Spirit, in the Revelation to John.[22]

[21] Matthew 5:27-48 (NRSV).
[22] John 16:12,13.

Abraham's words to the Rich Man in Jesus' parable do not falsify the Scriptural truth that Jesus not only has the keys to *Hades* but uses them. Abraham's words underline that only Jesus and His Church have this ability freely to enter and leave *Hades,* locking and unlocking whoever they choose. There is no general access to *Hades,* only the specific access which Jesus obtained through His death and resurrection. Only Jesus has the keys to *Hades.* Only Jesus and His Church use these keys to access *Hades* and the people in *Hades.*

Pictures of *Hades*

Like any good teacher, the Holy Spirit knows that illustrations reinforce theoretical points. We need not only to understand the truth but also to see the truth. We look to see the truth of *Hades* as Peter saw the truth that all foods are clean in his midday lunchtime vision on the roof. Here we commend certain pictures of *Hades* to the wider Church, for the Church to weigh and, we hope, receive.

New Testament Prison

In Acts we see how the Spirit of Jesus acts through leaders of His body when they are in prison. The Spirit of Jesus healed people through Peter and Paul in a way remarkably similar to how Jesus healed people. As we see how the Spirit of Jesus acted through Peter and Paul in first century prisons we, similarly, gain insight into how Jesus acts in the prison of *Hades.* We can be on even more sure ground in expecting that the Church of Jesus will act in *Hades* in a way similar to how Peter and Paul acted in prison. We focus particularly on Paul and Silas because Luke gives us more detail about them than about Peter.

After they had given them a severe flogging, they threw them into prison and ordered the jailer to keep them securely. Following these instructions, he put them in the innermost cell and fastened their feet in the stocks.
About midnight Paul and Silas were praying and singing hymns to God, and the prisoners were listening to them. Suddenly there was an earthquake, so violent that the foundations of the prison were shaken; and immediately all the doors were opened and everyone's chains were unfastened.

When the jailer woke up and saw the prison doors wide open, he drew his sword and was about to kill himself, since he supposed that the prisoners had escaped.
But Paul shouted in a loud voice, 'Do not harm yourself, for we are all here.'

Acts 16:23-28 (NRSV)

We see Paul and Silas sharing for a while the same conditions as their fellow prisoners, with no rational expectation of release. They are as securely locked in as anyone. They are not immediately released. For a while, they are simply alongside the other prisoners. Not until about midnight did anything different happen. The same is true of Peter when Herod imprisoned him, as recorded in Acts 12. Peter was kept in prison, while the church prayed fervently for him, until the day before he was to be brought out and judged. This was a substantial period of waiting and hoping. We are not told how the other prisoners responded to Paul and Silas, or to Peter, alongside them in prison. Some may have mocked and insulted them; some may have respected them.

Jesus in *Hades* could well be simply sharing the conditions and the fate of people in *Hades* as the Lamb looking as though slain. He may be mocked and insulted as He was on the cross; He may be respected by one person as He was on the cross. He will probably be waiting and hoping. His Church, the successors to Peter, Paul and Silas will be alongside the prisoners in *Hades* allowing them to respond as they want to respond. The Church, in *Hades,* will be waiting and hoping.

We also see Paul and Silas praying and singing hymns in prison. Hymns lift people's hearts and minds to have faith in the goodness and salvation of God. Paul and Silas' hymns helped awaken or build faith in their fellow prisoners. Jesus in *Hades* could well be helping to awaken or build saving faith in people there. The Church of Jesus in *Hades* will be helping to awaken or build faith in Jesus, encouraging people there to call upon the name of Jesus and be saved.

We also see an earthquake which releases the prisoners. The keys which locked the prisoners in were the only keys which could release them. The earthquake overrode the need for keys in a remarkable way. The doors did not collapse, but they were forced open. The chains were not reinforced by falling rubble, but were unfastened. This was a targeted earthquake with the specific purpose of releasing prisoners. Jesus in *Hades* could well have caused a similar earthquake. Indeed Matthew tells us that, when Jesus died, there was an earthquake which had the sole effect of releasing people from death, from *Hades.* Jesus in *Hades* certainly has the ability to override all other keys, for He has The Keys, the master set. He will be trying to let people know that, in Him, there is freedom. The Church of Jesus will also be in *Hades* helping people to see that, because of Jesus, and by calling on His name, they are actually free to go. They may be singing hymns, or using other ways to evoke and build saving faith in the prisoners around them.

In Acts 12 and Acts 5, when Peter is in prison, we see not an earthquake but, on each occasion, an angel who caused doors to open and chains to fall off. The angel has the same targeted, limited, effect as the earthquake. Nothing and no-one else in the prison is disturbed, only Peter, with the other apostles in Acts 5, is released and guided out. Jesus is in *Hades* with His holy angels who are, with Him, releasing chains, opening doors and guiding people out. The Church of Jesus is in *Hades* encouraging people to welcome the ministry of these, sometimes initially frightening, angels.

We see Peter free to go and leaving prison and we see Paul and Silas free to go and staying in prison. Paul and Silas know that they will be more permanently free if they are declared free by the authorities and so they stay for official release. Peter has no hope of official release, so, guided by the angel, he leaves. Jesus is in *Hades* making people free to leave and also assuring them that He has the authority and ability to keep them free. All authority in heaven and on earth has been given to Him. When Jesus makes someone free, even someone in *Hades,* they are free indeed. The Church of Jesus is also in *Hades* encouraging people to know not only that Jesus can or has set them free, but that He has authority to keep them free forever. Once people have been released from *Hades* they cannot return, they are free for eternity.

The Harrowing of *Hades*

Throughout the Eastern European Church icons have been continually treasured, including 'Anastasis' icons showing Jesus fresh out of *Hades* robed in triumphant and living white, pulling people out of *Hades.* 'Anastasis' means literally 'Resurrection'. The Eastern European Church holds together the vision of Jesus walking out of his own tomb and the vision of Jesus rescuing people from *Hades,* in the same way that He declared through John in Revelation that He is the living one and He has the keys of *Hades.* Instead of the keys lying in Jesus' hands, they are usually lying at His feet in *Hades.* The Anastasis icons show that He has, or has had, the keys of *Hades.* More importantly, they show the effect of Jesus having and using the keys: they show Him dragging people out of *Hades.*

The Anastasis icons are today as popular as ever. The most famous, shown on the cover of this book, is in Istanbul where it is a 'must see' on the list of many tourists and copies are sold in their thousands.

As Jesus is alive, and the icon is a representation of Jesus alive now, so Jesus is pulling people out of *Hades* now. Anastasis icons do not only depict a historical Jesus, but a Jesus very much alive and active. His arms are active, drawing people out of *Hades*; His robes, flowing in the air, show the dynamic movement of His body. Here we have an illustration of Jesus using the keys of *Hades* to save the lost which the Holy Spirit has kept visible throughout the years of official doctrine perpetuating the lie of hell.

In the Anastasis icons, the people being drawn out of *Hades* are usually Adam and Eve. Sometimes we see the great Old Testament patriarchs leaving *Hades* with Jesus. Some people have concluded that Jesus rescues a very limited number of people from *Hades,* only those in Old Testament times who lived by faith in God. Yet the list of such people in the Bible, particularly in Hebrews 13, is extensive, including gentlies from outside the people of Israel. The Jesus who Christians know is not intent only on saving the lost from the people of Israel, although they were the people He was sent to first. As we see in the icons Old Testament figures leaving *Hades,* we can be certain that the same Jesus will continue to seek and to save all people from every tribe and tongue, nation and language. This humanity-wide ministry of Jesus is shown in those icons which depict Jesus rescuing Adam and Eve, the parents and representatives of the whole of humankind.

In the Western European Church, icons were not used and treasured as in Eastern Europe, but the Harrowing of Hell was portrayed in drama, as part of the mystery plays, performed extensively in the Middle Ages and often revived today, as in the *Lichfield Mysteries* quoted in the previous chapter. In these plays, the Holy Spirit kept alive for people an illustration of Jesus using His keys to release people from *Hades*. Hymns also, for a while, affirmed the truth of *Hades* in the Church, when official doctrine taught a much more hopeless fate for unbelievers.

Modern Visions

One of the most remarkable and affirmed series of visions from the Holy Spirit in recent years came to Pastor Roland Buck of Boise, Idaho who saw angels visiting him over a period of several months. He wrote the account of his *Angels On Assignment* in a book of that name. Pastor Buck described himself as a conservative Evangelical Bible-believing pastor, not exercising any 'charismatic' ministry. Other people have confirmed that he was indeed such a faithful, orthodox, level-headed, servant of the gospel. Beginning on 18 June 1978, angels visited Buck, talking with him mostly of Biblical truth. They helped him to understand more fully the significance of the Old Testament sacrifices and their details. The angels sent him to the Philippines with a list of names of people he would meet. He did meet them all, some locals, some visitors like himself. Some were converted, some healed, some both. Pastor Buck and the angels were shown to have impeccable credentials in Biblical orthodoxy and in carrying out the Great Commission.

Pastor Buck was reluctant to speak about the angels, but they told him he had to pass on the messages and how they came. One angel came to church to 'encourage' him to speak out. (Pastor Buck was not allowed to pass the buck!) Other people heard and asked him to write the book. Ronald Buck died about 18 months after the first experience. He never made any money out of it all. His character and his theological soundness have never been challenged. The most likely explanation for his story is that he really did talk with angels.

Pastor Buck was taken by the angels to see Heaven, or 'The Throne Room' as he calls it. On the way out, he saw 'an area between our permanent abiding place in heaven and this earth from which we can be brought back.' This puzzled him. He wrote,

> I have preached that once you quit breathing, if you are not saved, and do not know God, you have missed heaven. God said that was not necessarily so . . . He did not try to give it in a textbook fashion so you could prove it, or teach it as a subject, but just as a fact! I remarked to God that this was totally against my theology, and he simply stated that he wasn't trying to compare it to my theology![23]

Pastor Buck believed categorically that people's judgement follows immediately their death and was comfortable with that belief. It is unlikely that he subconsciously made himself see this waiting area. But he did see such an area. The Holy Spirit, through the angels, gave Pastor Buck a glimpse of *Hades*.

Bill Wiese is a similar man with a similar experience. His book *23 Minutes in Hell* is been reviewed in Chapter Six above. As a Christian, conservative in every way, Bill has believed and continues to believe in the traditional hell. What he saw, experienced, and described, however, is a place where Jesus can and does make His presence known, and from which there is a permanent way out: 'an upward tunnel, approximately thirty-five feet in diameter.'[24] This tunnel corresponds with the earthquake described by Matthew which caused some dead saints to return alive to Jerusalem: a seismic shifting of rock. The tunnel Wiese saw was lined with demons who had been chained, apparently permanently. Their ability to interfere with Wiese, or anyone else, leaving *Hades* had been taken away. Jesus had used His keys to chain them out of harm's way. They had to watch Wiese, and presumably others, leave *Hades* while they were unable to hinder these escapees in any way. No wonder Wiese describes them as having 'a hatred for mankind,' including for the Son of Man who has triumphed over them so completely.

Howard Storm was given an experience of *Hades*, or drawn into a picture of Hades, when he had no belief in Hades nor in any other life beyond death. His experience was remarkably similar to the experience of Jesus on the cross. Storm was mocked, derided

[23] *Angels On Assignment* (R. Buck Whitaker House, 1979, 2005), Chapter 4. A free electronic copy can be downloaded from www.angelsonassignment.org/.
[24] Wiese, *23 Minutes in Hell*, p. 30.

and 'set upon', in a way similar to Jesus. He was then rescued by Jesus when he called out to Him.[25]

George Ritchie was shown 'hordes of ghostly discarnate beings' in a torment he was sure was hell. He wrote, 'Yet I could see that . . . immense presences were bending over the little creatures on the plain. Perhaps even conversing with them. Were these bright beings angels?' Ritchie was then aware that Jesus Himself was also ministering with the angels. Ritchie was no Bible scholar. He never made the connection between what he saw and Revelation 14 describing people in torment 'in the presence of the holy angels and of the Lamb'. Yet this is an obvious connection, an illustration of the ministry, mostly rejected by people, of angels and of Jesus in *Hades*.[26]

The trustworthy character of these people who have described a descent to 'hell', as attested by others, encourages us to believe that they are honestly reporting what they saw. The fact that what they saw contradicted what they already believed is even more encouragement to believe that their visions did not come from inside themselves but from a reality outside them. Such visions, which connect so closely with what Jesus and the Bible teaches about *Hades*, and which subsequently produced noted fruit of the Spirit in the lives of each person, may well have come from the Holy Spirit.

Conclusion

It has been commonly stated that the Bible only vaguely hints at the possibility of people being saved after death. For example, *The Nature of Hell*, produced by and for the UK Evangelical Alliance, stated 'this argument . . . is seriously lacking in exegetical foundation.'[27] Francis Chan and Preston Sprinkle wrote: 'But there is no single passage in the Bible that describes, hints at, hopes for, or suggests that someone who dies without following Jesus in this life will have an opportunity to do so after death.'[28] Chan and Sprinkle could not be further from the truth. The opposite is true. No single passage in the Bible hints at or suggests that Jesus does

[25] See above, pp. 152–4.
[26] See above, pp. 157–60
[27] ACUTE, *The Nature of Hell*, p. 91.
[28] Chan and Sprinkle, *Erasing Hell*, p. 36.

and will refrain from using His keys to *Hades* to continue His ministry, until His Father decides it is time for Judgement.

The truth that Jesus has the keys of *Hades* and continues to use them has been asserted, often not strongly, by various people at various times. John Sanders describes it as being well established by the end of the first century. J. A. MacCulloch has shown that up to and including the early Middle Ages, the Harrowing of *Hades* was widely taught in the Church. A considerable number of modern theologians, as Sanders demonstrates, also hold the view that opportunities to receive salvation continue after death.

Hades is a indeed a distinct place, not to be confused with Gehenna. *Hades* contains gloomy waiting areas where some people go after death and also areas of 'outer darkness', of affliction, of 'weeping, wailing and gnashing of teeth'. *Hades* is to be avoided at all costs.

Jesus has the keys of *Hades*. With His Church, He uses these keys to continue to seek and to save the lost in *Hades.* He enlists His Church to minister with Him in *Hades* and He has angels working with Him. We do not know how many people will be forgiven and escape from *Hades* through Jesus and His Church, but the number will include people from every tribe and language and nation. Some people will continue to refuse the offer of forgiveness and escape. We do not know how many of these there will be. Jesus will patiently and lovingly continue this ministry until His Father decides the time has come for the Final Judgement. Then everyone in *Hades* will be taken out and *Hades* will be thrown into the lake of fire, probably to be destroyed, so that it is remembered no more.

CHAPTER NINE

RECOMMENDATIONS

When the Spirit of truth comes, he will guide you into all the truth.

John 16:13

Confession

The Church needs to confess, abandon, and renounce its holding to the Greek, Roman, Manichaean, Islamic lie of hell. The Church needs to welcome, embrace and promote Jesus' Jewish teaching of *Hades* and *Gehenna.* This is the chief, general, recommendation of this book. Other, more specific, recommendations follow.

The starting point, as so often in the Christian life, is confession of sin. Abandoning the lie of hell, teaching the truth of *Hades* and *Gehenna,* will not be effective unless it is preceded, or at last accompanied, by the Church confessing its part in the creation and dissemination of the lie of hell. Each individual denomination or church will have to look at this for themselves. Individual church members and leaders will need to do what they can to bring the call to confess the lie of hell through their respective decision-making procedures. Inter-Church bodies and fellowships can offer mutual encouragement for this confession. The process will take time, but it is worth engaging in, for only in this way will the Church become truly free to teach and preach the truth.

The Church's confession of having been seduced by the lie of hell, having promoted it and profited by it, will be a powerful witness to the world. Today, maybe more than ever, public acknowledgement of mistakes is rare across the world. There is a general pull, especially in the West, away from a truth-based culture to a shame-based culture. Dignity is seen as more important than honesty. The Church's humiliating confession of sin will proclaim the importance of truth and teach all the good that is contained in the Christian practice of confession and forgiveness. Confession recognizes that we all 'get it wrong', and ultimately, there is no shame in this. (There is, on the other hand, eternal shame for those who refuse to confess their sins.)

Confession underlines the importance of speaking of mistakes out loud, so that we, and others, hear. (The Greek word 'confess' means 'speak out loud,' as in Romans 10:9: if you confess with your lips that Jesus is Lord.) Confession separates clearly the sinners' deeds from their nature, as we acknowledge our wrong doing despite having been created good. Confession opens the way for forgiveness and a new beginning which otherwise remains closed.

The Church's confession of sinful involvement in the lie of hell will also need to be linked to a commitment to a reformed life. The recommendations which follow are practical out-workings of the Church's turning away from the lie and turning to the truth. These can also be considered by the decision-making procedures of the various churches alongside or following considering the call to confession.

Language

Every Christian should stop using the word 'hell'. 'Hell' has a widely understood meaning which is at odds with the truth of Jesus and the Bible. This common meaning is so entrenched that it is impossible to continue to use the word with a different meaning. 'Hell' conflates *Hades* and *Gehenna*, confusing and distorting the truth. The word and the concept of 'hell' should no longer have a place among Christians.

Edward Fudge quotes G. C. Berkouwer:

> 'Hell' can easily assume a magical, terrifying dimension that speaks only of the incalculable, all-consuming wrath of God, and says nothing of His love . . . It is not difficult to see why the word 'hell' has come to be associated only with cruelty and hatred if it is proclaimed without the preaching of the only way out.[1]

Berkouwer understates the case. 'Hell' always speaks only of the eternal wrath of God. In the Bible, God's anger is not eternal. Hell is always associated with cruelty and hatred. It will mar and distort any preaching of Jesus, for it did not come from Him and is incompatible with Him. Percy Dearmer was more correct: 'For all the detergents of the universe cannot disinfect that word. The

[1] C. G. Berkouwer, *The Return of Christ* (Eerdmans, 1972), p. 416.

whole conception is wicked, shocking, and monstrous, not a splinter of its nauseous wreckage can be retained.'[2]

Church doctrine, liturgy, hymns, and songs should no longer use the word 'hell'. The words '*Hades*' and '*Gehenna*' should be used instead. In the Apostles' Creed, congregations used to say 'He descended into hell.' This was rightly seen as needing correction and it is more common now for congregations to say 'He descended to the dead.' 'The dead' is closer to Jesus' *Hades* but it has nothing of the warning of fierce heat, weeping, wailing and gnashing of teeth, described by Jesus. 'The dead' is a more accurate translation of the Old Testament *Sheol* than of the New Testament *Hades.* It would be more faithful to Jesus and the New Testament for congregations to say 'He descended to Hades.' Many people will not understand this name at first. Because of the predominance of the lie of hell, *Hades* has not been taught. But *Hades* can be and will be taught, both as the place of the dead where there is affliction, and as the place to which Jesus has the keys. When people speak or sing of *Hades,* they will recall both the warning and the saving grace of Jesus.

Bible translations to English should no longer use the word 'hell', but the words *Hades, Gehenna or Sheol* as in the original languages. The Greek-using writers of the New Testament concluded that they could not translate Jesus' *Gehenna* into a Greek word. No word existed in Greek to convey the concept of ultimate irreversible destruction. Guided by the Holy Spirit, they transliterated Jesus' word into the Greek alphabet. English is similar to Greek in this respect, having no word which can convey the meaning of *Gehenna.* 'Gehenna' should be used instead, Jesus' word in the English alphabet. Once we have rightly discarded the word 'hell', we similarly have no English word for *Hades.* Similarly, then, we should use the Greek New Testament word in the English alphabet: 'Hades'. The logical continuation for the Old Testament would be to use the Hebrew word 'Sheol' in the English alphabet.

Bible translations to other languages should be careful about the words they use for *Hades* and *Gehenna*, and, if there is any doubt, continue the New Testament practice of transliterating *Gehenna* into the local language and, probably, *Hades* as well. I

[2] *The Legend of Hell,* p. 20.

know a Bible translator working in an Asian country who has translated both *Hades* and *Gehenna* into a local term that means 'place of eternal torment'. This is a distortion of Biblical truth. Better is the advice of F. W. Farrar writing to a member of the Revision Committee of the English Revised Version in 1881:

> By retaining the word 'Hell' they will inevitably stereotype, in the minds of the ignorant, many conceptions which probably every one of them would reject as false; if they use the word 'Gehenna' *they use the word which our Lord himself taught them to use,* and follow the example of the Evangelists. Dare they do otherwise? More perhaps than any of us can at present decide may hang on the issue of their decision.[3]

The Character of God

Without the word and concept of hell, the character of the God of Jesus can be seen and grasped more clearly. Once the Church has repented of its part in the creation and dissemination of the lie of hell, the Church should proactively seek ways of teaching the true character of God. God is not the monster hiding being a caring veneer, as the devil wanted Eve to believe, and as the devil has succeeded in making many believe, even through the ministry of the Church.

C. E. Chandler wrote:

> Eternal conscious punishment speaks of a God who will for all eternity torture the unredeemed forever for sins committed in their brief time and space here on earth. Yes I believe that we shame our Holy God by upholding this doctrine that is not found to be in the Word of God. Our Holy, Righteous and Just God must not be tainted to the world because of a teaching that is unbiblical.[4]

Rob Bell put it in his engaging style:

> If your God is loving one second and cruel the next,
> if your God will punish people for all of eternity for sins no
> amount of clever marketing
> or compelling language
> or good music

[3] Letter to Troutbeck (20 Dec. 1881) in Rowell, *Hell and the Victorians,* p. 145.
[4] *Immortalizing Evil,* p. 176.

or great coffee
will be able to disguise
that one, true, glaring, untenable, unacceptable, awful reality.[5]

Christians, and others, have lived far too long in fear of the eternally angry God who is a myth and a lie. We need to grasp afresh the true character of God as the one who is eternally 'kind to the ungrateful and wicked.'[6] This God does give all people true freedom to accept or reject Him and His loving ways. This God has appointed a time and a way for those who persistently reject love, choosing instead self-righteousness, self-pity, and resentment, to be taken out of their miserable, afflicted, existence. This God postpones that time for as long as He possibly can so that every conceivable opportunity is given to every human being to be embraced by and to embrace grace, forgiveness and love. Such is His character. He is always, gracious, always forgiving, always loving. The Father of Jesus has always been and always will be the most loving Father imaginable, accomplishing 'abundantly far more than all we can ask or imagine, to him be glory in the church and in Christ Jesus to all generations, for ever and ever.' Amen?[7]

Preaching and Teaching in the Church

> In all discussions of Hell we should keep steadily before our eyes the possible damnation, not of our enemies nor of our friends (since both of these disturb the reason) but of ourselves. This chapter is not about your wife or your son, nor about Nero or Judas Iscariot; it is about you and me.

So wrote C S Lewis.[8] David Pawson also pointed out that 'the warnings of Jesus . . . were rarely aimed at sinners; they were occasionally directed at religious hypocrites (like the Pharisees) but usually at his own disciples, particularly the twelve.'[9]

There is an eternal 'Or else!' Christians are the first people who need to be aware of this and live in its light. *Hades* and *Gehenna* remain possibilities for Christians who only call Jesus 'Lord, Lord,' but do not do the will of His Father in heaven. This 'Or else!' of

[5] *Love Wins*, p. 175.
[6] Luke 6:35 (NRSV).
[7] Ephesians 3:20,21 (NRSV).
[8] *The Problem of Pain*, p. 116.
[9] *The Road to Hell*, p. 6.

Jesus is a sharp part of His teaching which we need to recover. In Mark 9 Jesus follows warnings about *Gehenna* with the enigmatic 'For everyone will be salted with fire.' We take this to mean that the possibility of *Gehenna* acts like salt for everyone: the 'Or else the fire' is like salt. It is a sharp message to be used widely but in very small amounts. Used properly, it enhances flavour and prevents rot setting in. Used too liberally it poisons and kills. Not used at all it makes food bland and liable to go off. 'Salt is good; but if salt has lost its saltiness, how can you season it? Have salt in yourselves, and be at peace with one another.'[10]

The effect, the impetus, of this salt is to enhance moral purity and peace among Jesus' disciples. Christian teachers and preachers should talk of *Hades* and *Gehenna* primarily to people within the church, as a warning to them to continue on the narrow road of loving God, and their neighbours as themselves. After his near-death experience of *Hades*, Howard Storm became a Christian minister. His message is

> You are given a life for only one purpose, which is to love God. You love God by learning God's will and doing God's will by loving one another. Anything else is immaterial to the purpose of your brief life experience in the world.[11]

Teaching about *Hades* and *Gehenna* should include the vital importance of right action as well as right belief. Rob Bell states 'in reading all of the passages in which Jesus uses the word "hell" what is so striking is that people believing the right or wrong things isn't his point.'[12] Francis Chan and Preston Sprinkle, remarkably, agree:

> In the light of this truth and for the sake of people's eternal destiny, our lives and our churches should be – no, they must be! – free from the bondage of sin, full of selfless love that overflows for neighbors, the downcast, and the outsiders among us.[13]

[10] Mark 9:49,50 (NRSV).

[11] *My Descent Into Death*, p.37.

[12] *Love Wins*, p. 82.

[13] *Erasing Hell*, p. 146.

Christians especially, who have grasped the right belief, need to know the continuing importance of right behaviour, including not saying to a fellow Christian 'you fool'.[14]

Teaching about *Hades* should also include the comforting assertion that, after death, Jesus does not give up, neither on Christians, nor on anyone else. *Hades* is a place of such affliction that no one would choose to go there. It is to be avoided by turning to and adhering to Jesus. But those who were never able before death to turn to Jesus, either through no witness or through bad witness from Christians, will be able to be reached by the one who has the keys of *Hades* and whose Church cannot be kept out of *Hades.*

The Message about Mission

Some, particularly Evangelical, writers have stated that it is necessary to believe in hell in order to have the required urgency for proclaiming the gospel. The potential damage to world mission and to support for world mission has been a major criticism of annihilationist and escapist views. David Pawson writes 'It is safer for the evangelist to have hell more frequently in his heart than on his lips. This will fuel his fervency, increase the urgency of his appeal.'[15]

The trouble with such a view is, simply, that this is trying to use a lie for a good purpose. The end does not justify the means. Bringing the gospel to people, or supporting others to bring that gospel, while motivated by a lie will lead to a distorted gospel. There is enough urgency in the reality of the affliction of *Hades* and the annihilation of *Gehenna* to inspire any evangelist or supporter of missions. Any more urgency will mean that too much fear is communicated and the new Christians will suffer from this distorted beginning. The very early Church did not, generally, believe in nor teach hell as we have known it. Yet they took part in the most successful period of mission in history, converting the Roman Empire. George Lindbeck pointed out 'Christians in the first centuries appear to have had an extraordinary combination of relaxation and urgency in their attitude towards those outside

[14] Matthew 5:22.

[15] *The Road to Hell*, p. 81.

the church. Relaxation in knowing that their pagan neighbours died without knowing Jesus, and urgency in proclaiming the gospel.'[16] A true grasp of *Hades* and *Gehenna* will give us a similar, soul-winning attitude.

Jesus never told Christians to bring the gospel to others in order to save them from *Hades* or *Gehenna.* In His command at the end of Matthew's Gospel, commonly called 'The Great Commission', Jesus instructed His disciples to 'Go therefore into all the world and make disciples' The 'therefore' was not 'people will perish, therefore go', not 'you will be responsible for people perishing, therefore go', but 'All authority in heaven and earth has been given to me. Go therefore . . . ' In Jewish, Biblical, thinking, as we have seen from Paul's letter to Ephesians, *Hades* is the lowest parts of the earth to which Jesus descended.[17] Jesus' complete authority in all the earth includes authority in the lowest parts of the earth, that is, *Hades*. Jesus told His disciples to go and make disciples on the basis of His authority in heaven above, in this life, and in *Hades.* Knowing that Jesus has the keys of *Hades,* and the authority and willingness to use them, is not a disincentive to mission, but part of the motivation for mission as Jesus gave it to us. It is because Christians know that Jesus can open every door, unlock every chain, in this life and in *Hades,* that they go proclaiming that release and inviting people to live in the freedom of following Jesus.

The other motivation for mission, which is the motivation for the whole of the Christian life, is love. Christians cannot truly love Jesus and His Father without joining in His great invitation to everyone to become part of His family. Michael Green writes,

> Believers do not evangelise because they have carefully calculated the probabilities of universalism, annihilation or unending torment. They go because they have fallen in love with the great Lover. They go because they have been set free by the great Liberator. They love him and they want that love to reach others. It is far too good to keep to themselves.[18]

The message that Jesus has the keys of *Hades* is far too good for Christians to keep to themselves. Christians who try to bring the

[16] *The Nature of Doctrine* (Westminster Press, 1984), p. 58.

[17] Ephesians 4:9.

[18] Michael Green, *Evangelism Through the Local Church* (Hodder and Stoughton, 1993), p. 78.

message of Jesus to others without saying that Jesus has the keys of *Hades* will not truly be loving Jesus nor their neighbours. Unfortunately, the Church has done precisely this. The message has been given that all who have died without a commitment to Jesus are suffering eternally. This lie has rightly been rejected by many people. The Church needs to consider how much the gospel that has been presented, without Jesus having the keys of *Hades* as an integral part, is, in fact, a distortion of the true gospel. The word 'gospel' is used in Matthew, Mark and Luke, to describe both Jesus' message about the Kingdom of God and the writers' message about the whole life and teaching of Jesus. The gospel is meant to proclaim and explain the authority of God as given to Jesus, including authority in *Hades.* The gospel is meant to proclaim and explain all Jesus did and said, including 'I have the keys of Death and Hades.' If the proclamation and explanation have omitted part of the message of the kingdom of God, omitted part of the truth of Jesus, it cannot truly be called 'the gospel'.

A letter of Francis Xavier, Roman Catholic Jesuit missionary to Japan in the 16th century, illustrates how the lie of hell has hindered mission:

> One of the things that most pains and torments these Japanese is that we teach them that the prison of hell is irrevocably shut, so that there is no egress therefrom. For they grieve over the fate of their departed children, of their parents and relatives, and they often show their grief by their tears. So they ask if there is any hope, any way to free them by prayer from that eternal misery, and I am obliged to answer that there is absolutely none . . . They often ask if God cannot take their fathers out of hell, and why their punishment must never have an end. We gave them a satisfactory answer, but they did not cease to grieve over the misfortune of their relatives.[19]

Concern and care for dead relatives, concern and care which was apparently not shared by the Christian God, led many Japanese to reject this God. This is probably a major hindrance to the Gospel, even today, in Japan and other nations.

[19] Letter from Cochin, 29 Jan. 1552 (Xavier, *Life and Letters*, ed. Coleridge, 1881, p. 347)

In the UK too, Christian pastors often encounter people with a concern and care for dead relatives, which the lie of hell has told them is not shared by the Christian God. Steven Jonathan writes:

> As a church pastor engaged in regular evangelistic conversations for over twenty years, this author would suggest that it is restrictivist theology that acts as a greater hindrance to the gospel message than any disincentive apparently caused through Wider Hope theologians diminishing the urgency for mission.[20]

The Message for the World

> One of the greatest benefits to come by recovering the scriptural teaching on hell will be to loose preachers' tongues to make very clear this alternative to salvation in the power of the Holy Spirit and in the wholesome and truthful language of the Word of God.[21]

Edward Fudge here is thinking not of preaching to Christians but of bringing the message of Jesus to everyone. This message is a message of forgiveness and salvation, which necessarily involves explaining why people need forgiveness and what they need to be saved from. People need forgiveness because they will be judged on their deeds, including minor injuries to other people. People need to be saved from ending up in *Hades* and *Gehenna.*

In the book of Acts we read that the coming judgement of all people by Jesus was a key part of the original Christian message. To the God-fearing Roman, Cornelius, Peter explained:

He commanded us to preach to the people and to testify that he is the one ordained by God as judge of the living and the dead. All the prophets testify about him that everyone who believes in him receives forgiveness of sins through his name.

Acts 10:42,43 (NRSV)

The dual message is that everyone has both a need for forgiveness and the opportunity to be forgiven by Jesus. People are invited to believe in Jesus, not primarily to swell the ranks of Church members, but because they will meet Him one day as judge and need to be forgiven by Him sooner or later; the sooner the better.

[20] *Grace Beyond The Grave* p166

[21] *The Fire That Consumes*, p. 208.

This forgiveness can be found nowhere else but through Jesus. The foundation of the Christian life is not that I have made a commitment but that I have needed Jesus' forgiveness and He has brought it to me.

Howard Storm summarises the message he tries to give: 'We create our eternal judgment by what we do in this world. The truth judges us. In the light of God there is no deception . . . Thank God there is a way to change our lives and be forgiven our mistakes.'[22]

The message of Jesus includes the 'Or else!' of judgement. It also includes the amazing grace and patience of Jesus and His Father who want no one to be lost, who are kind to the ungrateful and the wicked. This grace and patience never ends; it lasts well beyond this life into and throughout *Hades*. It is much easier and better to respond to the grace of Jesus and seek His forgiveness in this life. In *Hades*, with all the weeping, wailing and gnashing of teeth, people are more entrenched in their self-justifying ways. It is harder to turn to Jesus in *Hades* than in this life. If we are forgiven by Jesus now and led by Him through death to Paradise, rather than being brought down to *Hades*, we not only avoid considerable distress, but can live in hope rather than fear. This is the message which the Church needs to bring afresh to the world.

The Message to the Bereaved

'Do not let your hearts be troubled. Believe in God, believe also in me. In my Father's house there are many dwelling-places. If it were not so, would I have told you that I go to prepare a place for you? And if I go and prepare a place for you, I will come again and will take you to myself, so that where I am, there you may be also. And you know the way to the place where I am going.'
Thomas said to him, 'Lord, we do not know where you are going. How can we know the way?' Jesus said to him, 'I am the way, and the truth, and the life. No one comes to the Father except through me.'

John 14:1-6 (NRSV)

[22] *My Descent into Death*, p. 104.

These words are frequently read at funerals for the encouragement they give in the wide availability of rooms in Jesus' Father's house and in the ability of Jesus to shepherd people through death. Yet there is also the stark assertion that only Jesus can do this for us.

It is good for Christian ministers to explain that Jesus' offer of guidance through death does not expire when we breathe our last physical breath but continues into the world of the dead, into *Hades.* At a funeral there will probably not be the time to explain all about *Hades*. Even the unfamiliar name is best avoided until it is better known. For those who have shown no obvious commitment to Jesus in this life, we can confidently say something like: 'We trust and hope today that N will look to Jesus, will accept Jesus' help and forgiveness, and come through to a new life.' A slightly longer version, referring to Psalm 23, would be 'We hope and trust that N will come through the dark valley. We hope and trust that Jesus, the Good Shepherd, will guide and lead her through as she welcomes and trusts Him. Jesus, the Son of God, will come alongside N in a way that we cannot, offering to guide her through. This is a guidance that all of us need. Today we commend N to God, to Jesus, and God to N, that N may come through to join the great multitude in the house of the LORD, for ever.' If, later, the close family are given a copy of the funeral address, they can pick up what is said should they wish, or should the Holy Spirit draw them that way.

In further conversation with the bereaved it will be possible to explain more about *Hades* and Jesus having the keys, as much as people are interested to know. Once people understand that there is an 'intermediate state' and that Jesus has the keys to this state, they will draw comfort from the hopeful conclusions which will naturally follow. Jesus' presence in *Hades*, along with His angels and His Church, will also bring comfort.

Christian ministers will do well also to explain that only Jesus has the right of access to those who are dead. For everyone else, a 'great chasm' has indeed been fixed between this life and the next. We cannot and we should not attempt to communicate directly with those who have died. Spiritualism is not a Christian option. Instead we ask Jesus to take any message that we have to those who have died. He has the keys, He has the ability to reach them.

'Please, Jesus, will you let my Grandad know that I do love him, and I am grateful for the way he provided for us all, and I wish I had told him properly before he died.' This sort of prayer is good and healthy and Biblical. If there is concern that the person who has died was never, in this life, properly open to Jesus and His forgiveness, this concern too can be told to Jesus, asking Him to keep reaching out to the person now. This kind of praying for the dead has been controversial in Churches but fits well with both the truth of *Hades* and the practice of the earliest Church.

If a response from the person who has died is wanted, this too comes safely only through and from Jesus. 'Jesus, please will you let me know that my Mum is OK now,' is also a good prayer, as long as we allow Jesus to answer it in His way and His time. Often people who have spent much time and effort making sure that those they love are OK in this life find it hard suddenly to know so little about them once they have died. Jesus knows and understands the effect of this 'great chasm' and will do what He can to comfort and reassure people. Jesus brings this message in various different ways, appropriate to each person. Any more detailed request for help or information should be made to Jesus and not to any dead person. 'Jesus, please show me how to treat my niece as Grandma would have done,' is much better than trying to ask Grandma direct. All the help and guidance we need in life can come from Jesus. We should not trouble those who have died with requests, nor trouble ourselves by opening ourselves to the voices of unclean spirits pretending to speak for those who have died. Only Jesus is the way, the truth and the life.

Renunciation of Torture

'As the souls of heretics are to be eternally burning in hell, there can be nothing more proper than for me to imitate the Divine vengeance by burning them on earth.' Queen Mary is reported to have given this justification for torturing Protestants to death.[23] Percy Dearmer argued that the practice of torture in Europe was derived largely from the lie of hell, referring to the *History of the*

[23] W. R. Alger, *The Destiny of the Soul* (Roberts Bros, Boston, 1880), quoted in Powys, *'Hell': A Hard Look at a Hard Question*, p. 18.

Rise and Influence of the Spirit of Rationalism in Europe by W. E. H. Lecky (1865)

> Lecky has shown at length how persecution and torture, to an extent unexampled in heathen times, were due to the 'Last Things' being the habitual object of the thoughts and imaginations of men. If you tell men, he says 'that the Being who is the ideal of their lives, confines his affection to the members of a single Church, that he will torture for ever all who are not found within its pale, and that his children will for ever contemplate those tortures in a state of unalloyed felicity, you will prepare the way for every form of persecution.' It was as a matter of fact Augustine who really fixed the doctrine of hell upon the Church and suggested that of purgatory, and it was he who was the first Christian theologian to advocate the use of force against heretics and schismatics.[24]

The God of Jesus is not a torturer. The followers of Jesus must not be torturers, nor must they ever support or condone the use of torture. The Church needs to repent of its encouragement of torture and to campaign with a fresh vehemence against all torture. Historically opposition to torture has come from the opponents of the Church. The Church needs to make up now for not opposing torture in the past.

Renunciation of torture includes renunciation of torturous imprisonment for criminals. The punishment of prison is to be withdrawn from freedom and normal human society. Harsh conditions and harsh treatment of prisoners are unacceptable additions to that basic punishment. Unfortunately, however, such punitive conditions and treatment have been encouraged and justified by the lie of hell. Geoffrey Rowell recounts how prison reform in nineteenth century Britain was led by Jeremy Bentham and the Utilitarians, specifically linking their arguments with a non-traditional view of hell. Others argued for punitive imprisonment based, at least partly, on the example of hell.

> Fitzjames Stephen asserted that it was morally right to hate criminals, and it was not surprising that, in another context, he proclaimed that Christian love stopped short at the gates of

[24] Dearmer, *The Legend of Hell*, p. 67.

hell, and hell as 'an essential part of the whole Christian scheme.'[25]

The God of Jesus is 'kind to the ungrateful and wicked.'[26] The followers of Jesus must also be kind to criminals, including those in prison. Jesus' followers are told to visit those in prison, not to reinforce their guilt, but to bring care and relief, as they bring care and relief also to those who are strangers, naked, or sick.[27] Jesus' Church visits those in prison in this life as a foretaste of their ministry in *Hades* with and for Jesus. Jesus' followers are to encourage and support kindness to criminals wherever they are found. It is this kindness, Christians believe, which will draw people to true confession and forgiveness. Beating criminals is more likely to 'beat the devil into them.' The alarming failure rate of British prisons to reform criminals, despite holding them for longer than most other Western countries, shows these simple words to be true.

The lie of hell has not only justified torture and punitive imprisonment, but also a range of other abusive behaviours. Wess Stafford is President of the US charity Compassion International. In his book *Too Small to Ignore* he describes spending part of his childhood in a boarding school run for the children of American missionaries in West Africa. Humiliating abuse was a routine practice of the school, including sexual abuse. Stafford writes that part of this hell on earth was the doctrine of hell – that the Africans were going to burn for eternity, that any misdemeanour could diminish mission and send more Africans to hell, that 'we were little sinners in the hands of an angry God.'[28] It is vitally important, especially for all our children, that we proclaim that the God of Jesus is not angry for ever, not even for two days at a time, and that no human should ever allow their anger to be expressed in violence. God's wrath is expressed mostly in allowing people to experience the natural consequences of their own actions: His wrath makes Him step back from His usual practice of gracefully protecting us from our own mistakes. The worst that

[25] *Hell and the Victorians*, p. 14.

[26] Luke 6:35

[27] Matthew 25:31-46

[28] Dr Wess Stafford, *Too Small To Ignore* (Waterbrook Press, 2007).

humans can do is to copy this stepping back. We also need to remember the salt-like warning of Jesus:

If any of you put a stumbling-block before one of these little ones who believe in me, it would be better for you if a great millstone were hung around your neck and you were thrown into the sea.

Mark 9:42 (NRSV).

Care for all People

The chief lesson of learning the truth about *Hades* and *Gehenna* is, simply, the importance of love in action. Practical care for others, especially fellow Christians and the poor, is to be the warp and weft of Christian life, not a colouring to be added onto the core duties of worship and evangelism. The Church has too often warned people of the dire consequences of missing Sunday worship or of not taking every possible opportunity to tell others the gospel. Jesus warned people of the consequences of not doing the will of His Father in heaven, not loving their neighbours as they love themselves. This love in action has to be the priority of Christian life. Pastor Buck reported that the *Angels on Assignment* told him how important it is to show love in action, more important than 'giving our testimony' or trying to talk people into faith. In other words 'Let your light so shine before others that they may see your *good deeds* and give glory to your Father in heaven.'[29]

Loving our neighbours as ourselves affects everything Christians do or think. Our neighbours include everyone whom we see to be in need, as the Good Samaritan saw, and the priest and Levite failed to see.[30] Christians who know that God never turns His back on anyone, should be at the forefront of care for the whole of humanity. The lie of hell has encouraged some Christians to turn their backs on 'the heathens'. The truth of *Hades* and *Gehenna* will encourage all Christians to show love to everyone.

All our actions need to be infused with the concern that people feel loved by us and by our God. Most Christians will express this love in practical, individual, care for others, meeting their physical

[29] Matthew 5:16.
[30] Luke 10:30-37.

and other needs. Some Christians, who have the gift and call of being evangelists, will express this love in praying with others and explaining to others the love of Jesus and His Father for them.[31] This ministry of evangelism will need to be caring, patient, and individual, as Jesus instructed. In Luke 10 and Matthew 10 Jesus gave clear instructions to those whom He sent out as evangelists to the villages where He was soon to go. In Matthew 28 Jesus extended the remit of evangelists to going 'into all the world', but He did not change the previous instructions. These instructions apply to evangelists today. Evangelists are to care for others by spending time with them and graciously receiving what is offered. Evangelists are to learn the individual needs of others for healing and pray for Jesus and His Father to meet these needs. Evangelists then, and only then, are to explain the will, the kingdom of Jesus' God for people's lives. Knowing that Jesus has the keys of *Hades*, evangelists are not impatient to move on to 'win another soul' but take time with each individual and community. Knowing that Jesus has the keys of *Hades*, evangelists graciously leave those who have refused to accept their message. The truth of *Hades* and *Gehenna* will encourage evangelists to renounce formulaic or threatening presentations of the gospel.

The truth of *Hades* and *Gehenna* encourages all people to live lives of active love and forgiveness, inspired by the forgiveness and fellowship of Jesus.

[31] Luke 10:1-12.

CHAPTER TEN

FINAL WORD: JESUS TODAY

My sheep hear my voice.

John 10:27 (NRSV)

The Holy Spirit leads us into all truth. He leads us through logic, through illustrations, dreams and vision, and also through prophecy. In Acts 2 Peter explains that the dramatic coming of the Holy Spirit at Pentecost was to fulfil the promise that 'your sons and you daughters shall prophesy.' Prophecy is the ability to hear and to speak out what God is saying. It is not foretelling the future, but forth-telling the living word of the living God. Prophecy is part of the guidance of the Holy Spirit. Words of prophecy need to be weighed and tested by the wider Church. With this assessment by the Church, prophecy is to be welcomed as from the Holy Spirit.

As I have prayed about all the matters, and particularly the Bible verses, in this book, over several years, it has seemed to me that words of prophecy have come. I have heard the voice of the Good Shepherd and been able to record what He has been saying. This chapter presents what has come to me. It is for others to discern how much these words are true Holy Spirit prophecy.

My listening to God has been enabled and enhanced through the teaching of Mark Virkler. Mark is an American Church leader who found himself wanting to hear the voice of Jesus directly, believing that this is possible, but not knowing how to listen. He dedicated a year to asking anyone who seemed to be able to hear Jesus, how exactly they did it. Some responses were unhelpful: 'It just comes to you and you just know it's Jesus.' This would make Mark think, 'No, it doesn't come, and I have no idea if it's Jesus or just me.' Some practical insights did come, from a range of people, from Jesuit Roman Catholics to Independent Pentecostals.

Towards the end of his year of enquiry, Mark could see how the various insights fitted together in the prophet Habakkuk's description of how he listened to God:

I will stand at my watch-post, and station myself on the rampart; I will keep watch to see what he will say to me, and what he will answer concerning my complaint. Then the Lord answered me and said: Write the vision; make it plain on tablets, so that a runner may read it.

Habakkuk 2:1,2

The prophet did four things:

- He went away to a watch post, a place apart from his normal activity and work.
- He kept watch, looking, expecting to see something. Although he wanted to hear, he began with seeing.
- He initiated a conversation. He made a complaint expecting an answer to come.
- He wrote down what came to him, what he saw and what he heard, while it was being revealed to him.

Mark Virkler saw in Habakkuk's description four integrated parts of the process of listening to God. Mark calls these 'The Four Keys to Hearing God's Voice'.

- Be still. Take yourself away from normal activity and routine.
- Open the eyes of your heart. Picture yourself in the presence of Jesus.
- Welcome the flow. Expect communication to come from the Holy Spirit within you, in thoughts, impressions, words, pictures.
- Write out what comes, while it is coming.

Mark has written a book called *How to Hear God's Voice*. He leads seminars across and beyond North America teaching people to hear God's voice for themselves. He has an international network of other trainers who are authorised to teach his material.[1]

One of the insights of Mark Virkler, and others who teach about listening to God, is that God speaks through the Holy Spirit within us so that His voice comes through our personality. The Holy Spirit does not bypass us in some impersonal way, using us as a dictation machine. The Holy Spirit delights to flow in us, including using our characteristic turns of phrase. The Holy Spirit, speaking the words of Jesus through me, will sound like me, but will be kinder and wiser than I tend to be. The words I record here therefore are expressed through my distinctive personality. It is

[1] Mark Virkler, *How to Hear God's Voice* (Destiny Image, 2006). See also cwgministries.org/Four-Keys-to-Hearing-Gods-Voice.

for others to assess whether they are from me alone or, in some measure, from the Holy Spirit in me.

All that is written here has come as I have followed Mark Virkler's teaching. Mark has not seen any chapter of this book. Nothing in this book, including this chapter, has been in any way endorsed by him.

Words from Jesus are indicated by a + at the beginning. Words from me do not have this +.

Gehenna

A

What if God, desiring to show his wrath and to make known his power, has endured with much patience the objects of wrath that are made for destruction; and what if he has done so in order to make known the riches of his glory for the objects of mercy, which he has prepared beforehand for glory - including us whom he has called, not from the Jews only but also from the Gentiles?

Romans 9:22-24 (NRSV)

Some perish, in Israel and beyond, some have life. You are more patient for the sake of those who will have life. Seems hard to us, but then we are too soft? How important it is to proclaim that the alternative to life is death indeed.

+ Yes indeed there is blessing for those who turn to me and the possibility, the strong possibility, of destruction for those who don't. That is, as it has always been, my message, in a nutshell, that you need to keep to. But don't make it the certainty of destruction for there is no such certainty in my love. And people can easily find themselves in the wrong side of my welcome!

B

I tell you, my friends, do not fear those who kill the body, and after that can do nothing more. But I will warn you whom to fear: fear him who, after he has killed, has authority to cast into *Gehenna*. Yes, I tell you, fear him!

Luke 12:4,5 (NRSV alt.)

Fear God! It must be. Still seems strange to fear your power to dump us in *Gehenna*.

\+ That is because you do not know the half of it! There is power to dump people in *Gehenna*, as you say, but there is equal and greater power to save! One goes with the other. There cannot be salvation like that without the possibility of allowing you to go your own sweet way to destruction. So don't worry, and know that the power to save is greater than the power to condemn, but both are held together in the end by the one who holds everything in love and knows all the details.

\+ Yes, my Father and I know all the details of your life and enjoy looking upon you in this way. We rejoice when we see you, we enjoy what we see. Why would we want it to be burnt up unless you forced us to do it? There is love in what we see and the way we see you always.

C The Parable of the Sheep and Goats (Matthew 25)

The fire is definitely for the devil and his angels. Is the experience of punishment eternal, or more irrevocable for eternity?

\+ Yes the punishment is eternal in the sense that it lasts for ever, burns for ever and burns up all who are committed to it. It is an eternal fire which will never go out which will remain even when the devil and his angels are burnt up! The fire has a good purpose in my kingdom too, part of my glory which you will enjoy. The fire has a great role to play for my people, it will be a glorious fire of victory and warning and challenge and triumph.

There is a kingdom prepared for us and a fire for the devil and his angels! Yes indeed! Thank you Jesus.

\+ There is a grand opening of heaven to see and witness the coming of my people into their kingdom, into their inheritance which will last for ever. Rejoice that you see and understand something of this inheritance!

\+ This is good that you see that the fire is not for people. The fire is not for people, never intended to be for people, for my chosen ones who respond to me and my love.

Thank you that the fire is eternal and has a part in your purposes, a great good fire, a fire of your love, prepared in love like everything else?

\+ Yes indeed! The fire is a good fire, a bright and glorious fire. Just don't go into it, like any child would be warned to keep away, so I warn you to keep away. Generosity, your generosity, will keep you away from the fire.

D

\+ I do choose whoever I want to choose, which is why it is not right that there should be eternal punishment for those who are not chosen. I make some pots for ordinary use, some to hold richer, more lasting treasures. The ordinary pots are destroyed when they have fulfilled their purpose. I love them and use them, but in a different way. And few people want the discipline and the firing necessary for a highly glazed, lasting pot. It's easier, as you know, to be an ordinary pot!

E

So will all be saved?

\+ No, only those who are drawn to me by my Father allowing me to draw them, allowing themselves to be drawn and paying the price for this, as you know.

This is different from how I have been thinking.

\+ Yes I know! Hell is where the ordinary pots are burnt up along with the devil. He cannot touch the treasure pots though. They just get stronger in the fire! Stoking the fire is his job and he is very good at it. He just wants more power, more say over who goes in, without realising that in doing this he has prepared his own place there, burning furiously and painfully for him, for he is eternal, more than you are.

F

\+ I love all that I have made and I do not want it to perish. You know that. But there has to be freedom too, freedom to reject me. The way into life is clear. That is the most important thing.

G

You were dead through the trespasses and sins in which you once lived, following the course of this world, following the ruler of the power of the air, the spirit that is now at work among those who are disobedient. All of us once lived among them in the passions of our flesh, following the desires of flesh and senses, and we were by nature children of wrath, like everyone else.

Ephesians 2:1-3 (NRSV)

The bad news, all going astray.

\+ Yes there is truth here that needs to be said loudly too, that the life of sin is heading for destruction, severe and painful destruction which you can see coming which makes you weep and wail and gnash your teeth. Be serious about sin and punishment, punishment firstly for the evil one and then for those who are linked inextricably with him. Now there are loose ties, but these can be confirmed in the end as people keep refusing the offer of life in me and in my Father's grace. There is truth here that needs to be said to the people of this generation so that there can be true repentance.

H Isaiah 34

Fierce judgement against Edom, more even than the nations generally. So those hills are barren today . . . What to say about this Jesus?

+ Rejoice my people that my word is true. There is destruction, an end, a full and complete end, for those who are entrenched in wickedness, in opposition to my people and eventually to me. That is indeed their fate, destruction is decreed and foreshadowed in the fate of Edom. Take this as a warning to all nations and all people, that the nation which I choose and which honours me in some way, even if not at all perfectly, survives and can flourish with me, while the nation which stands in my way and bars my passage and harasses my people and wants to live off their prosperity will come to nothing. Nothing at all. No people truly. Where are the Edomites now? Not languishing in sorrow and misery but no more, wiped out as my prophet saw for their wickedness. This has to be said, unfashionable though it is, that judgement does come even on this earth to those who fail to follow me fully.

I

If you see your brother or sister committing what is not a mortal sin, you will ask, and God will give life to such a one - to those whose sin is not mortal. There is sin that is mortal; I do not say that you should pray about that. All wrongdoing is sin, but there is sin that is not mortal.

1 John 5:16,17 (NRSV)

Pray as well as telling them? Or is the telling them only for sins committed against us? This is how they prayed for Saul – even his sin was not 'mortal.'

\+ As for the verse, yes indeed, this is mostly about sin not committed against you, or about sin for which the person refuses to repent.

\+ And there is a sense in which all needs to be forgiven in the end but there are certain attitudes which get seriously in the way of this, even the sensual ones! Those who, as Revelation says, are continuing unrepentant idolaters and fornicators etc. will not be able to come into the new Jerusalem, sad but true. Pray for such people . . . whose sin is so ingrained that they will have to stay outside until the time is right for them to be destroyed indeed.

The Devil

A

And the tongue is a fire. The tongue is placed among our members as a world of iniquity; it stains the whole body, sets on fire the cycle of nature, and is itself set on fire by hell.

James 3:6 (NRSV)

The tongue is set on fire by *Gehenna*? How is this?

\+ This is good to note, yes indeed! *Gehenna* is a place and an atmosphere, a place of the devil, a place of the evil one who knows that his time is short! That is why he wants to drag as many people as possible into his fire. He doesn't want to go alone, he wants to be able to say that it was worth it to take a few people away from me. Yes, the evil one, who knows his time is short, wants to drag as many people as he can with him. He loves to exercise power in this way, to use his power against my power. That makes him feel wonderful, so big. It is like a drug which once tasted cannot them be forsworn. You see the similarity with the tongue. When the tongue has tasted the power it can have over people by what it says, it enjoys and wants that power still. And this is just what the devil wants, the evil one. It is like him and from him, a fire of *Gehenna*, a fire that tries to exist in opposition to me and my Father and the Holy Spirit, but cannot, a fire of rebellion that will consume itself eventually.

B

\+ Yes there is a power in blessing which is my power working through you, not the power of the devil. The power of the rain, which is stronger than the power of the sun and the fire.

Which seems stronger, the fire which rages from time to time and destroys in a night, or the rain which renews and renews all the time and which brings new life from the earth again? My power is the power of the rain with you and for you. I am the Lord of Blessing, and my blessing is seen in the rain!

C

When a strong man, fully armed, guards his castle, his property is safe. But when one stronger than he attacks him and overpowers him, he takes away his armour in which he trusted and divides his plunder.

Luke 11:21, 22 (NRSV)

This is what you did in the desert?

\+ It is what I did in coming to the world, including to the desert. I came in and overpowered his needing to keep me out. I came in and disrupted all his plans, turning round his anger into his own judgement. I tied him up in his own legality so that he is under the sentence of death himself. I am the victor and all his spirits need to know, to be told, that he is heading for death, and I am the only way that they can live. If they stay with him they will die. People and unclean spirits need to know this for it is true. I have tied up his home, plundered it and set it alight, prepared it for burning. All those who want to live need to get out of his domain so that they can live for ever with me. This is the true deliverance for all people everywhere!

D Parable of the Sheep and Goats (Matthew 25)

The eternal fire is for the devil mostly but will swallow those who are too close to him. Will they be tormented for ever or consumed with no return?

\+ As for the devil and his angels, their hearing the praise of me for ever will cause them pain for ever. Then seeing the joy of my family will cause them anguish for ever. Because the kingdom is for ever, the enemies of the kingdom are for ever accursed and tormented by themselves because they do not stoop to become part of that kingdom!

E

\+ Yes indeed, the ruler has been condemned for killing me, trapped in the pit of his own making! So there can be no future for him and for those who are wedded to him.

F

\+ The devil has authority over death. That is his realm, to take people into death because of their sin. Authority has been given him to do this; this is his sphere of authority.

\+ In the end it is only me who has overall authority as the Lamb of God, God Saving. I have to be true to my name, and my name is God Saving. So you can see what happens! This is not what the devil wants. If Jonah was mad at me, the devil will be steaming spitting furious at me. But what can he do? All he can do is go into the fire himself. That is where he will end up, burning himself in his fury and indignation, burning himself up. Even now he is stoking the fires of *Gehenna* in *Hades*, stoking the indignation and violent mockery.

\+ Yes it is that serious. Everything that mocks me stokes the fires of Hell. Everything that praises me cools the fires of Hell. That is why praise is so powerful. I am good, and knowing that I am good, takes the heat out of the devil's plans.

G

\+ The evil one, as you call him, cannot stand the fire of love which reminds him of the lake of fire! Like the waters covering you now, the lake of fire is the way through to the Father's heart, but for those who are afraid, or determinedly unclean, they perish and do not come through! Try that as an image, the fires all coming together, including Paul's refining fire where the dross is burnt up and only the gold survives. Then you are golden in heaven!

H

Does Satan really have authority here, or did he before you took it away from him?

\+ This is complicated! Yes he rules through people but my Father places them there too! Placed by my Father, but the communication with heaven is interrupted by the rebellious confusers. So he has authority under God which he is abusing. He has some authority, authority to speak judgement, even accusation. He is now enlarging his authority by provoking people to sin so that he can have more legitimate targets. He is doomed to die himself, as you know and he knows, but he wants now to take as many as he can with him. He will not succeed anything like how he imagines. My will be done. My will and the will of my Father will be done and we will regain complete authority over heaven and earth.

Hades

A

While God has overlooked the times of human ignorance, now he commands all people everywhere to repent, because he has fixed a day on which he will have the world judged in righteousness by a man whom he has appointed, and of this he has given assurance to all by raising him from the dead.

Acts 17:30,31 (NRSV)

Message of judgement for idolatry. Your resurrection enthrones you as judge. What do you want to say about this, Jesus?

\+ There is truth here of course! I am judge who has been through the judgement. That you can proclaim, the judge has been through the judgement himself so he knows what it is like and what can come out of it and what there is that needs to be done for those who are facing judgement, mostly that they have a companion when the enemy wants them to be alone. .

B

\+ Carry on knowing that I have the keys. There are keys and they are in my hands. Alleluia! Indeed.

\+ What does it mean to have the keys except that you have access there? That seems to be the natural explanation of it. But it doesn't mean that everyone automatically comes out.

C

\+ The jailer thinks he has power forever. He doesn't. He is only the jailer. I am the judge and I have the power and the authority. And when his jail is empty, he will perish. Some may come to perish with him. Some may well. But he will perish because there is no longer any need of a jail! I can free them all. I can free them all if they will let me.

D

+ Know that I have the keys, I have control of the place of captivity! The Prison is mine, I am the key holder and I will decide who stays and who goes out, before it is thrown into the lake of fire! I am Lord of heaven and earth, through my Father's grace. I am Lord of Time and Lord of Love for you all.

E

+ Yes, I came down to the depths, the depths of earth, including the place of the dead under the earth, where they are captive still until the day of my appearing. Satan thinks he has charge of people there forever. That is his lie, and he knows it really, fooling himself as well as you. But I have the keys forever. I show them to him from time to time and he is enraged against me and my people.

F

(When it says, 'He ascended', what does it mean but that he had also descended into the lower parts of the earth? He who descended is the same one who ascended far above all the heavens, so that he might fill all things.)

Ephesians 4:9,10 (NRSV)

This only makes sense if the power that keeps us in captivity is over us, in the second heaven, not under us, in hell. You descended to earth, into the prison, so that you could then go to the Home Office, above the Prison Governor! From there you have the keys over all, you can see all and fill all! Anything else about the ascending and descending?

+ No, you know how they saw it then! That is the closest to how it is. I did choose that culture at that time to reveal myself as you have thought. That too is a thought from me.

G

+ Note this, that my people are punished but not destroyed, and Christians are my people. Even though they can be punished in Hades, Sheol, they will be spared the final judgement for there is enough in them to repent and turn to me again.

Even those who have tasted and turned away?

+ Yes indeed there is the first death they are liable to, but not the second death for that is my promise to them and to all my people.

H

The tombs also were opened, and many bodies of the saints who had fallen asleep were raised. After his resurrection they came out of the tombs and entered the holy city and appeared to many.

Matthew 27:52, 53 (NRSV)

The general resurrection beginning. Seems too much for modern minds, but it must have been so. What do you want to say about this Jesus? Why? And why so little made of it, no one else mentioning it?

+ This is my will, that all who see me come out of the grave, out of *Hades*, with me. These people were the few who came with me as I had the right of entrance to the prison of Hades. When I come through and out I bring people with me. That is what this says!

I

As for this worthless slave, throw him into the outer darkness, where there will be weeping and gnashing of teeth.

Matthew 25:30 (Parable of the Talents, NRSV)

+ Yes Roger, it is anger, spite against me for turning out the light. That's all I do, turn out the light and they curse and swear as if they owned the light. There is still light there but they are so angry that they can't see it! When they are exhausted in their spite they may see the glow, but rage that it is a cruel reminder of what they have lost. It is, but it is also a beacon for the future, steady, small and weak, although obscured by steamy clouds of rage and spite. So sad, sad like animals trapped in a cage, not knowing that if they quieten down and crawl they will find a way out! Yes this is all true, believe it! Keep looking and you will understand more!

J

And I know that such a person - whether in the body or out of the body I do not know; God knows - was caught up into Paradise and heard things that are not to be told, that no mortal is permitted to repeat.

2 Corinthians 12:3,4 (NRSV)

There is Paradise – a Persian idea but correct! What do you want to say about this?

\+ This is fine too. You know that there is a garden first and then the house! First the garden then the house. First the darkness and then the fire, with smoke coming through as a warning! Enjoy being able to talk of this as you know that there is a way out of the darkness for those who look to me and recognise me with them! Alleluia for there is a warning that I do want to bring to people, that the fire that consumes is real.

K

Whoever believes in the Son has eternal life; whoever disobeys the Son will not see life, but must endure God's wrath.

John 3:36 (NRSV)

When we see you, we will recognise what you have been saying to us through your people. Then we will have life. Otherwise God's wrath. But surely one of the characteristics of God's wrath is that it does not last forever?

\+ Alleluia, for I am good and kind to all, even those who disobey my word, for I love all that I have made and my mercy is stronger than even your disobedience. For a while there is wrath, but then the dawn from on high breaks with healing for all humankind and forgiveness in plenty. There is a darkness and a wailing and gnashing of teeth, but it is not the end, for there is a dawn beyond. Tell my people. Through the tender compassion of the Most High, the dawn from on high shall break upon us, even on those who walk in the shadow of death, stumbling over their own misdeeds, even on these, precisely on these, the dawn shall break.

Will there still be some who prefer darkness?

\+ Yes indeed, that is true too. There may be some who prefer darkness still, but we will have to wait and see, for my love is strong, my blood is shed for all, and there is still hope!

L

For Christ also suffered for sins once for all, the righteous for the unrighteous, in order to bring you to God. He was put to death in the flesh, but made alive in the spirit, in which also he went and made a proclamation to the spirits in prison, who in former times did not obey, when God waited patiently in the days of Noah, during the building of the ark, in which a few, that is, eight people, were saved through water.

1 Peter 3:18-20 (NRSV)

He seems to veer off the subject! He points to the good that comes from you, not retaliating even to death. Good which we maybe cannot see yet . . . Is that it?

\+ That's fine for now. Carry on a little. Yes I preached to the souls in *Hades*, or *Sheol*, and can preach to them still, for I have complete authority everywhere.

\+ There is a great message to be given to my people, that I am with them. That is so simple and yet so far-reaching – there is no place, no place here or anywhere, there or wherever, that I cannot be with my people. My authority is the authority to walk in anywhere, wherever I am welcome. That is complete authority in the world, everywhere.

M

And baptism, which this prefigured, now saves you - not as a removal of dirt from the body, but as an appeal to God for a good conscience, through the resurrection of Jesus Christ, who has gone into heaven and is at the right hand of God, with angels, authorities, and powers made subject to him.

1 Peter 3:21,22 (NRSV)

Don't see how this follows, how it connects with being ready to suffer. He seems to be saying that we are like those in the ark, safe from destruction. Is it that, as we know our souls are safe, we can be prepared for our bodies to suffer?

\+ This is strange to you, for it is not quite the same way of thinking as you know and are used to. Don't worry, for the meaning is plain: you are to be ready to suffer, knowing that I am the one who preaches even to the dead. The connection is that I have the power to rescue everyone. You are to leave those who do not respond to you! As you trust that even those who persecute you will have a chance to hear me directly in prison as Peter says, you are not too concerned if they reject you now. Rejecting you now does not mean the end of their salvation however much you may want to think that it does. You are not that important! So be ready to suffer, be ready to be persecuted and rejected, knowing that even for your persecutors there is another chance, whatever the Pharisees may say!

N

Transgression speaks to the wicked deep in their hearts; there is no fear of God before their eyes.

Psalms 36:1 (NRSV)

Temptation comes and the wicked relish it. What do you want to say about this Jesus?

\+ The wicked have no fear of me, no understanding that they are on a slippery path to destruction. Explain as much as you can that there is a path that leads to destruction and it is real.

\+ There is torment before you reach there, as you begin to see or to sense what is to come. That is why I came to save people, to save people from death and destruction. Proclaim this now with the freedom you have. For I am with you to lead you away from the paths of wickedness and into the path of life.

Yes, Jesus. How to explain that you are close and you can forgive?

\+ Speak of me, just of me, as much as you can and leave it at that for now. If they are thinking of me even a little, my work is so much easier!

O

So it will be at the end of the age. The angels will come out and separate the evil from the righteous and throw them into the furnace of fire, where there will be weeping and gnashing of teeth.

Matthew 13:49,50 (NRSV)

Judgement by the angels – under your command of course. But here the furnace does not consume but torment? Or is it only temporary? I thought it was the darkness of *Sheol* in which there is weeping and gnashing of teeth – in anger and regret and nastiness?

\+ Yes you are learning still! The darkness is a darkness of regret and separation from the light, not wanting to go into the light, holding back from the searing truth of the light. The furnace is that light-truth which separates the dross from the pure gold. But people need to see that there is dross there, and they hold back from that revelation. Yes, you do need to see that there is sin in all of you, and not one part of you is actually healthy enough to come through the furnace unchanged. So the furnace is similar to the lake of fire but it is not quite the same thing! The furnace is part of the purifying of *Sheol / Hades* but there is more immense heat to come for the dross that is left and is completely burnt up.

P

And I tell you, you are Peter, and on this rock I will build my church, and the gates of Hades will not prevail against it. I will give you the keys of the kingdom of heaven, and whatever you bind on earth will be bound in heaven, and whatever you loose on earth will be loosed in heaven.

Matthew 16:18,19 (NRSV)

It seems that the Church is to go into *Hades* and rescue people? In this life we do indeed free people from or heading for *Hades.* What about afterwards?

\+ There is a way to understand this that needs explaining: People do not know that they are in *Hades* necessarily and it can begin even now. When I called the dead or called people 'the dead', that meant that I saw the gates of *Hades* already around them. They were so fixed in their ways that they were not alive in their thoughts and attitudes, not flexible and growing. That is the mark of those who have already succumbed to the gates of *Hades,* where everything is fixed in their way. Keep asking to be shown the keys, which key for which person, and you will see the fruit of that prayer. Carry on thinking of this as in this life for that is where you are now. I would not talk of something that made no difference to you now!

Can we ask you to go and rescue a loved one if they have not repented? Or can the Church do this – it seems so from what you said here?

\+ Yes indeed leave the dead alone! That is the major message of the Old Testament and it should be practised in the New

Testament times too! There is a love which you know and which does last beyond death, but it is best to leave people with me once and for all.

Q

\+ Trust that I am all kindness as you experience my presence again and again. The judgement is real but not for now and there is a better way: to come to me and welcome me in my kindness.

\+ Yes indeed the nature of God, as shown even in the Old Testament, is to be kinder than we imagine, Jonah and Isaiah show that clearly, and this kindness means that I give people a second chance.

R

\+ As for beyond this life, yes indeed it is hard to tell in any great detail. But it just fits with me, with my character, which is the main thing. And what is my name? God Rescuing, as you call it. That is my name and my character, so what you believe must fit in with that name, for there is no other name that is higher than God Rescuing. God Punishing is lesser than God Rescuing!

S

\+ Carry on telling people the truth about my kindness being kinder than they can imagine. My treatment of the wicked gives them every opportunity to repent, but, in the end, when there are no righteous left, as they have driven them out, the collapse and destruction comes inevitably. All I have to do is give the word and the chaff is burnt up. But I take every pain to ensure that what is left is indeed 100% chaff.

T Isaiah 25

The end beyond judgement, although Moab remains broken down. Is the picture of Moab a picture of the judgement before the new earth, or an indication that not everyone enters the new earth, or something else?

\+ Yes indeed, as the rabbis pore over the text and ask each other questions, so you need to ask me, the great Rabbi! As for this text, yes indeed there is a hope for all peoples which will come to pass. As for Moab, yes indeed their walls are broken down, as Isaiah so much wanted to see, but where are the people? They too have, as many as possible, gone to worship and follow the God of

Zion! Yes indeed there is hope for all people, even the people of Moab in my eyes, even if it is not quite what the prophet and the people at the time wanted to see!

The Human Soul

Thus it is written, 'The first man, Adam, became a living being'; the last Adam became a life-giving spirit.

1 Corinthians 15:45 (NRSV)

No pre-existence of the soul? You are the exception, existing before becoming incarnate. OK?

\+ Yes that's fine and important! There is no way that you have all already existed before you were created. Where were you? It is a nonsense to say that you come into this life fully fledged in some way internally. No, you grow and develop and are nurtured, and the nurture you receive imprints your soul in vital and significant ways. Resist that semi-pagan teaching that tends to downplay the need to care fully for children, for their souls as well as their bodies.

\+ These things, these beliefs, are important indeed.

PERMISSIONS

Many thanks to various publishers who have given permission for extracts from particular books published by them, mostly on a 'fair use' basis: Review and Herald Publishing, IVP USA, OUP, Clairview Books. Thanks to E. W. Fudge for permission for excerpts from *The Fire That Consumes.*

Acknowledgements:

Hilborn, David (ed.), *The Nature of Hell – A report by the Evangelical Alliance Commission on Unity and Truth Among Evangelicals (ACUTE)*, Milton Keynes: Paternoster, 2000.

Wenham, John W., *Facing Hell: An Autobiography 1913–1996*, Milton Keynes: Paternoster, 1998.

MacDonald, Gregory *The Evangelical Universalist* (Wipf and Stock 2006, SPCK 2008) used by permission of Wipf and Stock, publisher.

Francis Chan, Preston Sprinkle. *Erasing Hell* pub. by David C Cook, publisher. Copyright 2011, Permission required to reproduce. All rights reserved.

Extracts from *The Problem of Hell* edited by Joel Buenting [Farnham etc:Ashgate,2010] Copyright 2010 reprinted by permission of the publishers.

Extracts from *The Light Beyond* by Raymond Moody published by Ebury Press reprinted by permission of the Random House Group Ltd.

Permissions awaited from other publishers will be included in future editions.

Also by Roger Harper

A British Crash

A young couple celebrate their relationship over a meal in a city centre restaurant. He is the son of a successful Asian Moslem businessman. She is a bright English girl, involved with the media.

They speed off into the city underpass. Their car smashes lethally into the concrete wall.

Who was responsible? A jilted lover? A racist?

This is Birmingham, September 1999.

David Jeffery is a solicitor who knows both families. Dismissing the obvious suspect, he searches for the truth.

David takes us with him for 10 days. He is an interesting companion, open about his thoughts and feelings, but not insisting on our immediate attention. He covers Christianity, Islam, and American coffee shops in England, the point of sermons, the ethics of air fresheners, and much more.

David is a practising Christian. He finds himself planning a dramatic funeral. His faith and sexual fidelity come under pressure as never before.

David keeps investigating until the truth comes out.

'A whodunit, a Christian story, and a book about racism? *A British Crash* really is all three, and more . . .

You'll find insights into Islam, the New Age, handling lust and grief, Britain as a Christian nation, and living in Birmingham. Reading this book is a rich and entertaining experience.'

Review in *Sorted* magazine.

'Definitely worth a read – will make you think and keep you gripped till the end.'

Review on Amazon

Ladder Media Ltd. is a Christian Equitable Company (CEC) – a company where investors and workers love each other as they love themselves.

A CEC is a company limited by guarantee and without a shareholding. Those who invest in the company and those who work for the company are equal partners in running the company and in benefiting from profits.

In a normal shareholding company, the shareholders appoint directors to run the company on their behalf and in their interests. Shareholders take any profit which is not reinvested in the company. Workers receive a salary but normally do not benefit from any increased profit. For workers it has been described as 'working to make other people rich'.

In a normal shareholding company, the shareholders own the company as a piece of property which they can transfer, with continuing entitlement to profit, through generations. This has been the main mechanism through which the gap between the rich and the poor has widened considerably, especially in recent years. Overall, capital is rewarded more than labour. This arrangement is not 'loving your neighbour as you love yourself'.

A cooperative seeks to reverse the inequality, with the workers controlling the company and benefiting from profits. This too is not 'loving your neighbour as you love yourself'.

Christians believe that it is supremely important to love God and to love our neighbour as ourselves in every aspect of our life. Hence the recent formation of the model of a Christian Equitable Company.

Ladder Media Limited is pioneering the development of Christian Equitable companies in the UK.

It is hoped that a Venture Capital CEC, Jerusalem Developments, will soon be formed to help set up further CECs in the UK and across the world.

For further details or to register an interest in helping with the development of CECs, please write to *lad1@abritishcrash.co.uk*